Assessment of Digital Librarianship

Assessment of Digital Librarianship

M. Ram

RANDOM

RANDOM PUBLICATIONS

NEW DELHI (INDIA)

Assessment of Digital Librarianship

ISBN 978-93-5111-488-8

Published in 2015 in India by

RANDOM PUBLICATIONS
4376-A/4B, Gali Murari Lal, Ansari Road
New Delhi-110 002
Phone : +9111-43580356, 011-23289044, 011-43142548
e-mail: sales@randompublications.com,
info@randompublications.com, randomexports@gmail.com

Reprint 2021

Type Setting by : Friends Media, Delhi-110089
Digitally Printed at : Replika Press Pvt. Ltd.

Preface

Digital libraries are an emerging concept, as today's libraries routinely provide information and services in digital form. As the nature and role of libraries have changed in response to the new digital environment, new applications and services have been developed. Many practitioners have reported on these changes in the digital workplace.

Digital libraries have unique characteristics that differ from traditional libraries and their approaches to information provision. The evolutionary view of digital libraries has been addressed by practitioners in the library and information fields. From a traditional librarian's point of view, digital libraries present a transformative model of a large scale, user-centric organization that is moving towards an integrated form with various components. However, the main purpose of digital libraries remains consistent with that of traditional libraries in that the purpose of digital libraries is to organize, distribute, and preserve information resources just as it is for traditional libraries.

Due to the changing nature of librarianship resulting from the increasing amount of information available in digital format, educating digital librarians has become an important agenda within library and information science schools. To design and offer appropriate courses and teaching approaches for training competent digital librarians, educators can benefit from feedback provided by current practitioners in order to accurately determine what skills and knowledge are really required for digital librarians to be effective in the digital work place.

This book is a collection of selected topics that highlight the application of information technology in the scientific management of collection, organization and dissemination of information in digital libraries. It will be a useful reference book for budding librarians, students, researchers, teachers and peer groups in the field of library and information science.

Author

Contents

1

Role of Librarians in Digital Age

A digital library is a distributed technology environment which dramatically reduces barriers to the creation, dissemination, manipulation, storage, integration, and reuse of information by individuals and groups. Information sources accessed via the internet are ingredients of a digital library. Today, the network connects some information sources that are a mixture of publicly available information and private information shared by collaborators. They include reference volumes, books, journals, newspapers, national phone directories, sound and voice recordings, images, video clips, scientific data, and private information services such as stockmarket reports and private newsletters. These information sources, when connected electronically through a network, represent important components of an emerging, universally accessible, digital library. Digital libraries' relationship with conventional or traditional sort is clearly of some interest. The function of conventional libraries has been described as fourfold: collection; organisation and representation; access and retrieval; and analysis, synthesis, and dissemination of information. Collection includes techniques for understanding what information resources are of use to a client population and for cost-effective storage and preservation of such resources. Organisation and representation have to do with classifying and indexing information resources in ways relevant to their potential users.

Access considerations include design of physical space and organisation of materials within such space to respond effectively to user needs and expectations. Information retrieval has been addressed, of course, in the design of systems specific to that task. Analysis, synthesis and dissemination functions include responding to reference questions, producing evaluative reviews, and devising community outreach programmes. Librarians and information scientists have developed techniques, procedures, and systems for addressing each of these functions for many kinds of data and presentation.

Digital library does not add any qualitatively new roles to these, nor does it omit any of these roles. Although DL implementation may well depend on the local context and technologies chosen, there are commonly accepted constraints which must be maintained to please users. DL research has focused on automating activities carried out by librarians, such as automatic indexing and classifying and expert systems for reference desks.

Conventional cataloguing presumes people are involved and can only assign a few keywords; digital catalogues can support long keyword and key phrase (or even word sense) sets with weights, long user queries, ranked retrieval, etc. Information search via hypertext illustrates that indices can be implicit rather than explicit, giving users a seamless blend of primary and secondary works. Further, some current library activities may become irrelevant; for instance, circulation problems originating in a fixed number of copies of each work simply disappear. Thus, DL involves not only automation of each traditional library activity and service, but also calls for redefinition of services, new groupings of services or replacements of groups of services with other solutions. Whether one judges the differences between digital and conventional libraries to be intrinsically qualitative or merely quantitative, the quantitative factors are so immensely different that it will often be better to treat them as qualitative. On the positive side, the potential ease of integration of information in different modes from mutually remote repositories creates new social possibilities; for instance, that the California death certificates are now being collected into a digital library enables a test of the conjecture that shipbuilding in 1940-45 led to premature deaths from asbestosis. So there are clearly new problems and new possibilities for which should seek new answers, develop new techniques, and create new institutions or significantly modify old ones. But we see no reason to believe that the novel elements constitute the entire digital library service, and feel should be careful to capture traditional values. To some readers, these comments might appear to be labour the obvious. They were, however, not uniformly agreed among the workshop participants, and are probably still not fully accepted.

A digital library is a machine readable representation of materials which might be found in a university library together with organising information intended to help users find specific information. A digital library service is an assemblage of digital computing, storage, and communications machinery together with the software needed to reproduce, emulate, and extend the services provided by conventional libraries based on paper and other material means of collecting, storing, cataloguing, finding, and disseminating information. A full service digital library must accomplish all essential services of traditional libraries and also exploit digital storage, searching, and communication. Public, private, professional, school, commercial, and other kinds of library emphasize different services, different kinds of information, and different service styles. While any digital library instance may thus offer only partial services, the technology suite from which library instances are assembled must permit assembly of a full service library. In addition, this suite must shield the user who wishes to draw on multiple libraries from inter-library differences which are irrelevant to him.

What distinguishes a conventional library from a heap of things to read is organisation provided by someone other than the authors of the collected materials. For a small, private collection this could be shelf organisation; for a large collection it is typically a descriptive catalogue which is distinct from the collection, with at least one catalogue record associated with each item held. Not every database is a library, but every library is a database. What distinguishes a library from an arbitrary database are certain data integrity and security rules that constitute an implicit contract between custodians and users. A few circumstances and characteristics for which expect DLs to emulate conventional libraries holding books, pictures, and other material objects communicate the flavour intended:

i) users are usually elsewhere than the information they want, and often want to correlate items from several sources;
ii) whoever wants to use a library must show permission to do so;
iii) different patrons are permitted different actions and to see different parts of each collection;
iv) the catalogue and the collected items are used differently and not necessarily housed in the same place;
v) to find specific information, each user must understand the catalogue structure;

vi) the catalogue may describe items in other libraries;

vii) documents contain cross references to other documents;

viii) documents are catalogued with text descriptors and also with conventional properties, such as author names;

ix) document identifiers are different from document names;

x) translations of a document may express essentially the same information;

xi) each stored item is valuable, often with part of its residual value owned by its authors or authors and assignees;

xii) part of the value provided by a library is the provenance information it holds for each item;

xiii) items are put into libraries because, while each is thought valuable for future reference, the specific individuals who will read it and the times when this will occur are not known.

Digital library is having the benefits of improved control and plasticity are not only improved data quality, but also more freedom and reduced bureaucracy for individual users. Only a librarian may add to the collection of a conventional library, because of the discipline essential to create a quality catalogue. In a digital library, cataloguing discipline and search restrictions to authorised data can be automatically enforced. It can thus allow each patron and author a wider range of services than is practical with a conventional library.

Digital Library Toolkits

Digital libraries are created by software which includes the following module classes:

i) *A document storage subsystem* is a resource manager that creates a library abstraction implementing all the essential data storage, retrieval, protection, communication, and search functions as primitive operations which do not depend on the interpretation of the data handled. It is middleware that integrates more basic resource managers, such as database managers, video servers, cache managers, and file managers.

ii) *Network directory and security servers* are intimately related resource managers which help users locate protected resources, limiting each user to what each resource and item owner permits. A name or directory service maps names to locations and other descriptors. Authentication and authorisation services combine to control access to what is permitted.

iii) *A billing subsystem* is a component or set of components which collects and validates subject and account information, rate information and resource consumptions, and submits these to a charge-back subsystem.

iv) *A source selector* and fuser is an application enabler which partitions a query among as many libraries as the query implies, calls on query managers to execute the queries, and assembles the results to hide those inter-library differences that the user considers irrelevant.

v) *A search engine* is a resource manager which accepts a query and returns item descriptors, but not usually copies of the items themselves. There may be primitive search engines that operate only on certain kinds of database and also more complex search engines which partition queries among simpler query engines and combine results using joins and selections which are beyond the simpler engines. Part of a search engine might be an external query optimiser intended to overcome the performance problems inherent in multiple, separated library catalogues.

vi) *A filter service* is a separately programmed bit-stream to bit-stream transformation that can be linked into a resource manager or an application enabler for functions like encryption, compression, and partial object access.

vii) *A link engine* is an application enabler which interprets a hypermedia link and calls on resource managers to manipulate a copy of the item indicated, possibly by launching separately-provided application programme, and possibly invoking library services to provide integrity holds on the primary copy of the item.

viii) *A preview/thumbnailer* is an application enabler which collects from one or more libraries a set of small data objects, or creates each such thumbnail from a library item, to present these to a user for selection. Each thumbnail remains bound to the associated item so that selecting it can be used to drive item retrieval or some other action.

ix) *A presenter or renderer* is an application enabler which prepares an object for manipulation in a client machine, possibly assembling item parts from one or more libraries. Each tool is specific to an object class, i.e., is selected when the user asks to render an item of the class at hand. There is no clear boundary with a filter or a format converter which edits a set of files to create another set of files representing a subset of the same information, typically executing close to the data source or sink.

x) *Data analysis tools*, browsers, navigators, and authoring and editing services are application enablers.

xi) *Source/sink servers* are resource managers such as scan servers, print servers, and fax servers.

xii) *Indexing tools, document analysers, and other tools* to recognise patterns and structure are application enablers for creating search indices automatically. An actor or active agent is a persistent process which monitors database state and sends to principals filtered information about changes. Alternatively, an active agent is a network process which creates other active agent instances at remote locations, with each instance collecting filtered information from databases.

Resource managers and application enablers are essentially passive and cannot distinguish active agents from human users. Triggers, a database feature in which an incoming message causes not only database changes and/or responses to its source, but also messages to a third party, share some of the characteristics of actors. Both triggers and actors are dependent on store-and-forward network services because the message target may not be active when the message is ready for delivery. Some of these components can and must be adopted from activities not labelled DL. Such components certainly include those for naming, authentication, and many kinds of search engine.

Protection of Digital works

Technological solutions exist today and improved means are being developed to better protect digital works through varying combinations of hardware and software. Protection schemes can be implemented at the level of the copyrighted work or at more comprehensive levels such as the operating system, the network or both. In the past few years, there has been an explosion in the popularity and volume of use of the internet. The internet serves today, through electronic mail and remote access, to connect people to information and to deliver information products and services. An almost incomprehensible variety of information has been made widely and easily accessible through this system. Since the internet and applications which use it, like the electronic mail and "world wide web," have exploded in popularity and use, systems used today and being designed for short term implementation are likely to serve as the foundation for communications.

The internet provides individuals many different ways to disseminate and retrieve information. The basic concept of communications underlying the internet is that a user with his or her personal computer or workstation can 'connect', either directly or through a succession of intermediary computers, in a uniform manner to a 'remote' computer that acts as a 'server' of information. The user attaches to the remote computer and uses the services offered by the remote computer system. The service may provide for immediate transfer of information or eventual transmission. For example, a user can direct a remote computer to send data through an established connection to the user's computer. Alternatively, the user can send information to the remote computer that will eventually result in information being sent back to the user's computer from that remote computer. In either sense, there is a 'connection' established between the two computers that permits the flow of information, typically at the request of the user. The simplest type of connections use a character-based 'dumb terminal' interface. This type of scheme consists essentially of the user using his computer to do nothing more than type commands which the computer executes.

Many of the established protocols have been integrated and enhanced using tools that can access what is termed the world wide web. The world wide web is a scheme whereby organisations use graphical 'front ends' to provide remote users with point and click access to information stored on their servers, as well as access through 'links' to information stored on other remote servers. Web 'browsers' are programmes that run on a personal computer or workstation that enable a user to establish connections to these graphical front ends, view, retrieve and manipulate data provided by those remote servers. At the root of the web are several of the established protocols, a file format for embedding navigational information in graphical and text-based documents; the Hypertext Transfer Protocol (HTTP), a communications protocol for communicating navigational information and other data between the remote server and the requesting computer; and the

Uniform Resource Locator (URL) scheme for identifying the location of web-accessible documents.

A number of organisations and groups are also working to develop additional protocols to enable secure communications. Some of these protocols have been published as draft specifications at this point, including the Secure Sockets Layer (SSL), the Secure Hypertext Transfer Protocol (SHTTP) and the Enhanced Mosaic Security Framework. The integration of these various protocols into a single, easy to use, understandable interface has led to a tremendous increase in the popularity and use of the world wide web and, correspondingly, of the internet as a means for providing and retrieving information.

Access and Use Technological Controls

Technology will likely play a central role in implementing controls on the access to and use of protected works at both the file and server level. Distribution of digital works can be regulated by controlling access to the source of copies of the works—information or data servers. Access to these servers can vary from completely uncontrolled access to partially controlled access to completely controlled access. Access control is affected through user identification and authentication procedures that deny access to unauthorised users to a server or to particular information on a server. Nearly all service providers, including commercial online services, private dial-up bulletin board systems, and servers accessible through the internet, control access to their systems.

Some information providers grant full unrestricted access to all the information contained on their servers, and use control simply to comport with physical limitations of their servers. Other information providers restrict access to users with accounts or grant only limited access to unregistered users. Of course, an information provider can elect not to provide uncontrolled access, and permit only those with pre-established accounts to access the server. This is more common with commercially-oriented online service providers. Control over access to a server containing protected works will typically be the first level of protection a content provider will look for before making their protected works accessible through the server. A second level for controlling access to and use of protected works can be exerted through control measures tied to the electronic file containing the work.

Restrictions on access at the file level can be implemented using features in 'rendering' software. For example, a content provider may develop specialised software products or implement features in general purpose software products that would control by whom, and to what degree, a protected work may be used. Such restrictions could be implemented using features in the rendering software, a unique file format or features in an established file format, or a combination of both. 'Control' measures could also be implemented to determine if the content provider had authorised certain uses of the work, as well as some means to control the degree to which a user would be able to subsequently 'manipulate' the work.

Encryption

Encryption amounts to a 'scrambling' of data using mathematical principles that can be followed in reverse to 'unscramble' the data. File encryption thus simply converts a file from a manipulable file format to a scrambled format. Authorisation in the form of possession of an appropriate 'key' is required to 'decrypt' the file and restore it to its manipulable format. Encryption techniques use 'keys' to control access to data that has been 'encrypted'. Encryption keys are actually strings of alphanumeric digits that are plugged into a mathematical algorithm and used to scramble data using that algorithm. Scrambling means that the original sequence of binary digits that constitute the information object is transformed using a mathematical algorithm into a new sequence of binary digits (i.e., a new string of 1s and 0s).

The result is a new sequence of digital data that represents the 'encrypted' work. Anyone with the key can decrypt the work by plugging it into a programme that applies the mathematical algorithm in reverse to yield the original sequence of binary digits that comprise the file. Although most commonly thought of as a tool for protecting works transmitted via computer networks, encryption can be and is used with virtually all information delivery technologies, including telephone, satellite and cable communications. Of course, once the work is decrypted by someone with the key, there may be no technological protection for the work if it is stored and subsequently redistributed in its 'decrypted' or original format.

A widely publicised technique for sending secure transmissions of data is 'public key' encryption. This technique can be used to encrypt data using an algorithm requiring two particular keys—a 'public' key and a 'private' key. The two keys are affiliated with the recipient to which the information is to be sent. The 'public' key is distributed publicly, while the private key is kept secret by the recipient. Data encrypted using a person's public key can only be decrypted using that person's secret, private key. For instance, a copyright owner could encrypt a work using the public key of the intended recipient. Once the recipient receives the encrypted transmission, he could then use his private key to decrypt that transmission. No secret (private) keys need to be exchanged in this transaction. Without the private key of the intended recipient, the work cannot be read, manipulated or otherwise deciphered by other parties. Of course, if a decrypted copy is made and shared, then others could manipulate the work unless other means are used to protect it. There may be instances where someone other than the communicating parties needs access to the encrypted data.

A key escrow system is one way such access might be obtained. A key escrow system would hold the key needed to decrypt an encrypted transmission in 'escrow'. Such a system could be maintained by a private organisation or the government, and anyone seeking access to an encrypted transmission would have to demonstrate their need for the key through a process, such as obtaining a search warrant, that ensures the legitimate privacy and security needs of users of encrypted transmissions.

Digital Signatures

Mathematical algorithms can also be used to create digital 'signatures' that, in effect, place a 'seal' on a digitally represented work. Generating a digital signature is referred to as 'signing' the work. The algorithms can be implemented through software or hardware, or both. The digital signature serves as means for authenticating the work, both as to the identity of the entity that authenticated or 'signed' it and as to the contents of the file that encodes the information that constitutes the work. Thus, by using digital signatures one will be able to identify from whom a particular file originated as well as verify that the contents of that file have not been altered from the contents as originally distributed. A digital signature is a unique sequence of digits that is computed based on:

i) The work being protected,
ii) The digital signature algorithm being used, and
iii) The key used in digital signature generation.

Generating a digital signature uses cryptographic techniques, but is not encryption of the work; the work may remain unencrypted so it can be accessed and used without decryption. In fact, digital signatures and encryption can be used simultaneously to protect works. Generally, a signature is computed for a copyrighted work first and then the work (including the seal) is encrypted. When the work is to be used, the work is decrypted, then the signature (i.e., the seal) is verified to be sure the work has not been modified (either in its original or encrypted form). If the work is never changed, the seal need never be removed or changed. If the work is changed, a new seal must be computed on the revised information. Typically, the digital signature is incorporated in some manner in the transmission that constitutes the work. Often, the sender will also distribute his public key as well.

The signature serves as a 'seal' for the work because the seal enables the information to be independently checked for unauthorised modification. If the seal is verified (independently computed signature matches the original signature), then the work is a bona fide copy of the original work, i.e., nothing has been changed in the file that constitutes the work.

Steganography

Innovative new techniques are being developed to address security or management-driven concerns relating to dissemination and use of digitally-encoded information. In essence, using steganographic techniques, a party can embed hidden messages in digitised visual or audio data. The embedded information does not degrade or otherwise interfere with the audio or visual quality of the work. Instead, the embedded information can only be detected if specifically sought out. More advanced steganographic techniques based on statistical or entropically-directed encoding are proving to be difficult to defeat. For example, one system modulates a known noise signal with the information to be embedded and adds the 'scaled' signal to the original data. Once encoded in this fashion, the steganographically encoded identification data is distributed throughout the work as subliminal noise and, like noise, cannot be fully eliminated from the work. Thus, one can ensure detection of an embedded message even after substantial corruption of the data, such as might occur through compression/decompression, encoding, alteration or excerpting of the original data. By providing a means to indelibly tag a work with specific information, steganography is likely to play a complementary role to encryption as well as authentication techniques based on digital signatures.

Content providers will rely on a variety of technologies, based in software and hardware, to protect them against unauthorised uses of their information products and services. The hardware is programmed to read certain coding information contained in the 'digital subcode channel' of digital sound recordings and broadcasts. Based on the information it reads, the hardware circuitry will permit unrestricted copying, permit copying but label the copies it makes with codes to restrict further copying, or disallow copying. The serial copy management system allows unlimited first generation copying-digital reproduction of originals, but prevents further digital copying from those reproductions.

Systems for managing rights in works are being contemplated in the development of the NII. These systems will serve the functions of tracking and monitoring uses of copyrighted works as well as licensing of rights and indicating attribution, creation and ownership interests. A combination of file- and system-based access controls using encryption technologies, digital signatures and steganography are, and will continue to be, employed by owners of works to address copyright management concerns. Such security measures must be carefully designed and implemented to ensure that they not only effectively protect the owner's interests in the works but also do not unduly burden use of the work by consumers or compromise their privacy. And measures should be studied to ensure that systems established to serve these functions are not readily defeated. To implement these rights management functions, information will likely be included in digital versions of a work (i.e., copyright management information) to inform the user about the authorship and ownership of a work (e.g., attribution information) as well as to indicate authorised uses of the work (e.g., permitted use information).

For instance, information may be included in an 'electronic envelope' containing a work that provides information regarding authorship, copyright ownership, date of creation or last modification, and terms and conditions of authorised uses. As measures for this purpose become incorporated at lower levels (e.g., at the operating system level), such information may become a fundamental component of a file or information object. Once information such as this is affiliated with a particular information object (e.g., data constituting the work) and readily accessible, users will be able to easily address questions over licensing and use of the work. For example, systems for electronic licensing may be developed based on the attribution or permitted use information associated with an information object. Electronic contracts may be used. Providers may inform the user that a certain action—the entering of a password, for instance, to gain access to the service or a particular work, or merely the use of the service—will be considered acceptance of the specified terms and conditions of the electronic licence.

Education

The average citizen has only the most general understanding that there are patents, copyrights and trademarks, let alone an understanding of the legal, economic and trade issues involved. Indeed, many lawyers do not have an understanding of this highly specialised area of the law. However, as the convergence of computer and communications technology brings the capability of high speed computers and communications networks into homes, all have the possibility to become not only authors and users of copyrighted works, but printers, publishers, exhibitors and distributors as well. Most people do not have a very clear idea about the role of intellectual property law in encouraging creativity and the importance of intellectual property to our economic well-being.

Intellectual property law is typically perceived by non-lawyers as being incomprehensible with its own 'technical' jargon and legalistic terminology that do not provide clear-cut rules in many circumstances. Many often resist learning such 'legalese' and want to see clearer and more easily understandable rules. Unfortunately, a mere recitation of 'dos' and, 'don'ts' is not enough to explain to NII users how the copyright system affects their interests, and why certain activities are not allowed by the law. It is not only intellectual property law that presents complexities for the NII user. The underlying information technology is also difficult to understand, and it is constantly evolving and presenting users with new capabilities. Just learning about these capabilities and how to use them is difficult enough for users. It is also difficult for users to understand that they may not be able to always use all of the new facilities to copy, perform and use works that the technology allows.

Overcoming these barriers is also difficult because the market for copyrighted works is complex with many participants. Individual users generally do not appreciate the impact that an unauthorised use of a protected work can have in that market. This is especially true when the unauthorised use has an immediate benefit to the user, and no immediately visible harm to others. How tempting it is to simply make yourself a copy of a piece of shareware and not pay its author, or to make just one copy of a sound recording that someone has put up on a bulletin board.

The first goal—raising public awareness of the existence of intellectual property—is a broad goal to which anyone may contribute. At present, few people understand what intellectual property is, or the types of intellectual property protection available. Generally, owners of intellectual property should strive to get the word out about intellectual property, whether individually or collectively, so that the public becomes more familiar with the concept. As people begin to associate intellectual property with public benefits, they will be more receptive to learning about and respecting intellectual property.

The second goal is to develop educational curricula about intellectual property. In addition to heightening public awareness, such curricula would reinforce the important role of intellectual property as an incentive to create and innovate, provide guidance as to legal use of protected works, and dispel the notion that intellectual property is a barrier to the public availability of works. The substantive components of the curricula may be broken down further into a number of elements. Initially, respect for copyright protection needs to be highlighted—intellectual property needs to become a 'household word'. This element will work in conjunction with the goal of public awareness, but should focus more on the importance of intellectual property, and not simply on its existence. Second, a comprehensive programme needs to be developed to target different educational levels.

Ideally, copyright owners, users, and educators will seek to develop broadbased 'model curricula' that incorporate all of the substantive issues that are required for useful education about copyright. Such model curricula could then be disseminated to state school boards, private schools, libraries, community centres and other educational institutions for incorporation into their programmes.

Certain core concepts should be introduced at the elementary school level—at least during initial instructions on computers or the internet, but perhaps even before such instruction. For example, the concepts of property and ownership are easily explained to children because they can relate to the underlying notions of property—what is 'mine' versus what is 'not mine', just as they do for a jacket, a ball, or a pencil. At the same time that children learn basic civics, such as asking permission to use somebody else's pencil, they should also learn that works on a computer system may also be property that belongs to someone else. Therefore, they should learn what one participant refers to as 'electronic citizenship', including how to determine the owner of a work, and how to go about asking for permission to use it. Similarly, they should learn that the taking of someone else's property, including copyrighted works, without permission is not right.

Other concepts of intellectual property should perhaps be introduced later. Soon after learning about property and ownership, students should learn more about the various forms of intellectual property, and why their protection is so important. Students should learn about the many valuable technologies that would not have been developed without protections of the patent system to recover costly research and development investments. Similarly, students should be aware of the substantial economic contributions of the industries that rely on copyright protection—including the computer, entertainment, publishing, and broadcasting industries.

Additional concepts regarding copyright may be explored throughout a person's education the economic rationale for granting authors and inventors exclusive property rights in their creative efforts for a limited period of time in order to foster creativity and innovation might fit neatly in a high school economics course. Similarly, a number of topics might be explored during social studies or history classes including the constitutional roots of patent and copyright law, the nature of a governmental grant of a property right, or the role of the copyright and patent systems in fostering the present-day information and communications revolution. Business courses could discuss the concepts of licensing intellectual property rights, the use of intellectual property as a marketing device, the concept of intellectual property as a corporate asset, and the trademark concept of goodwill. At the college level, concepts of intellectual property could be included in many programmes. Along with the initial consideration of the substantive component of what should be taught, a procedural component must also be determined.

The public should understand that copyright protection is specifically prescribed for a limited period of time, after which the underlying work becomes dedicated to the public. In order for the public to respect and participate in educational programmes, they must be able to rely on the information they receive. As many private organisations have already developed their own educational materials—often directed at specific audiences and applications—confusion may result on the part of the layperson based on perceived 'mixed signals' of what is and is not permitted. Therefore, as curricula and other educational programmes are developed, clear and consistent information must be ensured in order to avoid confusion and contempt.

The third factor is the form of communication used to deliver an education program. Clearly, audiences respond differently to varied methods of communication. Educators and media organisations can have tremendous impact on the procedural component because they possess the expertise required to determine whether a particular educational message is being effectively communicated. Through testing procedures, educators may determine whether certain concepts are comprehended by students. Similarly, through marketing surveys, media organisations can determine the forms of communication that are most effective for particular audiences. These methods of evaluation are already available for other educational and communication materials, thus requiring only minor adaptation for the evaluation of an intellectual property curricula. The final goal of the campaign is the establishment of a system that provides the public with easy access to accurate and uptodate information on copyright, including guidance on when and how to get authorisation to use copyrighted works. While educational programmes and curricula may raise public awareness, they cannot teach the public every facet of the law as it applies to new and previously unencountered situations.

Digital Library Development

There are many thousands of digital library projects currently underway, in all sectors of the library community. These projects have taken widely varying approaches, dependent on the needs of the different libraries, the sector in which they are based, and, in part, the definition of digital library that has been applied. This has led to a variety of digital libraries being developed, with no common model being available. The many existing digital library studies can give a useful pointer to the general development of digital libraries. However, the majority of published digital library research has occurred in the academic and public library sectors.

Watson and Streatfield were concerned that there has been a major focus on digital library developments in recent years, yet there has been relatively little attention paid to special libraries, especially those outside the "commercial" arena. Missingham concurred with this view, noting that the use of new technology in special libraries has been quite different to that of academic and public libraries. Government libraries usually fill a quite different role within their agency than their academic and public library counterparts.

The basic concept underlying the digital library is not new. In 1945, Dr Vannevar Bush of the U.S. Office of Scientific Research and Development discussed a device called a "memex". He envisioned this device being used by individuals as "a sort of mechanised private file and library". It would be able to store large amounts of books, pictures, periodicals, newspapers, correspondence, and so on, with material being indexed for easy retrieval. According to Saffady, the Bush vision is "one of the most influential and frequently cited precursors" of the modern digital library concept. He continued to note that although the digital library seems a revolutionary development, the concepts and technologies involved are more accurately described as evolutionary.

Although not a recent concept, in terms of actual development, digital libraries are still relatively new. Because of this, there is as yet no universally agreed terminology in place. In the literature, the digital library may also be called the library without walls, virtual library, electronic library, e-library, desktop library, online library, future library, library of the future, logical library, networked library, hybrid library, gateway library, extended library or information superhighway. Of these many terms, digital library, virtual library, hybrid library and electronic (or e-) library are most common. Just as there is no universally agreed upon terminology for digital libraries, neither is there a common definition for this concept. In the 1990s, terms such as digital library, virtual library and electronic library became widely used, but considerable uncertainty remains about what they actually mean.

The term digital library has been defined both broadly and narrowly. In the narrower form, a digital library is construed as a mainly, if not wholly, digital entity, although this fully digital scenario is dependent on the necessary materials being available in an appropriate format. In the broader construction, the digital library is defined as a hybrid of traditional library services and new electronic sources and methods.

One of the more comprehensive definitions by Gapen, who defined digital libraries as:

> ...the concept of remote access to the contents and services of libraries and other information resources, combining an on-site collection of current and heavily used materials in both print and electronic form, with an electronic network which provides access to, and delivery from, external worldwide library and commercial information and knowledge sources. In essence, the user is provided the effect of a library which is a synergy created by bringing together technologically the resources of many, many libraries and information services.

The broader definition of digital libraries offered by Gapen was adopted. No distinction was made in defining the various terms used to describe the digital library concept, and for the sake of clarity, the term digital library has been used throughout. Regardless of the wide variety of terms used to describe the digital library concept, it is clear from the literature that there are certain common elements, regardless of the terminology applied. There must be, in some sense, a collection, to which clients must be linked in an efficient and satisfying manner. There is also a set of services, either human or electronic, which link clients to the collections.

The technologies involved in providing digital library services should support document creation, retrieval, transfer, dissemination, manipulation and management. Finally, there must be an institution in which the digital library collections and services are embedded. A major study, conducted by the Association of Research Libraries (ARL) in 1992, identified series of different activities considered essential to the formation of digital libraries. These included:

— Use of, or development of electronic document delivery services;

— Policies, services, or reallocations that emphasise access [to information] over ownership;

— Participation in cooperative development or purchase of electronic files;

— Participation in the development of a campus-wide information system;

— A written plan that states its goal as access to information from a single workstation;

— Enhancement of the online public access catalogue (OPAC) to include the holdings of other libraries besides those held locally;

— Providing a gateway from the OPAC to other databases or networks, such as the Internet;
— End-user access to online files from on or off campus;
— Connection with the Internet;
— Training faculty and students:
— in the use of Internet sources; and,
— in end-user searching;
— Subscribing to electronic journals;
— Digitisation of text for electronic storage, retrieval and/or dissemination.

These elements, then, may be considered the basic building blocks of the digital library, although the nature and extent of the application of each component will depend upon the circumstances and needs of the library and/or organisation to which the digital library is attached.

There are number of activities that together make up digital libraries, so too does it show that the development of digital libraries is heavily dependent on a number of inter-related enabling (or hindering) factors. These include such issues as copyright, client attitudes, changes to funding and financial structures, the need for new organisational structures, technological issues, staff training, and so on. A study of Commonwealth library digital library developments was conducted in 1998-1999, with one of its objects to determine if the model developed from the general literature on digital libraries was appropriate to digital library development in the Commonwealth library sector. Libraries included in the study were libraries within those agencies, statutory and non-statutory authorities administered by the Commonwealth Government. Where an agency had more than one library, only those libraries that had policy and budgetary control over their individual library or network was included.

The National Library of Australia was excluded from this study as, although it is a Commonwealth library, it is also a national library, and as such, has different foci, programs and priorities than special libraries delivering information services to public sector organisations. An examination of the digital library activities undertaken in Commonwealth libraries showed that some activities were undertaken by far more libraries than were others. This suggests that the various issues that impact on the digital library environment have relatively equal importance, with none assuming much greater significance than another.

Content Management in Web Environment

The idea of "content management" is multifaceted. One's choice of a perspective on the idea carries with it distinctive terminology, particular alliances with facets of a complex information technology infrastructure, specific limits on what content is and is not, and implied commitments to organizational and administrative priorities. Each of the three perspectives outlined below attempts to deal with various aspects of the content management issue, ranging from digital content (as objects or assets), to the people who add value to the content, to the tools one uses to add support or manage the process of adding value.

For many people in the IT community, content management simply means WEB content. The key concept in Web content management is the creation of value through a reduction in "time to web." In practice, this concept translates into more dynamic web delivery systems built on the back of a relational database tied to a template-driven workflow process that allows fewer people to create and deliver more web content. A database-driven approach to web content management opens up new possibilities within an organization to share content across units and to share in the costs of creating and maintaining digital content. Some writers on content management have chosen to focus almost exclusively on protecting the asset value of digital objects, without regard to the purposes to which the objects may be put. From an asset management perspective, the organization of digital objects in well structured and well-documented databases is the most critical activity.

The digital preservation community in libraries has tended to emphasize asset management as a key value. The present movement to specify preservation metadata requirements within the construct of the Open Archival Information System reference model is the most dramatic example of efforts define content management in terms of the archival repository.

Knowledge management has traditionally suffered from the hubris of modernism: the belief that we can discover ultimate truths and organize the world according to rational principles using clever code. The idea was that we should capture and organize bits of "knowledge" in central databases. The people involved were relevant only as donors to the common ontology or as empty vessels into which knowledge could be poured. Therefore, postmodern KM can't be about management at all, because management implies external control of some definable resource. Its goal is simpler yet deeper: leveraging people. Postmodern KM operates within and on the basis of existing behavior patterns, mining conversation streams and relationships automatically to incorporate structure and context into the information human users already manipulate. It fosters human intelligence and interaction rather than trying to replace them.

This vision of content management suggests that librarians must reconcile the tensions between the structured and the dynamic, between "control zones" and empowerment, and between the Web that we access and the digital content that we provide. These tensions are not new or particularly interesting, except in so far as they help to extend the concept of "content" to encompass a much wider range of management responsibilities for digital content than we have heretofore chosen to consider appropriate.

Increasingly, libraries are being asked or expected to step up to the challenge of acquiring, organizing, and protecting digital content that they have neither created themselves (digitization) or licensed from publishers. Examples of new generations of digital content that are just beginning to flow into and through libraries include digital products produced and distributed or otherwise published by faculty, the output of research collaboratives, graduate student theses, the electronic records or the university's administrative offices, courseware content, and streaming audio and video resources generated from courses, conferences, and other campus activities.

In the Web environment, the business community has adopted the term "knowledge management" to refer to processes that use technology to leverage human expertise and know-how to create new value for the organization. In the higher education context, knowledge management constructs are most closely tied to scholarly communication processes. A critical issue for libraries is tension between possibly competing commitments to the process of scholarship as a discipline-based enterprise and the product of the process as an institutional imperative. Another critical aspect of considering "content management" to be an important but limited component of the scholarly communication process is the relationship of librarians and libraries to content creators, whether those creators are faculty/ authors or publishers/owners. Today's library is "all digital" in the sense that all services and content (digital and non-digital) are mediated via web gateways. Users begin and end their scholarly work with digital information, even if there is a considerable amount of paper in between.

Without some form of digital accessibility, library resources in any format are invisible and therefore unusable. Physical browsing for all but a vocal few has become a chimera. Libraries are already in the new business of digital product development by nature of their creation of digital resources, regardless of whether creation encompasses only digitization or extends to the development of specialized aggregations of digital resources. Libraries and archives cannot possibly assume full responsibility for preserving digital information, but rather must participate in a marketplace that itself has not come to terms with the idea of lost value. Librarians are critical players in the conception of the IT marketplace but have neither exclusive claim on content management concepts or a particularly strong share of the marketplace that is driving the development of content management tools.

Content management in the "all digital" environment within higher education can only function effectively at the corporate (i.e., university) level, even when the digital content itself is created and managed to support disciplinary or interdisciplinary scholarship.

Within the past four years, "new measures" has entered the lexicon of library performance and assessment literature. In the 1990s, escalating economic pressures and demands for accountability from governing boards, university administrators, and government agencies strongly encouraged ARL member libraries and many other libraries to find new ways to illustrate the contribution their collections and services provided to their constituencies.

Traditional, input measures (i.e., size of collections, budget, and staff) were not meeting institutional accountability needs. Although efforts were in place to measure some forms of output--e.g., activities such as circulation, interlibrary borrowing, and group presentations--these, too, did not always provide a good or complete indication of library performance and the cost effectiveness of their services.

Institutional Repositories in the Digital Age

The development of institutional repositories emerged as a new strategy that allows universities to apply serious, systematic leverage to accelerate changes taking place in scholarship and scholarly communication, both moving beyond their historic relatively passive role of supporting established publishers in modernizing scholarly publishing through the licensing of digital content, and also scaling up beyond ad-hoc alliances, partnerships, and support arrangements with a few select faculty pioneers exploring more transformative new uses of the digital medium.

Many technology trends and development efforts came together to make this strategy possible. Online storage costs have dropped significantly; repositories are now affordable. Standards like the open archives metadata harvesting protocol are now in place; some progress has also been made on the standards for the underlying metadata itself. The thinking about digital preservation over the past five years has advanced to the point where the needs are widely recognized and well defined, the technical approaches at least superficially mapped out, and the need for action is now clear. The development of free, publicly accessible journal article collections in disciplines such as high-energy physics has demonstrated ways in which the network can change scholarly communication by altering dissemination and access patterns; separately, the development of a series of extraordinary digital works had at least suggested the potential of creative authorship specifically for the digital medium to transform the presentation and transmission of scholarship.

A university-based institutional repository is a set of services that a university offers to the members of its community for the management and dissemination of digital materials created by the institution and its community members. It is most essentially an organizational commitment to the stewardship of these digital materials, including long-term preservation where appropriate, as well as organization and access or distribution. While operational responsibility for these services may reasonably be situated in different organizational units at different universities, an effective institutional repository of necessity represents a collaboration among librarians, information technologists, archives and records mangers, faculty, and university administrators and policymakers. At any given point in time, an institutional repository will be supported by a set of information technologies, but a key part of the services that comprise an institutional repository is the management of technological changes, and the migration of digital content from one set of technologies to the next as part of the organizational commitment to providing repository services.

An institutional repository is not simply a fixed set of software and hardware. While early implementers of institutional repositories have chosen different paths to begin populating their repositories and to build campus community acceptance, support, and participation, that a mature and fully realized institutional repository will contain the intellectual works of faculty and students—both research and teaching materials—and also documentation of the activities of the institution itself in the form of records of events and performance and of the ongoing intellectual life of the institution. It will also house experimental and observational data captured by members of the institution that support their scholarly activities.

At the most basic and fundamental level, an institutional repository is a recognition that the intellectual life and scholarship of our universities will increasingly be represented, documented, and shared in digital form, and that a primary responsibility of our universities is to exercise stewardship over these riches: both to make them available and to preserve them. An institutional repository is the means by which our universities will address this responsibility both to the members of their communities and to the public. It is a new channel for structuring the university's contribution to the broader world, and as such invites policy and cultural reassessment of this relationship.

Scholarship and scholarly communication are changing. These changes start with risky and bold acts of individual creativity. They will extend slowly to cultural changes at the disciplinary level and ultimately to new interdisciplinary standards that are expressed in the decisions of institutional tenure and promotion practices. Institutions of higher education have overlooked an opportunity to support our most innovative and creative faculty for at least a decade now, to the detriment of both the faculty members and the institutions themselves.

These faculty have been exploring ways in which works of authorship in the new digital medium can enhance teaching and learning and the communication of scholarship; such innovations are essential to keeping scholarship vital and effective, and they must not only be supported but nurtured. Indeed nurturing these innovations reaches to the core mission of our universities, and to the core values of our universities. A much broader and generally more conservative group of faculty have exploited the Net as a vehicle for sharing their ideas worldwide, whether these ideas are expressed in relatively familiar forms such as digital versions of traditional journal articles or (less commonly) in entirely new forms that begin to map out the future evolution of, for example, the scholarly monograph in the digital medium. This embrace of new dissemination opportunities is also important for what it says about the roles of scholars and universities in society and in a global environment.

Over the past few years, this has ceased to be a reasonable activity for most amateurs; software complexity, security risks, backup requirements, and other problems have generally relegated effective operation of Web sites to professionals who can exploit economies of scale, and who can begin each day with a review of recently issued security patches.

Institutional repositories can address both the near-term questions about continuity of access by providing an environment in which such new works of scholarship can be managed and disseminated—including such basic things as professionally managed systems and systematic backup procedures—and also the longer-term questions about preservation by creating an institutional commitment to such preservation. The revolution in scholarly communications is not limited to the development of new genres of scholarly works that are enabled by the digital medium; even traditional forms such as journal articles now frequently include supplementary datasets and analysis tools. Scholarship has become data intensive; it is supported and documented by data and tools that complement interpretive works of authorship.

Most scientific journals are now accepting what they characterize as "supplementary" materials as part of the publication of traditional journal articles, but it is much less clear what commitments these journals are making to actually integrating these supplementary materials into the permanent record of scholarship in the same way that they maintain the journal articles themselves as a part of that record. Journals will move too slowly and too unevenly to manage these resources, and disciplinary data repositories cannot be comprehensive. Institutional repositories can maintain data in addition to authored scholarly works. In this sense, the institutional repository is a complement and a supplement, rather than a substitute, for traditional scholarly publication venues. Institutional repositories also have roles beyond disseminating and managing the works of individual scholars that are part of the dialog of scholarly communications.

Institutional repositories are a place where they can put much of the material that research libraries identify as worth collecting. Finally, at least a few institutions themselves are changing their culture and are making commitments to globally disseminate extensive teaching and learning materials through the Net or, at a less systematic but still important level, to digitally capture and preserve the many of the events of campus life--symposia, performances, lectures.

Institutional repositories offer a framework for organized stewardship and accessibility of these materials. To summarize, institutional repositories can facilitate greatly enhanced access to traditional scholarly content by empowering faculty to effectively use the new dissemination capabilities offered by the network. This is also occurring on a disciplinary basis through the development of e-print and preprint servers, at least in some disciplines. In cases where the disciplinary practice is ready, institutional repositories can feed disciplinary repositories directly. In cases where the disciplinary culture is more conservative, where scholarly societies or key journals choose to hold back change, institutional repositories can help individual faculty take the lead in initiating shifts in disciplinary practice. Institutional repositories can encourage the exploration and adoption of new forms of scholarly communication that exploit the digital medium in fundamental ways.

Institutional repositories can support new practices of scholarship that emphasize data as an integral part of the record and discourse of scholarship. They can structure and make effective otherwise diffuse efforts to capture and disseminate learning and teaching materials, symposia and performances, and related documentation of the intellectual life of universities. Institutional repositories will succeed precisely because they are responsive to the needs of campus communities, and advance the interests of campus communities and of scholarship broadly. To the extent that they try to enforce behavioral or cultural changes--and particularly controversial ones--within the campus community they will and should fail. The theme is accepting responsibility, not exerting new levels of control. This is not to say that policies mandating the deposit of materials that are broadly recognized as part of the institutional record are inappropriate. But institutions should move very conservatively down this path.

Institutional repositories may legitimately serve as infrastructure to advance some of these interests—for example, groups might construct a peer-review process that certifies selected works that are accessible in various institutional repositories and even develop overlay systems that span a complex of institutional repositories and create a "virtual" journal. Such an effort would have to be extra-institutional and cross-institutional to have much scholarly credibility, for the same reason that university presses aren't simply publishing outlets for the faculty at their parent institutions, and the editorial boards of institutionally hosted journals are drawn from beyond the host institution.

Its extra-institutional nature should help to clarify that it shouldn't be confused with the development of individual institutional repositories. But this is not, to my mind, the primary point of institutional repositories. Indeed, it dramatically underestimates the importance of institutional repositories to characterize them as instruments for restructuring the current economics of scholarly publishing rather than as vehicles to advance, support, and legitimize a much broader spectrum of new scholarly communications.

But recognize that the institutional repository isn't a journal, or a collection of journals, and should not be managed like one. That's not the point or the purpose of an institutional repository. Institutional repositories are not a challenge or alternative to disciplinary repositories; rather, they complement them, just as they can complement existing venues of scholarly publication. The Open Archive Initiative Metadata Harvesting Protocol gives the tools for an institutional repository to act as an entry point for redistributing works to systems of disciplinary repositories. It is desirable to make this as simple as possible, and to insulate faculty from having to deal with the details of a constantly evolving multiplicity of disciplinary services. Better to present the faculty with a simple and stable submission interface to the institutional repository.

In this sense institutional repositories can be an infrastructure upon which disciplinary services and repositories can build. In the near future, many campus communities may expect and demand that such services be made available rapidly; creating institutional repositories may also become fashionable in some administrative circles. It's vital that institutions recognize institutional repositories as a serious and long-lasting commitment to the campus community (and to the scholarly world, and the public at large) that should not be made lightly. In establishing institutional repositories, institutions are both accepting risks and making promises; they are creating new expectations. In a budget crunch, the institutional repository may be one of the last things that can be cut, given the way that digital preservation demands steady and consistent attention and hence funding. Faculty who choose to rely on institutional repositories to disseminate and preserve their work are placing a great deal of trust in their institution and in the integrity, wisdom, and competence of the people who manage it.

An institutional repository can fail over time for many reasons: policy (for example, the institution chooses to stop funding it), management failure or incompetence, or technical problems. Any of these failures can result in the disruption of access, or worse, total and permanent loss of material stored in the institutional repository. As we think about institutional repositories today, there is much less redundancy than we have had in our systems of print publication and libraries, so any single institutional failure can cause more damage.

Institutional repositories make promises about stewardship and preservation. These promises are necessarily qualified. Institutions will make choices based on a balance of campus community demand and local assessments about technical feasibility, which will result in lists of file formats that they will commit to preserve in accessible forms (presumably through format migration); in other cases, they may preserve the bits that make up a file, but will offer no guarantees that these bits can be interpreted in the future without the development of specialized programs to read them.

These choices can then be collected into broader community consensus within the higher education and research community as a form of bottom-up standards development that benefits from active work in curation and ongoing faculty involvement. The ability to make persistent reference to materials in institutional repositories will clearly be critical as these materials will form an important part of the scholarly dialogue and record. This will have to include provisions to deal with issues like versioning.

Higher education and the library community have not been sufficiently active in this area, largely ceding the field to commercial interests and traditional publisher agendas. The deployment of institutional repositories will drive pragmatic solutions in this area. The management of rights for digital materials will be essential. The whole point of institutional repositories is to facilitate access, reuse, and stewardship (which may itself involve reformatting) of content, and we need methods of recording and documenting the rights and permissions associated with works that facilitate these goals of the research and education community.

Part of this is a technical problem involving metadata structures; the other part is building consensus around a relatively small number of sets of terms and conditions that can cover the majority of the materials in practice. University institutional repositories have some very interesting and unexplored extensions to what we might think of as community or public repositories; this may in fact be another case of a concept developed within higher education moving more broadly into our society. Public libraries might join forces with local government, local historical societies, local museums and archives, and members of their local communities to establish community repositories. Public broadcasting might also have a role here.

It is clear that the institutional repository is a very powerful idea that can serve as an engine of change for our institutions of higher education, and more broadly for the scholarly enterprises that they support. If properly developed, it advances a surprising number of goals, and addresses an impressive range of needs. Some of the results seem clear, though there are also likely to be any number of unexpected consequences.

Global Resource Programme

A globally oriented program is by definition ambitious, especially when it is focused on information and its dissemination. Despite an increasing reliance on electronic information, print book and journal publishing worldwide continues to expand dramatically. Accordingly, the strategies adopted to tackle the goals of the Global Resources Program are multiple and varied:

— providing seed money for an initial set of six diverse regional projects (on Africa, Germany, Japan, Latin America, South Asia, Southeast Asia);

— gathering information into a clearinghouse on ARL libraries' linkages with institutions abroad;

— building bridges to scholars who use international materials, and to the scholarly associations to which they belong, in order to develop a better understanding of the research resources they need and how libraries can facilitate access to them; and

— helping to create new models for recruiting and training future area specialists who have strong subject knowledge, initiative, and the right skill set.

The systematic identification of collection strengths of North American libraries will be another important step toward the Program's full implementation, and the launching of other area- and subject-specific projects as they are designed is an ongoing objective. The overarching strategy for the Program is to scale up from the projects by selecting, from among the models they are testing, the elements that will contribute to a comprehensive, cooperative, distributed program of access to international resources, regardless of their format or location.

The eventual goal is to move beyond a set of discrete, area-specific projects to an interconnected, globally oriented program in which "lead institutions" provide users throughout North America with both physical collections and access points to diverse resources published in or relating to a given world area. Another long-term goal of the Program–essential for making the vision into reality–is to develop a system of financial incentives that will benefit a broad range of institutions, as well as sustain the Program well into the future.

The six regional projects currently underway offer an impressive array of approaches to addressing some of the most urgent information needs of scholars researching individual world regions. These approaches range from the creation of a web-based union list of sub-Saharan African newspapers to an international document delivery service between North American and German research libraries, from a Latin American table-of-contents database with direct, user-initiated article requesting capability to the digitization, in India, of South Asian reference works and periodicals, and the creation of an image database of Thai journal literature.

The full impact of the Program, however, extends beyond this set of projects. For example, awareness of the factors that negatively affect the ability of libraries to provide the materials that users need, that litany of pressures with which librarians are all too familiar, has been heightened among faculty and within scholarly associations.

Librarians with responsibility for one region of the world are finding common ground with those whose principal focus is another. The Overseas Offices of the Library of Congress are key participants in many of the projects and are uniquely prepared to address directly the key issue of access through the expansion of the services they provide in Cairo, Islamabad, Nairobi, New Delhi, Jakarta, and Rio de Janeiro. The Center for Research Libraries has launched the International Coalition on Newspapers (ICON), an ambitious and much-needed effort to identify, preserve, and make accessible as wide a range of foreign newspapers as possible. Collaboration with institutions outside North America, both formal and informal, has been stimulated by the identification of reciprocal relationships for collection development, interlibrary lending and borrowing, and document delivery.

In short, the AAU/ARL Global Resources Program has been a catalyst in stimulating interest and action to strengthen international library resources. This new Department of Education program has stimulated the development of projects that bring together librarians and faculty in creative joint undertakings whose goal is exactly consistent with that of the Global Resources Program: to expand access to international resources through the use of new technologies. The initial focus of the Global Resources Program was on cooperative collection development. This is arguably the necessary first step toward a distributed network of interdependent collections, and yet the Program has since shifted focus within some of the regional projects to concentrate on document delivery. At first glance, this would seem to be a major change; however, they are part and parcel of the same theme.

For years, at meetings of collection development librarians and other conferences, inadequate document delivery and interlibrary loan capability has been pinpointed as a major obstacle to successful cooperative collection development, whether it be on a relatively small, regional scale, or at the national or North American level. Certainly, to gain faculty acceptance of a distributed collection it is critical to guarantee rapid access to needed materials that are not held locally. And since engaging faculty as supporters of the premises of the Global Resources Program and illustrating for them the potential of structured interdependence are among the Program's original goals, a focus on rapid delivery of the resources they need seems logical. It is important to demonstrate to faculty that the Program and other cooperative collection-building structures will expand access, not decrease it. They are gaining, not losing.

An acute awareness of the importance of building collections cooperatively still characterizes the Program, although several current efforts focus on disseminating information about what is held where rather than on orchestrating firm cooperative agreements. In order to distribute responsibility for collecting, it is important to know who has what, a need that has promoted the development of projects to establish union lists of journals and newspapers, or periodical indexes, for example.

Nevertheless, the Program will only achieve its goals and realize its full potential when participants take the difficult steps of redefining collecting policies to focus on local strengths and reallocating resources accordingly, while simultaneously moving toward a more inter-reliant network of research libraries. An emphasis on cataloging and preservation is inherent in all of the activities of the Global Resources Program.

The American Council of Learned Societies (ACLS) featured a special session on the AAU/ARL Global Resources Program. Executive directors of area studies scholarly associations and delegates to each organization, along with other interested participants, responded to a presentation about the Program and expressed their views on its future development. The environment, human rights, migration, popular culture, ethnic studies–these are examples of areas of scholarship with a significant international dimension, in which research requires access to a multiplicity of resources that may be ephemeral, difficult to locate, poorly preserved, and undercollected in North America.

A Global Resources project that takes a topical rather than a regional approach would encourage links among library collections that are not based on the traditional area studies model, that span national boundaries, and yet still address the core challenges of the Reed-Scott book and the studies that preceded it. There are many nonaffiliated projects underway that bear a relationship to the Global Resources Program. Similarly, any distributed collection development structure will take advantage of existing consortia and work in progress. Links among libraries and scholars, and the active involvement of faculty in helping to imagine and anticipate future needs, will be critical to the Program's continued success. Just as important will be a practical vision of a new interdependence among libraries.

Although it has focused on projects that expand access to international research materials, in many cases vernacular resources, the lessons of the Global Resources Program are not limited to the acquisition and distribution of foreign materials. The Program is also raising issues with broader, more general implications. In this way, the Program contains a microcosm of the newest challenges and concerns for research libraries, issues that are not peculiar to area studies.

These include, of course, the creation of cooperative structures for collection development and document delivery services that are rapid, efficient, and international. The Program is built on the need to discover ways to stretch budgets so that libraries collectively can offer access to more than they currently do individually. The Program has stimulated new thinking about service to users, especially those who are remote but rely on specialized collections held in our libraries, and has shifted focus to a user-based model of distributed collection development and away from an emphasis on amassing collections locally.

Participation in large-scale collaborative endeavors requires a significant commitment of staff time and energy, and this in turn requires a re-thinking of the collection development librarian's job description. The success of the Global Resources regional projects would have been impossible without the ideas, initiative, and action of a number of area studies librarians. Such energy and creativity will continue to be prerequisites for achieving the goals of multi-institutional collaboration, whether international or not.

To achieve the goals of the Global Resources Program, and any program based on cooperative collection development, we must view "collections" as a wide array of resources, some held locally but many found elsewhere–even outside North America–and not necessarily in libraries, or in print form. We do not need to own the physical object to consider it part of our "collection." Technology makes it feasible to consider remote collections to be local resources as long as it is reasonably straightforward for users to gain access to these materials. It is apparent that university administrators, faculty, library administrators, and collection development librarians need a new vision for their local library collection, and new ways of measuring its strength as part of a shared North American collection.

The Global Resources Program forces a redefinition of "collections" if we are to meet the needs of current users of our libraries and anticipate those of future generations. Bringing about the change in perspective that is necessary for distributed collecting to succeed will require progress in several interconnected areas:

— an understanding on the part of faculty that it is in their long-term interest for their university's library to have an interdependent relationship with other institutions, so that someone, somewhere, is collecting the materials that they, and their colleagues within North America, need;

— the autonomy for collection development librarians to craft cooperative policies that share responsibility for collecting and commit their institutions to a particular set of areas, the will and authority to cancel journals that are widely held elsewhere in favor of more specialized acquisitions in their areas of collecting responsibility, and the political sensitivity to explain these decisions to library users in compelling and convincing terms;

— an acknowledgment of the critical role of document delivery and interlibrary loan in making distributed collections feasible, and a commitment to invest in the redesign of systems of access;

— the necessary determination and support for rapid cataloging of international materials, which will not only make these resources more accessible to users but will also provide bibliographers with important information on holdings that may influence their acquisitions decisions; and

— a firm commitment on the part of library and university administrators to a new vision of interdependent collections, acknowledgment of the benefits of the strategy, and adequate, long-term financial support to continue building and preserving the collections for which their institution has accepted responsibility.

The Latin Americanist Research Resources Project is experimenting with distributed collecting responsibilities through its "Distributed Resources" component, in which each participating institution commits to redirecting a minimum of either $3,000 or 7% of its monographic budget for Latin American materials towards an area of locally established collection strength. By implication, they will rely on other Project libraries for materials they will no longer be acquiring.

Participating bibliographers have confirmed that, through reallocation, they have been able to acquire items that enrich their local collections in areas of emphasis while also providing access to these materials for users anywhere. In the division of responsibilities among the participating libraries, based on local strengths and local choice, nearly all countries are represented. Thus, the Project is demonstrating broad coverage and balance.

This element of the Latin American project is a significant step towards strengthening North American collections of Latin American publications. The Project has succeeded in large part because it is allowing individual institutions to emphasize local strengths (thereby eliminating the tension between local program needs and national-level commitments) and because it is focusing on materials that do not generally receive high use.

Role of Bibliographer

An expansion and redefinition of the role of the collection development librarian, or bibliographer, has been underway for some time as the job has required more contact with the public and advanced technological skills. In the Global Resources arena, bibliographers have the opportunity to serve as intellectual leaders in crafting new models for access and new structures for cooperative collection building.

Rather than being marginalized, bibliographers have become even more central to the success of complex international projects. They play a visible role in fund raising, including drafting proposals and administering grants. Designing area- and subject-specific projects to address the goals of the Global Resources Program also brings bibliographers together with faculty to think strategically about the variety of future scholarly resource needs. Working with a much broader definition of "collections" than ever before, bibliographers are collaborating with colleagues at other libraries and in other countries to ensure that research libraries are together providing access to the widest range of resources possible. The creation and maintenance of web pages with detailed collection descriptions and links to many other carefully selected and vetted resources is increasingly part of the bibliographer's job.

As the Global Resources Program moves toward the identification of a network of lead institutions, bibliographers' knowledge and experience will become even more important. The Global Resources Program has opened positive new lines of communication within individual libraries as well. The implementation of the regional projects, particularly those with significant document delivery components, encourages a closer relationship between collection development librarians and interlibrary loan staff. ILL librarians are in an excellent position to help identify where there may be gaps in local collections coverage. They are also key players in determining the nature and usefulness of new document delivery mechanisms that are at the core of enhanced access. Additional intra-institutional collaboration will flourish as cross-regional projects are developed, and subject and area studies bibliographers begin to work together to implement and publicize the projects and to evaluate their effectiveness.

Role of Library in Education

Today, the library and education community faces a series of fast-paced copyright and other intellectual property issues. The issues addressed in The

Digital Millennium Copyright Act (DMCA), PL 105-304, that are of utmost importance for libraries and the education community are: access to and fair use of copyrighted works issued in encrypted form; the liability of online service providers for infringing behavior by a user of the service; the proper uses of copyrighted works in distance education programs; and the use of digital technology to preserve library and archival materials. In the case of all but the last of these issues, major questions remain about application of the new statutory provisions in educational settings.

Many electronic works are distributed in encrypted form and the DMCA established stiff penalties for anyone accessing a copyrighted work protected by "technological protective measures" (TPMs) without the consent of the copyright owner. The law also bans equipment or services whose primary purpose is for use in defeating technology that limits access to a copyrighted work. Taking effect in two years, the new anti-circumvention and access rules will encourage publishers to distribute digital works online; by CD, CD-ROM, or DVD; or in other formats in either encrypted or protected form by providing greater assurance to copyright owners that those who abuse access barriers will be subject to severe penalties.

Legislators and content owners both hope that the severity of the penalties will discourage widespread piracy. The new law does provide for certain exemptions to the anti-circumvention penalties. However, the one exemption included for nonprofit libraries, archives, and educational institutions is solely for the purpose of determining whether to acquire the work or not. A central question not answered in the new law is how a library, archive, or school may obtain the means to circumvent, since the selling of such equipment is prohibited in the law. It also remains unanswered in law whether any fair use can be made of a work protected by TPMs, absent a future rulemaking.

The TPM and anti-circumvention provisions of the DMCA will most likely ensure that more works come with licenses and with an obligation to pay for each use or access. This change could hit libraries particularly hard because it challenges the way in which libraries function as archives of our published history. Libraries must be prepared to review contracts for the acquisition of digital works more closely than ever before and bargain for full access rights. Libraries must be alert to limitations on access and use of works that are licensed. In short, they must be prepared:

— to bargain for the right to a hard copy;
— to realize that digital access means limited access, unless you own a copy of the work;
— to pay for the cost of access; and
— to understand that equipment that decrypts works may be illegal to acquire or use.

The library and education community needs to organize itself and understand how it is using digital works today, how it is likely to use them in the near term, and what the economic and social impacts of the new regime will be. As with many agency rulemaking proceedings, active participation in the initial case will be very important, because procedures will be established for managing the record and early precedents will carry forward for years to come.

All issues raised by the legislation will be novel for the Librarian in the first rulemaking case. The central focus of these proceedings will be to determine (1) the "adverse affects" of the rules upon library and educational users, the significance of licensing alternatives ("pay per use"), and, ultimately, (3) the particular classes of works that should be exempted from the scheme. Since the burdens of obtaining relief fall on the proponents, library and educational institutions will have to make a persuasive record that justifies appropriate relief. It will be a challenge, but one that will help shape the future role of libraries in the digital age.

ONLINE SERVICE PROVIDERS

Creation of a new limitation on liability for online service providers (OSPs) was perhaps the most complex task of the DMCA legislators. The new rules establish certain procedures and conditions that grant OSPs, including libraries and educational institutions, an exclusion from monetary liability for copyright infringement by a user of the service.

Balancing a myriad of interests and fashioning legislation for technology that is arcane and evolving are no simple tasks. Thus, the OSP limitation of liability represents a very important contribution of the DMCA to copyright law. Also, the process used to develop this statutory limitation-congressional committee supervised negotiations-may also serve as a model for preparing legislation on other issues that require discreet balancing of concerns of contentious but politically powerful interests.

For libraries, the initial issue is whether to assert status as a "service provider" and register with the Copyright Office. This is not an easy question to resolve. Certainly, the definition of "service provider" is broad enough to encompass many of the libraries' online activities. However, the legislation's complex rules will require very careful compliance practices, including the use of sophisticated software and systems and the development of notification and termination policies.

Although monitoring of sites is not required, once a service provider receives notice of an infringement, actions such as "notice and take down" or "counter notice and put back" must also be taken. In weighing the benefits of coming within the statutory limitation terms, libraries should appreciate the reduction of potential damages for innocent, but contributory, infringements.

For libraries that are part of larger, educational institutions, exposure to money damages from cyberspace violations by patrons, students, and faculty-as well as third parties-must be deemed a real threat. It should be understood that online copyright infringements are a "hot button" issue for publishers. It should also be anticipated that a test case or two would be brought in the near future.

Further, it must be underscored that even though monetary damages may be avoided, all service providers are subject to all other copyright legal remedies, including injunctive relief. It is not known whether content owners will use the website list of service providers maintained by the Copyright Office as the "go-to group" that receives all the infringement notifications.

Since each OSP is an online ramp to the cyber-violations, whether more than a limited group will receive infringement notices is not yet known. If many owners adopt an approach that blankets the potential universe of OSPs, then those identified OSPs could be flooded with requests for take down. Such a situation could render operations at small- to medium-sized libraries into an immediate state of chaos. Then, too, how much technological support in terms of advanced software and personnel is required to satisfy the legal strictures is unknown.

Although DMCA did not include explicit expanded protection for educational activities involving the Internet, the creation of a congressionally-mandated study of the subject by the Copyright Office is important and deserves immediate and active attention by the library community. From its inception, copyright law has balanced owners' rights with users' rights.

Despite copyright owners proclaiming the need for fair return on their creative works and the importance of securing economic rewards in a global economy, principles like fair use and exemptions for classroom teaching and library preservation survive. Distance education is the latest major battleground in the effort to balance educational interests in a federal law that increasingly emphasizes the commerce of copyright.

Extending the face-to-face and transmission exemptions to Internet education will not happen without aggressive and active participation by the library and educational communities. In the initial hearings held in January 1999 by the Copyright Office, owners have already asserted there is no need to change the law. They argue licensing and other permissive approaches to incorporating works into course content will suffice.

Moreover, they claim to be the primary producers of course texts and thus any exemption hurts their markets and damages them competitively. Unless educators are energized by the opportunity to create a new and important expansion of principles embodied in the current classroom and closed circuit transmission limitations, no change will occur. The central points to be made include the following:

— Obtaining clearances for spontaneous use of copyrighted works in online courses is virtually impossible.

— Identifying copyright owners of certain works, like photographs, is so daunting as to make it a task not worth pursuing.

— Licensing is not an acceptable alternative because, when offered, the price is often far too high to justify the use.

— Unless the copyright law is modified, the playing field for parties negotiating licenses is out of balance. Libraries and educators will find they have less leverage to negotiate fair terms for digital use within their communities.

— The transaction costs associated with clearances and licensing requirements threatens to perpetuate or exacerbate the traditional disparities between "have" and "have-not" communities that distance education and the Internet could otherwise help to mitigate.

But if the library and educational communities are unified in their desire to update copyright law exemptions so that online education is treated on a par with classroom learning, then there is a chance that reform can be accomplished in the near future. With congressional and presidential elections coming in the next year, education will be a very important electoral issue and distance education should be a central topic in all races.

The DMCA provides the most significant updating of library and archival preservation rules since procedures to cope with photocopy machines were established in 1976. The changes permit preservation and storage of a copyrighted work in a digitized format and describe a mechanism for handling preservation of works originating in outmoded formats.

The updating of Section 108 to enable libraries to work in digital preservation was surprisingly hard fought. Even with the endorsement of the authors of the White Paper3, it required extensive negotiations in the House and Senate. The content community is very nervous about allowing digital copies of works to exist anywhere without explicit authorization. In the end, this update is a modest, yet important, change for libraries that will make their task of maintaining collections easier in a technologically advanced environment.

Moving in tandem to the DMCA legislation was another copyright reform bill-term extension. For the past three years, there was a drumbeat by certain copyright proprietors, especially those owning movies and musical works, for extension of the copyright term. Although the legislation had strong support, it was held hostage to a debate over the demand of certain groups-notably restaurants, bars, and religious broadcasters-to be entitled to relief from the high charges for use of music on their premises and in their broadcasts.

For the library community, concern about extension of the copyright term was expressed early in the debate. It was posited that the overwhelming majority of works are neither commercially exploited nor readily accessible in the marketplace after several decades, much less 75 years. Yet, for researchers and scholars, access to such works from the library's collection are important and no limitation should be made on such noncommercial uses. Moreover, with regard to already-existing works, no "extra incentive" is needed to spur creativity.

In an effort to resolve the concerns expressed by library interests, an understanding was reached regarding the ability of nonprofit libraries, archives, and educational institutions to exploit older works during what constitutes the extended copyright term. Suggesting that libraries should be able to exploit works that have lain fallow for decades should not strike one as an explosive proposal.

The Copyright Office, through the vehicle of regulations, will help determine the reach of the new exception that permits libraries to continue to freely use old works in the last 20 years of the extended term, just like public domain works. This is a vital concern for the library and education community, because maintenance of the public domain assures the role of libraries as archivists of history, not licensees of commerce.

Participation in the regulatory process that will define the terms and establish rules is a relatively efficient way to get one's key points across. Just as was noted with regard to the anti-circumvention rulemaking and the distance education study, active participation in these administrative proceedings assures that the library and education community's voice will be heard at the opportune time and its views not ignored.

References

Conway, Paul, *Preservation in the Digital World,* Washington, D.C.: Commission on Preservation and Access, 1996.

Fox, E. A., *Source Book on Digital Libraries*, Virginia Tech, Department of Computer Science, TR 93-35, 1993.

Hulser, Richard P., Digital Library: Content Preservation in a Digital World, *DESIDOC Bulletin of Information Technology*, 17, 1997.

Gopal Krishan, *Digital Libraries in Electronic Information Era,* Authorspress, New Delhi, 2000.

Rajashekar, T.B., *Digital Libraries, Information Studies,* October, 1995.

2

Digital Library Classification

Libraries and archives play a critical role in organizing, preserving, and providing access to the cultural and historical resources of society. In the relatively stable world of printed, hand-written, and mechanically reproduced information, repositories managed to preserve a rich array of scholarly communications, documentary evidence, and useful information for specialized scholars and for the general public.

The introduction of digital technologies into the processes of production, distribution, and storage of information challenges the capacity of libraries, archives, museums, and other cultural institutions to carry out their responsibilities for preservation. This problem has been the focus of numerous reports designed to raise awareness of digital preservation issues and to propose general strategies for addressing them.

The general outline of digital preservation challenges is well established. Digital materials are especially vulnerable to loss and destruction because they are stored on fragile magnetic and optical media that deteriorate rapidly and that can fail suddenly from exposure to heat, humidity, airborne contaminants, or faulty reading and writing devices. Even if the media are preserved intact, digital materials become unreadable if the playback devices necessary to retrieve information from the media become obsolete or if the software that translates digital information from machine- to human-readable form is no longer available.

Libraries, archives, and other repositories that traditionally have assumed responsibility for preserving information face technical, legal, and organizational challenges in responding to the new demands of digital preservation. Repositories need access to technical resources — both information systems that support digital preservation and the technical expertise to use these technologies effectively.

Institutions also face legal obstacles in fulfilling their mandates to preserve valuable information when copyright or licensing agreements prohibit duplication or local storage of digital information. Institutions can take action on their own, but there is a strong consensus that coordinated strategies and shared resources are essential to achieving broader solutions to digital preservation and enhancing the success of local efforts.

Digital Archiving by Research Libraries Group (RLG)

In early 1998, the Research Libraries Group (RLG) funded a study of digital archiving needs and requirements in RLG member institutions. RLG is an international consortium of close to 160 members, including universities and colleges, national libraries, archives, historical societies, museums, independent research collections, and public libraries.

The purpose of the study was twofold: (1) to gather baseline data on the nature and extent of digital preservation problems in member institutions and the status of their digital preservation programs, and (2) to identify needs and requirements of member institutions in meeting their responsibilities for preserving digital information.

Methodology

The methodology used for the research was a combination of a survey distributed to all RLG member institutions and follow-up interviews with one or more administrators at 15 institutions. This combination of data collection methods was used to gather and analyze data on the nature and types of digital collections in member institutions, the policies and programs in place for digital preservation, digital preservation needs and requirements, and future plans for developing digital preservation programs. The interviews with administrators provided additional qualitative insights into the problems they face and their perceptions of various strategies for digital preservation.

Libraries, archives, museums, and other repositories acquire digital materials through several different channels, which include purchasing digital information from publishers or distributors, legal deposit or transfer, donations, and licensing access to online databases. Many institutions also are creating digital information through programs or projects that convert print, photographic, and manuscript material to digital form. Libraries and archives do not necessarily assume responsibility for long-term preservation of all these materials. Some print-to-digital conversion projects exist primarily to improve access to materials, and some institutions consider the originals or a microfilm copy to be the preferable version for long-term preservation. Online databases that are updated regularly may only be useful in their current version. Licensing agreements and copyright restrictions governing online digital resources and hand-held digital products might prohibit institutions from maintaining copies of digital works for preservation purposes.

For the purposes of the project, the survey focused on digital materials for which an RLG member institution assumes long-term preservation responsibility. The materials within the scope of the study include: (1) information created originally in digital form and acquired by a repository through purchase, transfer, or legal deposit; and (2) digital materials that are created when repositories convert print, photographic, and manuscript materials to digital form, provided that the institutions considered it their responsibility to preserve the information.

The term "digital preservation" refers to both preservation of materials that are created originally in digital form and never exist in print or analog form (also called "born-digital" and "electronic records") and the use of imaging and recording technologies to create digital surrogates of analog materials for access and preservation purposes. While this broad use of the term digital preservation can cause confusion, data on both aspects of digital preservation were analyzed. Digital materials, regardless of whether they are created initially in digital form or converted to digital form, are threatened by technology obsolescence and physical deterioration.

The survey was designed to gain an understanding of member institutions' current holdings of digital materials and to gather data on present and near future needs related to preservation of digital materials. The survey questions were grouped into the categories of:

— digital materials policy,

— digital holdings,

— storage methods and formats,

— digital knowledge/training, and

— future needs for services and training.

A survey was distributed in late April 1998 to the designated member representative in all 158 RLG member institutions. E-mail was the primary distribution method, but copies were distributed in print form via fax or express mail to institutions without e-mail access.

A test survey consisting of the scope, definitions of terminology, and 25 questions had been distributed by RLG in March 1998. Based on feedback from eight individuals, the survey was revised and simplified to its final form of 18 questions, a statement about the scope of the survey, and definition of six key terms used in the survey. The survey was designed for ease of completion on a computer screen and reply via e-mail, with provision for returning the survey via fax or postal service. Although a May 6 deadline was specified, all surveys received by the end of August 1998 were included in the data analysis.

A total of 54 completed surveys were received between April and August 1998 for a response rate of 34%.

Interviews were conducted to gain additional insights that would supplement the quantitative data from the surveys. The interview script consisted of six open-ended questions designed to encourage spontaneous and reflective responses. Three questions focused on the current situation within the institution regarding:

— the impact of digital preservation demands on the interviewees and their institutions,

— experience(s) with outsourcing services, and

— availability and effectiveness of technical support within the institution.

One question asked administrators for feedback on the major issues that their institution will be facing with digital materials during the next four years; another focused on their insights regarding consortial arrangements for preservation of digital materials. The final question was a wish-list scenario, situating respondents "outside the box" to voice concerns about a particular problem regarding preservation of digital materials that they would like to see "magically solved."

RLG provided a list of 25 member representatives who were targeted for interviews. An e-mail message was sent to all, requesting their participation in individual thirty-minute interviews. Representatives of 16 institutions responded, and it was possible to schedule interviews with 14 of these. A test interview was also done, and as it was determined that no changes to the script were necessary, this was included in the final compilation for a total of 15 interviews. All interviews were conducted over the telephone, with the interviewer typing responses immediately into Microsoft Word. Fourteen interviews were completed between April 21 and May 7; the final interview was completed on June 15. Three interviews were conducted as conferences with two or three representatives from different departments in one institution. Interview length was determined by the interviewee, and ranged from approximately 15 minutes to one-and-a-half hours, with the average being about 25-30 minutes. At the end of each interview the interviewee was asked to return the institution's survey so that complete data would be represented in the analysis. The non-respondents in this interviewed group were the only institutions to which follow-up appeals were made to return surveys. Of the 15 institutions that provided interviews, 12 institutions are represented in the survey data.

The survey data was compiled in a database in Microsoft Access. This database was then exported into a Microsoft Excel spreadsheet, and all statistical comparisons were made using formulas in a series of spreadsheets. Owing to their qualitative nature and unstructured format, the interviews were more challenging to record. While complete interview responses were available in their entirety, for ease in comparison the major components of each response were distilled into abbreviated phrases (maximum 75 characters), coded by institutional identifier and question number, and arranged in an Excel spreadsheet. This produced a brief document that could be quickly scanned, with the responses arranged in columns by question number, and in rows by institution. Based on analysis, 10 major themes were then identified, and a second spreadsheet was created in which the coded, abbreviated phrases were matched with the themes they represented. This again produced a document in which responses could be easily scanned by theme, as well as by institution identifier and question number.

The data gathered and analyzed in the research permits drawing several conclusions about the current state of digital preservation in RLG member institutions and about their perceptions of needs and requirements for digital preservation. There are three aspects of the research that may limit broad generalizations from the results.

The sample was drawn from RLG member institutions to provide RLG with analysis of conditions and needs of its member institutions. It has the advantage of gathering data from a variety of institutions with digital preservation responsibilities, including research libraries, archives and historical societies, special research collections, and museums. However, there may be systematic differences between RLG member institutions and similar institutions that are not RLG members; and consequently, findings from the survey may not apply to all libraries, archives, museums, and special collections with digital preservation responsibilities.

Although 34% is a reasonably good response rate for a survey of this sort, there are two potential problems with the number of respondents and the nature of the response rate. The total of 54 responses allows detecting patterns and drawing certain conclusions across the entire data set. However, when one breaks the data into smaller categories by type of institution, location, whether or not the institutions have holdings or policies, etc., the small number of cases in some categories makes it difficult to draw statistically significant conclusions. Given this limitation, many of the findings are descriptive of the entire population, and trends within categories are suggested where the data supports such conclusions.

The potential bias in response is toward institutions with some digital materials in their holdings for which they assume preservation responsibility. Although there is no way of comparing the characteristics of non-respondents with institutions that responded, it is possible that institutions which consider digital preservation an important problem because they have digital materials in their holdings were more motivated to respond to the survey. This cautionary note is reinforced by anecdotal information gathered from respondents while they were completing the surveys and through informal feedback received after the surveys were completed. Several institutions reported difficulty completing the survey because there was no single individual or source of information for answering all of the questions on the survey instrument. Compiling all of this information and answering the questionnaire thoroughly required a significant amount of time on the part of member institutions, suggesting that a high level of motivation was necessary for member institutions to respond.

Digital preservation is a multi-faceted problem that is viewed differently by different institutions and different professionals. The broad umbrella of digital preservation includes preserving both materials created and acquired in digital form and digital files generated when institutions convert analog materials to digital form. The survey instrument took special measures to explain the scope of the survey and to define the technical terminology used. While acknowledging that there are different interpretations of the terminology used, it requested the respondents to refer to and use the definitions provided. Nevertheless, one cannot be certain that all respondents shared exactly the same concepts and terminology in all of their responses.

Findings

Digital Preservation Responsibilities

Digital preservation is not an isolated problem affecting only large libraries and archives. Two-thirds (36) of the institutions in the survey have some digital materials in their holdings for which the institution assumes preservation responsibility. In fact, the 30 research libraries, which tend to be larger than the 24 archives, museums, and special collections, are not quite as likely to hold digital materials as the other types of institutions. About two-thirds of the research libraries assume responsibility for preserving digital materials, whereas 71% of the other types of repositories hold digital materials. A higher percentage of institutions outside the US have digital preservation responsibilities — 83% as compared to 62% of the institutions in the US.

Most repositories with digital holdings both acquire material in digital form and create digital files through conversion. Two-thirds of the institutions with digital holdings both acquire and create digital materials. One-quarter of the institutions are responsible for preserving only information that they create through conversion. Two institutions acquire information in digital form, but do not create digital files through conversion. In the survey overall, almost half of the member institutions acquire digital materials and nearly two-thirds are involved in conversion activities. Through both acquisition and conversion activities, RLG member institutions are taking on responsibility for preserving unique digital materials that appear not be duplicated elsewhere. Twenty-eight institutions reported that irreplaceable information would be lost if the digital materials in their holdings are not adequately preserved for future use.

The digital holdings that member institutions are responsible for preserving vary in size, age, and the types of formats used for storage. Taken together, RLG member institutions that responded to the survey hold a minimum of 275,000 digital files and a total of at least 4.1 terabytes of information. These estimates are stated as minimum values because complete information on the quantity of digital materials was not available. Many institutions do not know how much digital material they hold and those that do use different measures to keep track of the quantity of digital materials in their holdings.

The survey asked institutions to report the number of digital files, the number of volumes (reels of tape, CDs, etc.), and the total storage volume (in MB, GB, etc.). Only 26 of the 36 institutions with digital materials were able to estimate the quantity of material using any one of these measures. Holdings range in quantity from less than 200 files at one institution to 96,600 files in another repository. Three repositories account for almost 75% of the total number of files and 90% of the total volume of 4.1 terabytes. In the 19 institutions that estimated the quantity of their holdings in megabytes or gigabytes, storage volumes range from a low of 500 megabytes in one institution to a high of 2 terabytes.

Many file formats and storage media are present in the digital holdings of these institutions. Among the 36 institutions with digital holdings, the most common formats are image files (97.2%), text files with mark-up (75.0%), and ASCII files (66.7%). More than one-third of the institutions had digital information in at least one of the following formats: word processing files (55.6%), audio (50.0 %), video (38.9%), and spreadsheets (38.9%), while fewer than a third of the institutions maintain digital information in geographic information systems, vector graphics, databases and other miscellaneous formats. When institutions create digital information through conversion, they also create archival master files in a wide variety of formats for preservation. The most common formats for archival master files of converted images are TIFF (80.6%); text files with mark-up (55.6%); JPEG (38.9%); and PDF, GIF, and ASCII (30.6% each). The survey shows that at least 24 different storage formats are present across the 54 responding institutions. Many institutions are maintaining digital information in several different formats. 24 of the 36 institutions with digital holdings maintain digital information in at least six different formats, and 13 of these institutions have 10 or more different formats.

Most of the institutions with digital holdings maintain relatively recent material, with some notable exceptions. The oldest digital materials reported were written to their current storage medium in the late 1970s, but the vast majority were generated in the last one to three years. Of 33 institutions reporting on the age of their oldest digital materials, 15 have materials created since 1995; only seven have materials created prior to 1990. Institutions with recent acquisitions and those that started conversion projects only in the last few years are just beginning to confront problems of long-term management of digital information.

In spite of the relatively young age of digital collections in most institutions, 15 institutions reported that they lack the operational and/or technical capacity to mount, read, and access some digital materials in their holdings. The most common storage media for which institutions lack access capability are floppy disks (five institutions) and open reel nine-track tape (three institutions); there are also scattered problems with CD-ROMs, magneto-optical disks, DDS DAT tape, 3480 cartridges, and various audio and video formats.

The research on digital preservation responsibilities and the nature and extent of digital holdings provides concrete evidence about digital preservation problems facing libraries, archives, museums, and other repositories. Digital preservation is a widespread problem in RLG member institutions. Typically, institutions with digital preservation responsibilities both acquire materials in digital form and create digital files through conversion. While a few institutions have large collections of digital materials, most are modest in size but growing rapidly. Most member institutions began acquiring or creating digital materials during the last one to five years. Nevertheless, 15 of the 36 institutions with digital holdings cannot access some of their materials because they lack the operational or technical capacity to mount, read, or access files stored on some of the storage media in their holdings. Three-fourths of the institutions with digital holdings report that irreplaceable information will be lost if the digital materials in their holdings are not adequately preserved for future use.

Digital Preservation Policies and Practices

Digital preservation policies and practices are not well developed in member institutions. Two-thirds of the institutions do not have written policies for digital preservation. One common reason that institutions appear not to develop digital preservation policies is that they have not yet assumed responsibility for preserving materials in digital form. However, taking responsibility for digital preservation does not necessarily mean that institutions use policies to govern their digital preservation activities. Only half of the institutions with digital materials in their holdings have written digital preservation policies.

Fourteen institutions with policies considered their policy adequate, two institutions said it met the institution's needs poorly, one said well, and one was not sure. Most of the policies govern the acquisition of materials in digital form, but less than half of the policies govern storage of digital information, conversion of materials from print to digital form, refreshing, and migration. Only five institutions have policies that cover acquisition, storage, migration, and refreshing. Of the 34 institutions that are generating information in digital form through conversion, only seven have policies governing conversion. This data and additional information gathered through interviews allows speculation about the lack of written policies. Most institutions that have not yet acquired materials in digital form or created digital materials through conversion have not yet experienced the need for written policies.

The interviews suggest that among those institutions with digital preservation responsibilities, the lack of good models for digital preservation and confusion about the most appropriate methods and approaches are major obstacles to developing effective policies and practices. Several administrators who were interviewed believe that policy development is important, but they do not yet see stable standards or effective models that can be used as the basis for institutional policy. Some expressed concern over competing strategies and the wide variety of approaches being advocated or followed by different institutions. At the same time, there is little information available on the costs or the effectiveness of different strategies. For some institutions, the perceived lack of a consensus in the community serves as a disincentive to policy development.

Effective digital preservation requires life-cycle management of digital information from the point of creation through storage, migration, and providing access on a continuing basis. Only 13 institutions reported that they have established methods in place for digital preservation. Some of the institutions in the survey have adopted practices that limit the formats of digital information that they must manage. Two institutions limit the acceptable formats to flat files while others accept several different formats such as PDF, TIFF, SGML, and word processing formats. Only seven of the 34 institutions that create materials through conversion have adopted a standard format or formats for preservation master files, and there are a wide variety of formats present across the institutions.

The institutions in the survey use a wide range of methods for storing the digital information in their holdings. It appears that a majority of institutions store some materials on the media in which they are received and transfer some materials to another digital medium, most commonly magnetic tape or cassette (68%), a hard drive (64%), or CD-ROM (52%). One-quarter of these institutions transfer some files to open reel magnetic tape. The use of rewritable magneto-optical disk and WORM optical disks is uncommon. One institution reported using a robotic tape storage system,5 while another prints its digital information on paper for preservation. Four institutions contract with a third party for storage. While there are several different storage methods in use, most institutions are avoiding proprietary and highly vulnerable media, such as magneto-optical and WORM disks.

Most institutions do not have established methods for digital preservation beyond transferring some material to new storage media. Eighteen institutions "refresh" digital materials, which the survey defined as copying digital materials in their original digital format from old to new media. A wide variety of practices are used for refreshing digital information. Nine institutions have refreshing cycles that range from as often as daily or weekly as part of the routine operations of a hierarchical storage management system to as infrequently as once every 10 years. The most common refreshing cycle is in the range of once every three to six years. One institution cleans and rewinds magnetic media on a yearly rotation and copies those files that exhibit access problems or physical deterioration. Two institutions reported that they refreshed digital materials only as a by-product of a larger system upgrade, while two others reported that the problem of refreshing had not arisen yet because of the newness of digital activities. One institution reported that refreshing services were provided by centralized information technology services and that the details of their practices were not available.

Seventeen institutions also reported that they migrate digital materials. The survey defined migration as the periodic transfer of digital materials from one hardware/software configuration to another, or from one generation of computer technology to a subsequent generation. Migration practices also vary among institutions and they do not appear to be well integrated into regular digital preservation processes. Rather, migration has mostly occurred on an ad hoc or project basis. Most institutions that described their migration methods indicated that they performed migration as necessary to ensure continuing access or as a by-product of a larger system upgrade. One institution reported that they had migrated digital images from a Xerox proprietary format (XDOD) to TIFF 5.0/6.0 and another institution was launching a similar project. When migration takes place, it appears to occur in response to impending technological obsolescence or in conjunction with larger system upgrades.

The policies and practices for digital preservation are underdeveloped in member institutions, especially given the increasing prevalence of digital materials in their holdings. Those institutions with the largest digital collections also appear to have the most developed policies and practices, and those without holdings have not yet experienced the need to address digital preservation issues.

Most institutions have not adopted policies that limit the variety of digital formats and storage media and few have adopted standards for the master files of materials that they generate through conversion. As a consequence, there are a significant number of institutions that maintain digital materials in many different formats. Many of these files are relatively new and the institutions have not yet confronted problems of technology obsolescence or systems upgrades. When migration is necessary or when the systems are upgraded, these institutions may face a complex and expensive task of converting files from many different formats, including proprietary formats. While more than half of the institutions with digital holdings refresh and/or migrate digital materials, these activities are not well integrated into digital preservation programs and tend to occur on an ad hoc basis or in conjunction with system upgrades.

Digital Preservation Staffing and Expertise

Lack of staff expertise is a common problem both in institutions with digital preservation responsibilities and in institutions that have not yet assumed responsibility for digital materials. Only eight institutions ranked the highest level of digital preservation knowledge on their staff as expert, while 21 ranked the highest level of in-house knowledge at the intermediate level. The largest group of institutions reported that the level of staff expertise was at the novice level, and two reported that they had no expertise available.

There is a relationship between having responsibility for preserving digital materials and levels of expertise. All institutions with experts available and 80% of the institutions with intermediate-level expertise have digital materials holdings in their holdings. This is true of only half of the institutions with novice-level expertise available and neither of those with no expertise. It is not clear from the data, however, whether taking responsibility for preservation encourages institutions to develop the requisite expertise, or whether institutions are reluctant to assume responsibility for digital preservation until at least a modicum of expertise is available in their institutions.

The telephone interviews gathered data about additional sources of support and about the experience of institutions that had used third-party services for some aspect of digital preservation. Some institutions get technical support from centralized institutional computing services such as the campuswide computing services in universities.

Interviewees were asked about the role of institutional computing services in meeting digital preservation needs. About two-thirds reported that they used institutional computing services, most often for backup, telecommunications, setting up systems, and as a source of expertise. Several of the interviewees mentioned that although they have access to centralized computing services, these services do not meet the needs of the repository. One interviewee pointed out that the computing services organization is responsible for meeting the institution's business needs and not the special requirements of digital preservation. Another mentioned the "intermediate view" of computing services, but a lack of awareness of long-term preservation.

Several respondents reported that, as organizations, the centralized computing services are also small or understaffed and lack technical expertise, while two people mentioned a "lack of imagination" and a conservative orientation among centralized computing staff. It appears that centralized computing services are potential sources of support for some digital preservation programs, and several people reported that they had initiated or established relationships with these organizations. Nevertheless, centralized computing organizations usually cannot meet all of the digital preservation needs of repositories.

Twenty institutions also use external sources such as consultants or contracts with third-party vendors to gain access to expertise in digital preservation or to outsource certain digital preservation functions. Interestingly, those institutions with the highest levels of staff expertise are most likely to acquire expertise from outside sources three-fourths of the institutions with in-house digital experts do so, as well as almost half of those with intermediate-level in-house expertise and one-fifth of those with novice-level in-house staff. Neither of the institutions with no in-house expertise available use outside sources for digital expertise. Interviews also yielded some insights into the experiences of member institutions that had outsourced preservation activities or contracted with third parties. A few institutions had outsourced digital conversion and preservation microfilming, but no institutions have experience with outsourcing digital preservation activities. Several interviewees expressed an interest in outsourcing conversion and one mentioned services related to access.

The interview research suggests some of the concerns about outsourcing. A few interviewees mentioned the need for quality services and for agreements between the institution and the vendor about acceptable quality. Others mentioned that the third-party services have to be flexible, affordable, and beneficial to the institution. Several respondents also discussed the potential for a consortium of institutions to share leads and experiences with vendors and to develop quality services without redundancy. The lack of expertise in digital preservation appears to be a significant obstacle to developing digital preservation programs. The programs with the highest levels of staff expertise also tend to have significant holdings of digital materials. Those institutions with expert staff also are more likely to take advantage of outside experts by hiring consultants with expertise to supplement that available on their staffs.

Although the research did not collect quantitative data specifically on the expertise available from centralized institutional computing services, the information gathered through interviews suggests that centralized computing services provide needed expertise and services only in exceptional cases. Some institutions have developed or are starting to form effective relationships with centralized computing services, but computing services often lack the staff, specific knowledge of digital preservation requirements, and vision to meet the digital preservation needs of many institutions. Finally, institutions have limited experience using third-party service providers for digital preservation. This may be due primarily to the lack of service providers in this area, but concerns over quality control and cost are also deterrents to outsourcing digital preservation services.

Needs and Requirements

The survey and interviews captured information about administrators' perceptions of digital preservation problems, their anticipated changes in digital preservation responsibilities in the next three years, and their sense of the most important issues facing their institutions. The research also gathered data on plans for increasing the institutions' capacity for digital preservation and respondents' perspectives on various types of services that consortia and/or third-party providers might develop to assist member institutions to implement sound digital preservation programs.

Threats to Digital Preservation

Respondents were asked to rank the significance of four issues as threats to digital preservation: technology obsolescence, insufficient resources, insufficient planning, and physical condition of materials. Member institutions ranked technological obsolescence as the greatest threat to loss of digital materials, followed closely by insufficient resources and an insufficient policy or plan for digital preservation. Only one institution ranked physical condition of the materials as the most serious threat. The lack of resources for digital preservation is ranked as the greatest threat by institutions that have policies in place for digital preservation and by the institutions that have digital materials in their holdings. Although the size of the sample is too small to reach statistically significant conclusions, this suggests that as institutions assume responsibility for preserving digital materials and as they develop policies, they then confront the resource requirements in concrete terms.

The interviews with managers of digital collections provide additional insights into how this problem is perceived and which strategies institutions are using to address it. When asked about the impact of digital preservation on their institutions, the interviewees mentioned changes in the way information management and preservation are organized and carried out, additional resource requirements, changing relationships with other professionals and specialists, and the need to hire new staff with digital preservation expertise. Several digital collection managers mentioned the lack of standards, planning, infrastructure, and models for digital preservation as significant problems for their institutions. Several administrators in archival repositories expressed concern about the changing nature of institutional memory, where paper records are disappearing but the repositories are not prepared to handle electronic records.

Another common theme is the strain that digital preservation places on resources, including staff, equipment, and funds. Several administrators mentioned the need to hire staff with technical expertise and a few had plans in place to do so. Cooperative efforts with experts in technology or with other individuals responsible for digital preservation were also mentioned as strategies to share expertise and learn from others. Several administrators mentioned the increasingly complex relationships between libraries or archives and information technology and service providers.

As responsibility for digital preservation becomes spread across several different divisions there is a need for more coordination. Two interviewees also raised lack of awareness and support from top administrators as a problem for dealing with digital preservation in a concrete manner. Some interviewees felt that administrators paid lip service to digital preservation issues but were not willing to support serious institutional efforts to address the problem. Finally, a few interviewees mentioned the positive impact of digital initiatives on their institutions, especially in the way that conversion of materials to digital form offers new means to deliver information to users and to preserve the originals.

The respondents had mixed reactions about the impact of digital preservation on them personally and professionally. They were fairly evenly divided between those who found digital preservation interesting and stimulating and who had made large personal investments to keep up with the issues, and those who were concerned about the challenges, the absence of clear guidance, and the need for greater expertise. Many of the interviewees said that digital preservation was forcing them to re-examine traditional practices, change the way they administer their departments, develop more interdepartmental relationships, and learn new skills.

Anticipated Changes in Responsibility

Member institutions appear to take digital preservation seriously. Almost all of the institutions in the survey anticipate an increase during the next three years in the quantity of digital materials that they are responsible for preserving. Fifty-two institutions expect an increase in digital materials from conversion projects, while 47 institutions expect digital preservation responsibilities to grow as a result of new acquisitions or accessions of electronic records.

In the interviews with administrators, several mentioned new acquisitions or the increasing size of the collections as a major issue that they would have to confront in the next four years. An archivist in a state archives anticipates that with a change in administration, records in electronic form will begin to arrive in the archives for the first time. The institution needs to develop information systems immediately that can support cataloging, access, and preservation of this material. In a different state archives, the archivist considered the need for more staff and funding to deal with the growing number of digital records as a major issue facing the institution. In this case, developing a fairly technical system to describe, preserve, and provide access to digital materials is considered a priority so that it is possible to make access more self-service. The director of a university library that may be designated as a national repository for digital materials considers the problem very serious because the library will have to be able to take responsibility for digital preservation if required to do so through legislation.

When asked about the major digital preservation issues facing institutions in the next four years, the digital collection managers who were interviewed mentioned a wide variety of issues along several common themes. A few respondents stressed the importance of raising the level of awareness about digital preservation problems, especially among top administrators.

Some collection managers expressed concerns that institutions would sidestep the issue of long-term preservation by viewing digital technologies as a way to provide access to materials, but that at some point this approach would fail, leaving institutions with a preservation crisis. This presents a challenge of convincing administration to see digital preservation as a priority and to take some immediate steps to avoid even greater problems in a few years. Several interviewees discussed human resource implications, including the need for more staff to carry out labor-intensive digital work, the demand for staff with new and different skills, the challenges of "upskilling" and retraining, and the need to redefine job descriptions and skill requirements.

A third theme relates to the absence of standards, clear models and best practices, especially in the areas of migration and frequent updating of hardware and software. Several digital collections managers stressed the importance of working together as a community to drive the development of needed products, services, and international standards so that vendors will begin to create products that meet digital preservation needs. The interviewees also mentioned the need to address preservation in the context of materials that institutions license, but do not own; better coordination among the various parties involved in digital preservation; and the development of tools for appraisal and risk assessment.

Proposed Actions

Most member institutions are planning to take concrete measures to build up their capacity for digital preservation. Almost all of the institutions (51 of 54) anticipate developing new policies for preserving digital materials in the next three years. This includes all of the institutions that currently have written policies as well as 33 of 36 that do not currently have a policy.

Institutions also anticipate using a variety of methods to increase the level of available staff expertise with digital preservation. Thirty-one institutions hope to hire people with digital preservation knowledge or expertise.Institutions plan to use multiple sources for training and staff development, ranging from training provided by professional organizations (42 institutions) to hiring consultants (20 institutions.). Institutions also expressed an interest in using a variety of digital archiving services if they were made available at a reasonable cost. The broad interest in model policies, standards and best practices, training, and specific storage, maintenance and conversion services suggest useful roles for institutions, consortia such as RLG, and commercial service providers.

In the interviews the researchers also asked about attitudes toward the possibility of institutions pooling resources into a consortium or network for digital preservation, and how each interviewee would see his or her institution fitting into such a network. In general, the interviewees supported cooperative efforts, but they differed in their views of how such cooperative efforts should be organized and exactly which activities could be done best through a consortium. The strongest support was expressed for having a consortium that could provide leadership and coordination in best practices and standards, serve as a source of technical information and expertise, provide training, and bargain collectively with publishers and vendors for more affordable services. The response was mixed to the idea of having a consortium assume responsibility for storage, preservation, and access to digital materials. While a few interviewees said they would be relieved if a trusted organization were available for storage and management of digital materials, many interviewees expressed concerns about losing control over their material.

Interviewees favored the idea of pooling resources to eliminate redundant efforts and reduce preservation costs, but they expressed several concerns. One manager pointed out that outsourcing and pooling of resources is popular politically, but it is difficult to achieve. This represents a major change from the way institutions have worked traditionally. Some of the keys to developing successful cooperative efforts appear to be a clear definition of the role and responsibilities of any consortium-based service and a proven ability to provide a quality service at a lower cost than the institutions can achieve on their own.

The research also compiled a "wish list" of issues that digital collection managers would like to see solved. When asked to choose "one concern or problem to be immediately and magically solved," most interviewees had trouble limiting their response to a single issue. Interviewees provided a lengthy wish list of issues to solve, but some issues appear repeatedly among the top concerns. One request is for a clear, coherent set of guidelines and standards to follow.

Some respondents were frustrated by the multitude of competing strategies and the varied and confusing voices addressing digital preservation. Several respondents considered technology obsolescence the most important issue to resolve, but they proposed different priorities for resolving this problem. One interviewee wanted to avoid migration by using standards as a way to ensure continuing access to materials. Another stressed the need for cost models and process models to deal with migration and obsolescence issues. Two interviewees mentioned fast, reliable and stable storage media.

There was also considerable interest in dealing with the economics of and funding for digital preservation. First, there is an interest in better data on the costs of digital preservation and the need for cost and funding models which in turn might be used to increase institutional understanding and commitments to digital preservation. This is often coupled with a desire for more resources and for more reasonably priced services.

Finally, several respondents mentioned legal and organizational issues, including the changing nature of ownership of information, the role of publishers and their responsibility for preserving digital products, and the issues of access, licensing, and copyright. Several interviewees also stressed the need for a long-term vision oriented toward the future to avoid rapid obsolescence of guidelines, resources, and technology.

Digital Library Classification System

In this era of the Internet and distributed, multimedia computing, new and emerging classes of information systems applications have swept into the lives of office workers and everyday people. New applications ranging from digital libraries, multimedia systems, geographic information systems, and collaborative computing to electronic commerce, virtual reality, and electronic video arts and games have created tremendous opportunities for information and computer science researchers and practitioners.

As applications become more overwhelming, pressing, and diverse, several well-known information retrieval (IR) problems have become even more urgent. Information overload resulting from easy creation and transmittal of information via Internet and WWW, has become prominent in people's lives (e.g., even stockbrokers and elementary school students, heavily exposed to various WWW search engines, are versed in such IR terminology as recall and precision).

Significant variations of database formats and structures, the richness of information media (text, audio, and video), and an abundance of multilingual information content also have created severe interoperability problems. The conventional approaches to addressing information overload and interoperability problems are manual in nature, requiring human experts as information intermediaries to create knowledge structures and/or classification systems.

Such manually-created classification systems, which represent subject vocabularies and their relationships, are often used to index and/or organize collections or to suggest search terms during retrieval processes. But as information content and collections become even larger and more dynamic, thus rendering manual knowledge creation to become more difficult, if not infeasible, we believe a complementary system-aided, algorithmic, bottom-up approach to creating large-scale digital library classification systems is needed.

Knowledge Networking

In US, the Information Infrastructure Technology and Applications (IITA) Working Group, the highest level of the country's National Information Infrastructure (NII) technical committee, held an invited workshop in May 1995 to define a research agenda for digital libraries. The shared vision that emerged is an entire Net of distributed repositories, where objects of any type can be searched within and across different indexed collections. In the short term, technologies must be developed to search across these repositories transparently, handling any variations in protocols and formats (i.e., addressing structural interoperability). In the long term, technologies must be developed to handle the variations in content and meanings (knowledge) transparently as well.

In a new NSF Knowledge Networking (KN) initiative, a group of domain scientists and information systems researchers were invited to a Workshop on Distributed Heterogeneous Knowledge Networks at Boulder, Colorado, in May, 1997. They considered that scalable techniques to improve semantic bandwidth and knowledge bandwidth are among the priority research areas, as described in the KN report: The Knowledge Networking (KN) initiative focuses on the integration of knowledge from different sources and domains across space and time.

KN research aims to move beyond connectivity to achieve new levels of interactivity, increasing the semantic bandwidth, knowledge bandwidth, activity bandwidth, and cultural bandwidth among people, organizations, and communities. "Knowledge networking'' or, using a more general term, "knowledge management'' (KM), has attracted significant attention from academic researchers and even executives in Fortune 500 companies.

KM is formal in that knowledge is classified and categorized according to a pre-specified - but evolving - ontology into structured and semi-structured data and knowledge bases. Many commercial software systems are considered enabling technologies for KM, including Internet/Intranet search engines, groupware, electronic document management systems, full-text retrieval systems, database management systems, and electronic mail.

Major consulting firms, on the other hand, are promoting KM practices such as organizational development, strategic planning, performances metrics, and methodology. Despite of obvious differences in technologists and consultants views of what KM should be, their calls for advanced classification and categorization technologies to help analyze, organize, and present mission-critical information and knowledge are the same - turning information overload into knowledge assets.

In "Practical Digital Libraries'', Lesk describes knowledge representation methods by which people have tried to organize and arrange knowledge, with the idea of making searching simple. Library classification systems and thesauri often capture nouns or noun phrases and represent only limited relationships (e.g., broader terms, narrower term, etc.). The representations are often coarse, but precise, and they do support their practical goal of supporting indexing and searching, but significant human efforts are needed to create and maintain such large-scale classification systems.

Artificial intelligence representations such as semantic networks, expert systems, or ontologies represent another approach to capturing knowledge, e.g., Lenat's CYC common sense knowledge base. Their representations are often richer and more fine-grained and the goal of capturing human intelligence is ambitious and difficult. Due to the granularity required of such representations, knowledge creation is slow and painstaking. Only experimental prototypes in small, limited domains have been created. Their usefulness in large-scale digital library applications remains suspect. The traditional approach to creating classification systems and knowledge sources in library science and classical AI is often considered top-down since knowledge representations and formats are pre-defined by human experts or trained librarians and the process of generating knowledge is structured and well-defined. A complementary bottom-up approach to knowledge creation has been suggested by researchers in machine learning, statistical analysis, and neural networks.

Based on actual databases or collections, researchers develop programs which systematically segment and index documents in various databases (text, image, and video) and identify patterns within such databases. Analyzing databases which contain structured and numeric data (e.g., credit card usage, a frequent flyer program) is often referred to as data mining or knowledge discovery.

Generating knowledge algorithmically from multimedia databases (especially text, e.g., customer complaint email, machinery repair reports, brainstorming outputs) is considered the core of knowledge management. Two stages of such a bottom-up knowledge management approach are often required:

— Object Recognition,

— Segmentation, and

— Indexing:

The most fundamental techniques in IR involve identifying key features in objects. For example, automatic indexing and natural language processing (e.g., noun phrase extraction or object type tagging) are frequently used to extract meaningful keywords or phrases from texts automatically. Texture, color, or shape-based indexing and segmentation techniques are often used to identify images.

For audio and video applications, voice recognition, speech recognition, and scene segmentation techniques can be used to identify meaningful descriptors in audio or video streams. Many of these techniques have been developed previously in the six large-scale DLI-1 projects. Several classes of techniques have been used for semantic analysis of texts or multimedia objects.

Symbolic machine learning, graph-based clustering and classification, statistics-based multivariate analyses (e.g., latent semantic indexing, multi-dimensional scaling, regressions), artificial neural network-based computing (e.g., backpropagation networks, Kohonen self-organizing maps), and evolution-based programming (e.g., genetic algorithms) are among the popular techniques.

Most of these are computationally intensive and are particularly suitable for creating classification systems or knowledge structures from unstructured textual collections. Large-scale image (and video) based knowledge extraction is still at an early stage of development due to the difficulty of designing image-invariant content-based segmentation and indexing algorithms.

Digital South Asia Library (DSAL)

The Center for Research Libraries (CRL) proposes a three-year collaborative project to improve electronic access to vital resources for understanding South Asia. Through this project scholars, public policy officials, business leaders, and other citizens will benefit from an improved electronic information infrastructure and expeditious delivery of digital research materials directly to them from the South Asian subcontinent and England.

The Digital South Asia Library (DSAL) project will produce:

1) On-line information about contemporary and historical South Asia - including full-text documents, statistical data, electronic images, cartographic representations, and pedagogical resources for language instruction;

2) Delivery on demand of page images from South Asia, scanned from both paper and microform sources;
3) Internet-based indexes to highly select journals in the regional languages of South Asia;
4) Use of Unicode electronic character encoding for non-roman language data disseminated under the project;
5) An international cooperative venture whose contributing members will include leading universities in the U.S., Britain, and South Asia as well as libraries with a focus on South Asian studies; and
6) A detailed plan of operation for phase three of the Digital South Asia Library.

The Internet will be used to its full potential in facilitating full-text delivery of documents created under this project. A distinctive feature of the approach successfully tested under the current pilot phase of the Digital South Asia Library involves direct delivery from India of scanned page images to scholars in the U.S.

The wide-ranging collaborative base established for DSAL includes indexing for highly select periodicals, cataloging of vital official publications from South Asia, and access to electronic databases of bibliographic information via the Internet. The Digital South Asia Library program is committed to full implementation of the internationally recognized Unicode encoding standard as the means of displaying DSAL texts in the regional scripts of South Asia over the World Wide Web.

While this means of text encoding is beginning to be included in standard software packages, it is currently used only rarely for South Asian texts.

Collaboration in the use of technology is a hallmark of this proposed program. Evidence of this approach is presented throughout the proposal. The collaborative nature of the enterprise is reflected in the wide array of institutions joined together to enhance language instruction, expand resources for scholarship on South Asia, and improve the position of international studies.

Participants in the Digital South Asia Library include leading U.S. universities, the Center for Research Libraries, the South Asia Microform Project, the Committee on South Asian Libraries and Documentation, the Association for Asian Studies, the Library of Congress, the Asia Society, the British Library, the University of Oxford, the University of Cambridge, MOZHI in India, the Sundarayya Vignana Kendram in India, Madan Puraskar Pustakalaya in Nepal, and other institutions in South Asia.

South Asian studies encompasses the subcontinent which lies south of the Himalayan range and comprises India, Pakistan, Bangladesh, Nepal, Sri Lanka, Bhutan, and the Maldive Islands. This area has been the site of major civilizations since at least 2,500 B.C. Both in geographical area and chronological expanse, the intellectual domain is enormous. The size of the subject is matched by the American contribution to the study of this region.

Since 1960 scholars from North America have done more to enhance knowledge of South Asia than their colleagues from any region, save the subcontinent itself. This assessment is based on the number and quality of books and articles written, Ph.D.s awarded, courses taught, and language instruction offered. The growth of knowledge about the region has been supported by forty-one years of funding from the U.S. Department of Education for foreign language and area training.

This sustained support has produced an intelligent and demanding body of scholars and policy makers with demonstrable capacity to use the languages of South Asia and comprehend the nuances of South Asian civilizations. They expect and deserve more extensive and flexible access to electronic resources in order to train succeeding generations of researchers and leaders as well as to further their own inquiries.4 This project will address that need.

South Asian studies in the United States has historical roots in nineteenth-century philological and religious studies, both focused on classical India. In the aftermath of World War II, however, there was a marked change. The war highlighted America's profound ignorance about the civilizations of South Asia and systematic efforts were made to develop programs of study, first at a few universities, but at many more by the 1960s.

These new South Asia programs had distinctive intellectual characteristics and disciplinary orientations that were shaped by founding faculty. Yet, in general, there was a strong emphasis on the social sciences and regional rather than the classical languages. The social sciences have remained vital and continue to attract the interest of new students and of scholars without backgrounds in South Asian studies.

Some researchers have been engaged by the writings of South Asian scholars addressing traditional issues such as colonialism from varied perspectives. Others have been interested in more novel approaches to knowledge such as those surrounding popular culture (or public culture), cinema, and gender studies. During this period of economic liberalization and increased foreign investment, economics and political science continue to attract the attention of many.

The humanities are also vital areas of research related to South Asia. As an example, scholars of regional literatures are writing new histories of the enormous and varied literary traditions in the subcontinent that challenge presuppositions of literary and language boundaries, chronological divisions, nationalism, and canon that undergirded earlier publications.

While most researchers come from a discipline - both as a departmental home and also as a methodological disposition - there is increasing interest in interdisciplinary studies and trans-regional research on South Asia. In addition to their wide geographical scope, these inquiries often have a global impact. The need for this project on South Asia is acutely felt in research libraries.

More specifically, books and periodicals in South Asia's regional languages are often targeted for sharp reductions. In response to decreased acquisition budgets, consortia of U.S. research libraries are beginning to share collecting responsibilities in order to ensure that the aggregate national collection remains strong. This cooperation entails a greater reliance on inter-library loan. For less commonly consulted publications inter-library loan remains an acceptable alternative to widespread duplication in acquisition.

However, for many core resources widespread demand requires alternative solutions that can provide a number of readers with important works in a timely fashion. The direct delivery of selected documents to readers via the Internet as proposed in this project is such an alternative. Beyond the primary audiences of scholars and policy makers, other important bodies of readers will be well served by the electronic resources prepared and disseminated under the Digital South Asia Library. These include:

— businesses;

— outreach coordinators at National Resource Centers, Centers for International Business Education, and Undergraduate International Studies and Foreign Language programs;

— school teachers;
— governmental and non-governmental organizations (NGOs);
— cultural institutions, especially museums and libraries; and
— media.

Through this project, the needs of a wide array of U.S. citizens for ready access to new and unique resources will be met. They will be able to turn to the project's site on the World Wide Web for free and dependable access to information of the highest accuracy and integrity. This project achieves significance through effectively addressing needs registered by national foundations and associations of scholars and librarians.

Association for Research Libraries (ARL) and the Association of American Universities (AAU) inaugurated the Global Resources Program (GRP). Its principal goals are to improve access to international research resources and help libraries contain costs through the creation of cooperative structures, the use of new technologies, and the expansion of international document delivery. This approach ensures more focused collection development at individual institutions resulting in access to a broader array of these often difficult-to-acquire resources.

The GRP coordinates its efforts with those of other libraries and organizations that share common interests with AAU and ARL. Current GRP regional projects include: the Cooperative African Newspapers Project; the German Resources Project; the Japan Journal Access Project; the Latin Americanist Research Resources Project; and the Digital South Asia Library.

The Digital South Asia Library pilot project is the only one funded by the Association of Research Libraries for South Asia. During the pilot project DSAL has developed an Internet-based infrastructure for intercontinental electronic document delivery to and from selected South Asian libraries. DSAL's large target audience will be well served by the digital resources provided. The Association for Asian Studies lists more than 760 of its members as having South Asian countries as a major focus of academic interest.

In addition, many members of other scholarly associations have a primary interest in South Asia-the American Academy of Religion, the American Political Science Association, the American Anthropological Association, and the American Oriental Society, to name a few. Looking to the larger body of citizens, the 1990 U.S. census shows that slightly more than one million Americans trace their heritage to the cultures of South Asia.

DSAL resources will serve "heritage learners" among this population. Finally, those outside the U.S. will be well served by the resources freely available over the Internet. It is important to recall that the South Asian subcontinent encompasses more than 22% of the world's population and that access to the Internet is expanding rapidly in that region.

Scholars in virtually all disciplines of the social sciences and humanities will be able to consult the DSAL Web site for an array of documents, statistics, images, and bibliographic data supporting their research, teaching, and planning efforts. Economists and political scientists will use the periodical indexes to locate current articles, both in English and in the regional languages, in the on-line Bibliography of Asian Studies (BAS).

Beyond the art historical and museological uses of photographs scanned from the British Library's collection, anthropologist and historians will consult the finding aids for photographs made accessible under this project to locate images from the Anthropological Survey of India or street scenes of urban India. Professors of art will be able to project pictures of South Asian buildings in class from the DSAL Web site when discussing the architectural heritage of the subcontinent.

Businesses and government policy makers will rely on current data from the statistical abstracts of South Asian countries presented with accompanying programs for statistical analysis of the data. Criminologists with interests in jail populations, rates of crime, and size of police forces will be able to query the same abstracts to derive data from as early as 1840.

Language teachers will be able to direct their students to the pedagogical resources for instruction in less commonly taught languages, knowing that the best available materials created under Department of Education grants will have been converted for easy access. The same teaching resources will enable distance language learning by students not able to meet face-to-face with one of the few U.S. instructors for certain least commonly taught languages.

Carefully selected on-line dictionaries will complement the grammars and readers if our complementary proposal to support their conversion is awarded. These language resources will be valued by "heritage learners" as well as others. News reporters and others in the media will find it easy to consult background articles from full-text documents such as the Economic and Political Weekly and India Briefing.

Systems staff of ARTFL will implement the project's computational and Web delivery components in the U.S. ARTFL, an acronym for American and French Research on the Treasury of the French Language, is a University of Chicago program for humanities computing and one of the first large-scale digital libraries developed on the Internet.

ARTFL's involvement will ensure high quality results. Further, it is highly significant that work done under this program will draw upon the body of software previously created by ARTFL thus reducing project expenses. At the same time project funds will support development of new computer algorithms and modes of dissemination over the World Wide Web that will further augment the software library ARTFL maintains.

The electronic resources created by ARTFL are shared widely throughout academic computing and will therefore serve the needs of a larger audience than this specific project. Overseas implementation of the project is significant for its method as well as its objectives. The DSAL project builds upon and expands existing cooperative relationships, particularly in the United Kingdom and South Asia.

More than a decade of close collaboration between the Center for Research Libraries' South Asia Microform Project, the University of Chicago, and the British Library's Oriental and India Office Collections have led to the preservation on microfilm of nearly 10,000 publications at the British Library. This project will extend that relationship into the realms of digitization and delivery of electronic files - files containing textual, pictorial, cartographic, and bibliographic data - to readers.

While much of this work will be undertaken overseas, multi-directional flow of information is central to the DSAL model. In other words, benefits accrue in South Asia, the U.S., and elsewhere in the world. In addition to the electronic resources on the Web, one is already beginning to see the results in India of DSAL workshops held to train librarians and archivists in preservation and bibliographic access, topics inadequately addressed in university training programs for professionals.

Another element in DSAL's overseas implementation is taking concrete form as this proposal is submitted. Effective dissemination of the resulting digital resources and information about the project will enhance the project's significance. The free DSAL Web site will allow readers around the world easy access to the texts, images, and bibliographic data created under this project.

The Co-Directors will notify scholarly organizations, libraries, and the general public of progress during the course of this project by means of news notes and articles in relevant scholarly publications, academic news publications such as the Chronicle of Higher Education, postings to the listservers for South Asian scholars, and press releases to national news media. We will send information about this project to the all members of the Association for Asian Studies' Committee on South Asian Libraries and Documentation, a group including representatives of all significant North American research libraries with collections on South Asia.

The two original sister institutions in India will continue to grow under this project, expanding to provide a larger array of digital resources while also helping to train those at new DSAL sites in the subcontinent. One of DSAL's fundamental objective is building a "new library movement" in South Asia, a new library movement more responsive to local needs and also more capable of joining in international collaborations.

A commitment to international standards is central to the project's design. For a more detailed statement of those standards, please see Appendix 5 with extracts from relevant Web sites. Where display of text in non-roman characters is required, DSAL will use Unicode. Further, DSAL staff will report to the Unicode Consortium on how the character sets for South Asian languages could be usefully expanded through the inclusion of conjunct characters for a more felicitous display of texts.

All electronic resources delivered over the Internet will contain Dublin Core metadata. Where bibliographic files are created the project will follow the USMARC standard for bibliographic records. The Encoded Archival Description (EAD) will be the standard where finding aids are created. The statutory standard for equitable access under Section 427 of the Department of Education's General Education Provisions Act is met through free dissemination of the project's resources via the Internet and through wide publicity of the availability of the project's Web site.

Classification Systems in Modern Libraries

Classification experts and librarians have long recognized the potential of library classification schemes for improving subject access to information.

There are several uses for classification in online retrieval systems. They include:

— to improve precision or recall,

— to provide context for search terms,

— to enable browsing, and

— to serve as a mechanism for switching between languages.

In the Dewey Decimal Classification (DDC) Online Project, Karen Markey demonstrated the first implementation of a library classification scheme for end-user subject access, browsing, and display. Although many online catalogs provide call number browsing, few employ classification in the manner described by Elaine Svenonius or explored by Markey in her innovative use of the DDC in an experimental online catalog which enabled users to search and browse online classification data.

Only recently, some ten years after Markey's pioneering research, is online classification data once again being seriously viewed as a tool for providing advanced browsing and retrieval capabilities in online systems. One factor that has contributed to the slow adoption of classification as a retrieval tool is that the DDC and the Library of Congress Classification (LCC) have only recently been converted into machine-readable form. The computerization of the DDC began with the production of DDC 19 from computer-based photocomposition tapes. This development and the Markey study prompted Forest Press, in 1984, to commission Inforonics to develop an online editorial support system (ESS) for the Dewey Classification. The resulting system and database was used to produce DDC 20, the first classification to be produced using an online editorial support system.

A different path is being taken in the conversion of the LCC to machine-readable form. Recognizing the benefits of online classification data for maintenance and distribution of LCC, the Library of Congress began developing the USMARC Format for Classification Data in 1987. The format was given provisional approval in 1990 and shortly afterward the Library of Congress began converting the forty six LCC schedules. The LCC database is expected to contain over 450,000 classification records when complete.

Electronic versions of the DDC and LCC make it possible to realize the potential of library classification to improve subject retrieval; however, much of the renewed interest in classification as an organizing and retrieval device for information resources has been sparked by the growth in usage of the Internet and World Wide Web (WWW). Several WWW sites give users the ability to perform word or phrase searches to retrieve items of interest, with two popular sites, Yahoo and Infoseek, providing the additional capability of allowing users to navigate through a series of subject categories to discover potentially relevant documents. Although, Yahoo and Infoseek use essentially the same input as the basis for their subject structures, the resulting categories displayed to users are quite different. The broad subject "Education" is found at the top level of both Yahoo and Infoseek, however, the next level under "Education" reveals a very different organization of the topic in each system.

Library classification schemes have long provided a similar organizing tool for library materials. The subject categories found in the DDC and LCC are based largely on the topics expressed in monographic material in traditional book format. For printed books, the Dewey Summaries and LC Classification Outline are the library community's functional equivalent to the subject categories of Yahoo and Infoseek. In fact, several noncommercial WWW sites are using DDC and LCC to provide subject access to Web-accessible documents. At a time when both Internet-based classification schemes and traditional library classification systems are being used to provide access to Internet resources it is appropriate to review the major characteristics of DDC and LCC and to assess whether the electronic versions of these schemes can be successfully extended to the Internet.

DDC and LCC

DDC and LCC are general classification systems. The purpose of the Dewey Decimal Classification is to arrange a general collection of materials. The DDC aims to classify books and other material on all subjects in all languages in every kind of library. Similarly, LCC is designed to provide order for a general collection, the collection of the Library of Congress. Although based on the collection of a single library, the LC Classification has been successfully adopted by a majority of U.S. academic and research libraries.

DDC and LCC have a hierarchical structure. Hierarchical relationships are the essence of all classification. Enumerative classifications systems provide a systematic arrangement of subjects according to set of principles based on an accepted philosophy of the organization of knowledge, on patterns established on the basis of literary warrant, and frequently, on a combination of both. However, classified order is not self-evident. Some method or device is required to preserve the relationships among classes, subclasses, topics and subtopics. In some classification systems, for example DDC, these relationships are preserved and may be manipulated through the hierarchical notation. LCC does not fit this pattern. Its notation preserves order but does not reflect hierarchy some other means must be found to preserve those relationships. In DDC, the sequence of subjects from general to specific, is indicated by the number of digits that form the DDC number. For example, when the DDC number 663.223 for the topic "making of red wine" is shown in the context of its Dewey hierarchy it can be seen that "White Wine," "Red Wine," and "Sparkling Wine" are at the same hierarchical level. The DDC number 663.22 corresponding to the heading "Specific kinds of grape wine" is one digit shorter than those used to indicate exact kinds of wine and is considered to be broader or superordinate to those with longer numbers. Indentation is also used to indicate hierarchy. Through both notation and indentation, this example shows that each topic except for the main class 600 Technology is subordinate to and part of all the broader classes above it.

600 Technology (Applied sciences)
660 Chemical engineering and related technologies
663 Beverage technology
663.2 Wine and wine making
663.22 Specific kinds of grape wine
663.222 White wine
663.223 Red wine
663.224 Sparkling wine

In both the LC Classification and in Yahoo's category trees, hierarchy is indicated by the indentation of category or class labels. To illustrate, consider the following class numbers and headings listed in the LC Classification QA schedule:

QA76.33 Computer Camps
QA76.38 Hybrid Computers
QA76.4 Analog Computers
QA76.5 Digital Computers

Given only the notation (class numbers) and captions (headings), it is unclear what relationship exists among the ordered classes. When these classes are placed in the context of the LCC hierarchy structure in a display similar to what is found in the printed schedules, the indentation clearly indicates that Hybrid, Analog, and Digital computers are the same level of hierarchy and that QA76.33 is a subcategory under study and teaching and not a type of hybrid computer.

QA71-QA90 Instruments and machines

QA75-QA76.95 Calculating machines

QA76 Electronic computers.

Computer Science

QA76.27 Study and Teaching

QA76.33 Computer Camps

QA76.38 Hybrid Computers

QA76.4 Analog Computers

QA76.5 Digital Computers

Yahoo subcategory trees also use indentation to indicate hierarchy. For example, the following hierarchy is found under "Computers and Internet"

Computers and Internet

Internet

Entertainment

Interesting Devices Connected to the Net

Spy Cameras

Indoor Cameras

Outdoor Cameras

Pets@

Aquariums

The preceding examples demonstrate that both Internet classification schemes and library classification schemes provide hierarchical structures capable of supporting topic browsing. Library schemes would seem to have some advantage over Internet-based schemes because they are accompanied by notations that facilitate the manipulation of class relationships. Recall that DDC's notation can be used to navigate broader, narrower, and coordinate relationships among classes, while LCC's can be used to arrange related topics in order. Yahoo's hierarchy structure requires encoding to take advantage of relationships among classes. Links to other subject-oriented schemes

They contain links to other subject schemes: Library classification schemes are generally considered to be retrospective: classes are added or revised only after sufficient literary warrant is demonstrated and classes are removed with even greater caution. For these reasons much greater attention needs to be given to employing the implicit and explicit links between library classification systems and other subject oriented schemes. For example, Electronic Dewey, the electronic version of DDC20, includes a statistical mapping from the OCLC Online Union Catalog of up to five of the most frequently used LCSH to each Dewey number. This Electronic Dewey feature, which has been well received by users, provides additional indexing terms to lead users to appropriate topic areas in Dewey.

In addition to statistical mappings, the Electronic DDC21 database will include many DDC/LCSH links that have been reviewed editorially. Links similar to those made in Electronic Dewey can be made for LCC and LCSH by processing the in bibliographic records containing fields for both. For LCSH and LCC explicit links are also available in LC Subject Authority records that contain LC classification number fields. In an analysis of the LC Subject Authority file, Vizine-Goetz and Markey found that about 43% of topical subject heading records contain LC classification number fields. Science and technology classes account for almost half (47.72%) of the LC class numbers.

For example, the LC subject heading Microsoft Network (Online service), listed among the "Subject Headings of Current Interest" in CSB, No. 70, can be linked to (among others) DDC number 025.04 "Automated information storage and retrieval systems" and to DDC number 004.678 "Internet." This subject heading, however, has been assigned to only four LC MARC records with DDC number 025.04 and therefore may not be among the top 5 LCSH statistically mapped to this number. The ability to map current terminology into DDC and LCC is particularly important if library classification is to be used to provide access to Internet resources.

They contain links to translations in other languages: Classification experts have long recognized the potential of DDC to serve as a mechanism for switching between languages. With the recent publications of DDC in

French and Spanish and with a Russian translation scheduled for publication in December 1997, it may now be possible to realize this capability.

Despite these favorable properties additional improvements are needed if online classification data is to be used as a major tool for providing online subject access to traditional collections as well as to Internet-accessible resources. To improve much better the classification systems need to:

1. Evaluate DDC and LCC captions for expressiveness and currency
2. Decompose and code class number components to identify the specific subject and aspects represented
3. Continue to add new terminology as index terms even if each is not supplied with its own number
4. Expand links to other controlled vocabularies
5. Expand definitions of literary warrant to include Internet resources
6. Build demonstration systems

Over ten years ago, Karen Markey advocated similar improvements be made to the DDC to facilitate its use in online catalogs. Arnold Wajenberg proposed a scheme for encoding DDC numbers to enhance automated subject retrieval. Today, there appears to be both interest and resources to make needed enhancements to online classification data. For example, a project has been established to transform captions in the 1000 DDC summaries (the first three digits in Dewey) into end user language. The recast summaries will be used in the prototype of a Dewey-based subject browser for the NetFirst database of Internet-accessible resources. While a good first step, it will be necessary to look well beyond the first three levels of Dewey to captions at lower levels of the DDC hierarchy since many of the DDC numbers assigned to NetFirst records extend four or more digits past the decimal point.

Dewey editorial staff and OCLC research staff are collaborating on projects to enhance the electronic version of the Dewey editorial database with selected LC subject headings from the Weekly Lists and headings with high postings in the OCLC Online Union Catalog database. Editorial staff will also add coding to the Editorial Support System database to indicate links between Dewey Relative Index terms and LCSH and Sears headings.

Portals and Catalogues

The world's information resources are abundant, but time is a scarce commodity. The ideal discovery tool, therefore, is one which consults omnivorously, but which returns a selection of relevant results in rapid sequence. Searchers find what they need promptly without having to wade through a vast assortment of tangentially related, inaccurate, or otherwise deficient data.

It costs little to build and operate, and it yields a high degree of user satisfaction because it delivers reliable information in a timely manner with relative ease. Such a tool is still imaginary, although it could become a reality in the near future if librarians organize themselves appropriately and commit the resources to design it. One precursor of this discovery tool is the library catalogue. Over the past century, the catalogue has achieved a reputation as a dependable starting point for people seeking particular kinds of information: published information appearing chiefly in books or journals that has undergone a formal review and editing process. Libraries have further filtered these publications through their selection practices, in which collection policies guide the acquisition of texts to meet the needs of a particular community. The titles chosen by bibliographers represent quality because they have been at least twice vetted, once by professional editors and once by library subject specialists.

Once acquired, the volumes receive added value through their integration with other related materials held by the institution. Through the cataloguing of these chosen items, they gain in significance as trained experts distil their essence into a standard bibliographic description. Subject headings and classification contribute further to the access of these materials.

Widespread adoption of the Anglo-American Cataloguing Rules, Library of Congress Subject Headings, Library of Congress or Dewey Decimal Classification, and the MARC format has enabled the creation of virtual union catalogues with a number of superior attributes. The catalogue yields highly codified citations to quality publications in a predictable and dependable fashion. Names are usually authoritative and consistent. These features instill a strong degree of user confidence in the results of their searches. Libraries enhance this trust by ensuring that the materials cited are readily available for consultation, since titles catalogued are either locally held or obtainable through resource-sharing agreements. Furthermore, the library's commitment to preserve the documents in its custody guarantees enduring access.

Over the past few years, library management systems have matured and now present catalogue users with sophisticated online public access capabilities that include web access, improved keyword searching, relevance ranking, ability to limit searches by date or other fields, and reference linking. The catalogue's trustworthiness comes at a price. It depends heavily on human intelligence to apply principles of organization to bibliographic works, and the complex rules needed to exact consistency have proven expensive to apply. Original cataloging can cost $50 to $100 per title.

Although libraries have reengineered their processes to take greater advantage of cataloging copy and automated assistance in the creation of bibliographic records, the world's output of publications has outstripped the resources available to control them using traditional cataloging procedures. Compounding the situation, there has been a rise in interest in other formats, such as films, recordings, photographs, manuscripts, maps, and, now, digital objects.

At the same time that the aperture of scholarship has been widening, libraries have been diverting resources devoted to cataloging to other functions, as ARL statistics reveal: the percentage of the total professional workforce in ARL libraries employed as cataloguers has dropped by 25% from 1990 through 1998. The declining role of the catalogue was highlighted in a New York Times article headlined "Choosing Quick Hits Over the Card (sic) Catalogue."

While conceding that "libraries are organized and easily navigated," the author reports "students prefer diving into the chaotic whirl of the Web to find information." More and more students and faculty turn to the Internet as their first point of contact for information. Even deans at top-ranked universities have confessed that they get satisfactory results from "Ask Jeeves," or that they question the need for physical libraries since they find all the references they require for their writing available online. Over the past five years, there has been a strong trend in many quarters of the university to prefer electronic resources because of the ease and speed of access. More recently, the concept of portal has emerged as a unifying device for the wide variety of data made available on the web. The portal serves as a starting point for searching, and it usually offers an array of associated services such as news, related products, and reference tools, often clustered around a theme or discipline. Portals differ from the catalogue in a number of significant ways. They provide access to a wide range of materials, much of which would fall in the "unpublished" category. Harvesting of data occurs through the use of algorithmic programs, and there is little human cataloging effort.

The largest catalogue departments process 250,000 volumes annually, while Google's search engine indexes millions of web pages weekly and claims to hold links to more than a billion URLs. To cope with the effect of large response sets, portals have moved to include relevance ranking. Still it is common to experience duplicates, false drops, and dead ends in many searches conducted with the discovery tools popular on the web. In addition, the free service they provide in locating information is often subsidized through advertising, which sometimes even affects placement in search results. Proprietary information, such as licensed databases to which libraries often subscribe, is inaccessible through most commonly used portals.

Despite these deficiencies, portals offer many compelling features. They yield up-to-the-moment information, and they deliver a vast quantity and rich variety of resources, including full-text, images, and sound. The web's ability to support linking enables the searcher to move with ease from document to document, and to capture material for his own use and facile manipulation.

Customization and even personalization of searching and retrieval are other popular characteristics of search engines and portals. Looney and Lyman observe that "portals gather a wide variety of information resources into a single 'one-stop' web page, helping the user to avoid being overwhelmed by 'infoglut' or feeling lost on the Web." The enthusiasm with which people embrace the web, and the skepticism which many of these same digerati express about traditional libraries, has been sobering for some librarians. Information professionals note the flaws in search engines and in digital "library" content, which is often unstable, of dubious quality and authenticity, and incomplete. Their cautionary observations go unheeded among the hype and the reality of the flexibility of the web and the wealth of resources it encompasses.

It is unlikely that the catalogue—in its present incarnation—can ever be the tool that provides the principal mode of access to information for students and scholars. An alternative to both the dot-com portals and the catalogue is the scholars portal. A concept developed by a number of library leaders in 1999, the scholars portal, described at length by Jerry Campbell, would promise high-quality content of the type consistent with the support of research and scholarship, and it would incorporate the suite of services, such as reference, familiar to library users. It would build on the collaborative strength of libraries to create a destination for scholars that would convey the traditional values of careful selection, expert organization, skilled retrieval and delivery, interpretation, and endurance that have characterized libraries over the past century. The scholars portal has not yet come to fruition, but the energy and debate surrounding the proposal are healthy signs of the realization that libraries must transform themselves and create new services in the near future. One area that is ripe for review is the proportion of time dedicated to the cataloging of books and journals.

In the past decade and more, cataloguers have become increasingly productive, using copy cataloging and automated workstations to lower the cost of cataloging. Library administrators have seized resources previously devoted to cataloging and reallocated them to other, higher priority areas, such as technology development.

There is a chronic imbalance between the amount of work to be done and the resources available to do it, however, and in addition to backlogs of printed publications such as books and journals, the level of bibliographic control over sound recordings, photographs, films, and archival materials such as manuscripts remains poor. To this growing population of resources, which is increasingly considered important research territory, we now add endlessly proliferating electronic files. User expectations are expanding for timeliness, for in-depth access at the word or image level, for rapid retrieval, and for linkages.

To serve their clients well, libraries must blend the features of the catalogue with the virtues of the portal. This will require the use of a sophisticated search engine to deliver the quantity of resources, the hyperlinks, the customization and personalization, and the instantaneous access that provides the user with convenience, flexibility, and immediacy. Libraries can add value by promoting filtering and ranking which would prefer resources produced by universities, governments, and other sources that meet a set of established criteria, such as having a strong likelihood of authenticity, accuracy, or endorsement by others of standing.

Added to the content retrieved by the search engine should be material contributed by libraries through a reengineered cataloging process. This reformed activity should favour timely access to a wide variety of formats. To achieve this, libraries will have to reallocate funds presently devoted to describing books and journals to materials that are proportionately underrepresented in today's catalogues, such as films, music, photographs, and digital objects. This cannot be accomplished by fine-tuning, but will rather require significant compromise and change. Although certain titles may still receive full bibliographic description and analysis such as is conducted today using the Anglo-American Cataloguing Rules and the Library of Congress Subject Headings, the need to increase greatly the number of resources of interest to scholars that can be located through the library's access tool will result in the application of a different standard to many materials.

The emphasis should be placed on identification of many new resources of value to the scholar and researcher, rather than on the cataloging of only a few, relatively speaking, new items. By working collaboratively, libraries will ensure that they avoid redundancy, and they can aggregate their efforts to create a large-scale portal that offers access to a large quantity of high-quality resources of current interest. One of the salient distinctions of this portal will be that it will bridge the analog and digital worlds in a far more comprehensive way than most Internet search engines do, calling attention to the 96% of the world's published knowledge that does not exist electronically.

A critical aspect of the library portal is that for an individual library to serve its users successfully, it must connect and ally itself with other libraries and developers of commercial search engines in a highly integrated fashion. Libraries should seek to partner with developers of portals and search engines to share expertise in a constructive way, drawing on the best each has to contribute to the goal of effective access to information. Traditional libraries have much to learn from the commercial portals about attracting and satisfying users. At the same time, libraries can call attention to the value they have offered and continue to offer for today's and tomorrow's scholars.

References

Ackerman, Mark S., and Roy T. Fielding, "Collection Maintenance in the Digital Library", *Proceedings of Digital Libraries* 95, Austin, TX, pp. 39-48., June 1995.

Crowe, W. J. & Sanders, N. P., "Collection development in the cooperative environment," *Journal of Library Administration*, 15(3-4), 37-48, 1992.

Demas, S., "Collection development for the electronic library: A conceptual and organizational model," *Library Hi-Tech*, 12(3), 71-80, 1994.

3

Digital Library Preservation

The technologies we use to create and enjoy the digital heritage have many advantages that explain their extraordinarily rapid take up in many parts of the world. But there are very serious challenges in keeping our emerging, but already burgeoning, digital heritage usable and available. The media we use to carry and store it are unstable, and the technology needed for access is quickly superseded by newer technologies, wave after wave. As technologies lose support, access to the digital heritage that they fostered is also lost. These challenges are not only technical in nature; they have organisational and societal dimensions as we struggle with the responsibility of keeping access lines open over extended periods of time, often with insufficient resources and uncertain strategies. The interest of UNESCO in this situation comes as no surprise. UNESCO exists in part to encourage and enable the preservation and enjoyment of the cultural, scientific and information heritage of the world's peoples. The growth of digital heritage and its vulnerability could hardly go unnoticed.

Digital Heritage

Resources of human knowledge or expression, whether cultural, educational, scientific and administrative, or embracing technical, legal, medical and other kinds of information, are increasingly created digitally, or converted into digital form from existing analogue resources. Where resources are "born digital", there is no other format but the digital original.

Digital materials include texts, databases, still and moving images, audio, graphics, software, and web pages, among a wide and growing range of formats. They are frequently ephemeral, and require purposeful production, maintenance and management to be retained. Many of these resources have lasting value and significance, and therefore constitute a heritage that should be protected and preserved for current and future generations. This heritage may exist in any language, in any part of the world, and in any area of human knowledge or expression.

Access to the Digital Heritage

The purpose of preserving the digital heritage is to ensure that it remains permanently accessible. Accordingly, access to digital heritage materials, especially those in the public domain, should be equitable and free of unreasonable restrictions. At the same time, the security of sensitive and personal information should be protected from any form of intrusion. It is for each Member State to cooperate with relevant organizations and institutions in encouraging a legal and practical environment which would maximise accessibility of the digital heritage.

A fair balance between the legitimate rights of creators and other rights holders and those of the public to access digital heritage materials should be reaffirmed and promoted.

Guarding Against Loss of Heritage

The threat of loss

The world's digital heritage is at risk of being lost to posterity. Contributing factors include the rapid obsolescence of the hardware and software which brings it to life, uncertainties about resources, responsibility and methods for maintenance and preservation, and the lack of supportive legislation.

Attitudinal change has fallen behind technological change. Digital evolution has been too rapid and costly for governments and institutions to develop timely and informed preservation strategies. The threat to the economic, social, intellectual and cultural potential of the heritage - the building blocks of the future - has not been fully grasped.

Need for Action

Unless the prevailing threats are addressed, the loss of the digital heritage will be rapid and inevitable. Awareness-raising and advocacy is urgent, alerting policy makers and sensitizing the general public to both the potential of the digital media and the practicalities of preservation. Member States will benefit by encouraging legal, economic and technical measures to safeguard the heritage.

Continuity of digital information

The digital heritage is part of the wider continuum of digital information. To preserve digital heritage, measures will need to be taken throughout the information's life cycle. Preservation of digital heritage begins with the design of reliable systems which will produce authentic and stable digital objects.

Measures Required

Developing strategies and policies

Strategies and policies to preserve the digital heritage can be developed, taking into account the level of urgency, local circumstances, available means and future projections. The cooperation of creators, holders of copyright and related rights, and relevant institutions in setting common standards and compatibilities, and resource sharing, will facilitate this.

Defining what should be kept

As with all documentary heritage, selection principles may vary between countries, although the main criteria for deciding what digital materials to keep would be their significance and lasting cultural, scientific, evidential or other value. Selection decisions and any subsequent reviews need to be carried out in an accountable manner, and be based on defined principles, policies, procedures and standards.

Protecting the digital heritage

Member States need appropriate frameworks to secure the protection of their digital heritage. Market forces alone will not achieve this. As a key element of national preservation policy, archive legislation and legal or voluntary deposit in libraries, archives, museums and other public repositories should embrace the digital heritage. Copyright and related rights legislation should allow preservation processes to be undertaken legally by such institutions.

The right to permanent access to legally deposited digital heritage materials, within reasonable restrictions, should be guaranteed without causing prejudice to their normal exploitation.

Legal and practical frameworks for authenticity are crucial to prevent manipulation or intentional alteration of digital heritage. Both require that the content, functionality of files and documentation be maintained to the extent necessary to secure an authentic record.

Promoting cultural diversity

The digital heritage is inherently unlimited by time, geography, culture or format. It is culture-specific, but potentially accessible to every person in the world. Minorities may speak to majorities, the individual to a global audience.

The digital heritage of all regions, countries and communities should be preserved and made accessible, creating over time a balanced and equitable representation of all peoples, nations, cultures and languages.

Responsibilities

Roles and responsibilities

It is for each Member State to designate one or more agencies to take coordinating responsibility for the preservation of digital heritage, and to provide the necessary staff and resources. The sharing of tasks and responsibilities may be based on existing roles and expertise.

Measures should be taken to:

(a) urge hardware and software developers, creators, publishers, producers, and distributors of digital materials as well as other private sector partners to cooperate with national libraries, archives, museums and other public heritage organizations in preserving the digital heritage;

(b) develop training and research, and share experience and knowledge among the institutions and professional associations concerned;

(c) encourage universities and other research organizations to ensure preservation of research data.

Partnerships and cooperation

Preservation of the digital heritage requires sustained efforts on the part of governments, creators, publishers, relevant industries and heritage institutions. In the face of the current digital divide, it is necessary to reinforce international cooperation and solidarity to enable all countries to ensure creation, dissemination, preservation and continued accessibility of their digital heritage.

Industries, publishers and mass communication media are urged to promote and share knowledge and technical expertise.

The stimulation of education and training Programmes, resource-sharing arrangements, and dissemination of research results and best practices will democratize access to digital preservation techniques.

The role of UNESCO

UNESCO, by virtue of its mandate and functions, has the responsibility to:

(a) take the principles set forth in this Charter into account in the functioning of its Programmes and promote their implementation within the United Nations system and by intergovernmental and international non-governmental organizations concerned with the preservation of the digital heritage;

(b) serve as a reference point and a forum where Member States, intergovernmental and international non-governmental organizations, civil society and the private sector may join together in elaborating objectives, policies and projects in favour of the preservation of the digital heritage;

(c) foster cooperation, awareness-raising and capacity-building, and establish standard ethical, legal and technical guidelines, as a companion sourcebook to this Charter;

(d) determine, on the basis of the experience gained over the next six years in implementing the present Charter and the Guidelines, the need for further standard-setting instruments for the promotion and preservation of the digital heritage.

Preservation of Digital Heritage Materials

Digital preservation is used to describe the processes involved in maintaining information and other kinds of heritage that exist in a digital form. In these Guidelines, it does not refer to the use of digital imaging or capture techniques to make copies of non-digital items, even if that is done for preservation purposes. Of course, digital copying, may well produce digital heritage materials needing to be preserved.

Digital materials is generally used here as a preferred term covering items of digital heritage at a general level. In some places, digital object or digital resource have also been used. The terms have been used interchangeably and generically: they do not imply a particular kind of item unless that is clearly stated. Preservation programme is used to refer to any set of coherent arrangements aimed at preserving digital materials.

More commonly used terms such as digital archive and digital repository have been avoided because of their potential ambiguities: archive has different meanings for the records management community and the ICT community, whereas both archive and repository may imply a single storage site - not an appropriate implication where very distributed arrangements may be in place.

Of course, the term programme also comes with some baggage. It should be understood to cover all the aspects of preservation responsibility, including policy and strategy as well as implementation. Presentation, re-presentation are used to describe the processes of providing access to digital materials. The second term has been consistently (and idiosyncratically) hyphenised to emphasise the understanding that digital preservation seeks to re-present what was previously presented.

Not all digital materials need to be kept, only those that are judged to have ongoing value: these form the digital heritage. For those materials that warrant keeping, continuity of survival and accessibility is critical. The chances of recovering lost access to large amounts of data are very slim. Continuity requires sustained, direct action (called digital preservation) rather than passive 'benign neglect.'

Digital materials cannot be said to be preserved if access is lost. The purpose of preservation is to maintain the ability to present the essential elements of authentic digital materials. Digital preservation must address threats to all layers of the digital object: physical, logical, conceptual and essential.

Digital preservation will only happen if organisations and individuals accept responsibility for it. The starting point for action is a decision about responsibility. Everyone does not have to do everything; everything does not have to be done all at once. Comprehensive and reliable preservation programmes are highly desirable, but they may not be achievable in all circumstances of need. Where necessary, it is usually better for non-comprehensive and non-reliable action to be taken than for no action at all. Small steps are usually better than no steps.

Currently, preservation efforts have to work against the prevailing trend of digital technology and how it is developed and used. Digital materials are very often created without long-term preservation intentions in mind. Working with producers to influence the standards and practices they use, and to increase their awareness of preservation needs, are important investments.

Preservation programmes must clarify their legal right to collect, copy, name, modify, preserve and provide access to the digital materials for which they take responsibility. Digital heritage materials must be moved to a safe place where they can be controlled, protected and managed for preservation.

Digital heritage materials must be uniquely identified, and described using appropriate metadata for resource discovery, management and preservation. 18. Taking the right action later depends on adequate documentation. It is easier to document the characteristics of digital resources close to their source than it is to build that documentation later. Preservation programmes should use standardised metadata schemas as they become available, for interoperability between programmes.

The links between digital objects and their metadata must be securely maintained, and the metadata must be preserved. Authenticity is a critical issue where digital objects are used as evidence. It may also be important for other kinds of digital heritage. Data that underlies digital objects must be safely stored and managed if there is to be any chance of re-presenting authentic objects to users.

Digital preservation programmes are subjected to increased authenticity concerns because they so frequently have to use processes that involve change. Authenticity is best protected by measures that ensure the integrity of data is not compromised, and by documentation that maintains the clear identity of the material. Data protection is built on the principles of system security and redundancy.

For preservation programmes, redundancy must include securely stored backups designed around the long-term maintenance of data rather than a cycle of overwriting old data with new. The goal of maintaining accessibility is to find cost-effective ways of guaranteeing access whenever it is needed, both in the short-term and the long-term. Standards are an important foundation for digital preservation, but many programmes must find ways to preserve access to poorly standardised materials, in an environment of changing standards.

Preservation action should not be delayed until a single 'digital preservation standard' appears. Digital data is always dependent on some combination of software and hardware tools for access, but the degree of dependency on specific tools determines the range of preservation options. It is reasonable for programmes to choose multiple strategies for preserving access, especially to diverse collections.

They should consider the potential benefits of maintaining the original data streams of materials as well as any modified versions, as an insurance against the failure of still uncertain strategies. Strategies for preserving accessibility do not stand alone: they are supported by other responsibilities, and many strategies can be combined to good effect. Preservation programmes are often required to judge acceptable and unacceptable levels of loss, in terms of items, elements, and user needs.

Preservation programmes require good management that consists largely of generic management skills combined with enough knowledge of digital preservation issues to make good decisions at the right time. Digital preservation incorporates the assessment and management of risks programmes are usually faced with more material and more issues than they can cope with, so they must set priorities.

The costs of preservation programmes are hard to estimate because they encompass so much uncertainty, including evolving techniques, changing technologies and very long timeframes. Costs may well be lower per unit of information than for non-digital materials, but the amount of information to be managed in digital form is very large so total costs are also likely to remain high, including set-up costs and significant recurrent costs.

Preservation programmes may start as pilot projects but they eventually need to establish sustainable business models. While suitable service providers may be found to carry out some functions, ultimately responsible for achieving preservation objectives rests with preservation programmes, and with those who oversee and resource them. Working collaboratively is often a cost effective way to build preservation programmes with wide coverage, mutual support and the required expertise.

Types of Digital Heritage

Over time, new types of digital heritage can be expected to emerge: we have already seen the enabling power of the technology in forms as diverse as word processing, email, websites, relational databases, computer models and simulations, digital audio and video, space imagery and computer games. Electronic publications, being information that is made available for wide readership. Publications are distributed in various ways including online via the World Wide Web, or on portable carriers such as CDs, DVDs, floppy disks and various electronic book devices.

Some publications manage to combine both online and portable carrier access to different parts of the publication. As well as their means of distribution, digital publications may be classified by genres, some familiar from traditional publishing formats like monographs and serials, and others less easily defined like websites and e-zines. Some publications are released as complete items, but others evolve over time, their creators taking advantage of the interactive potential of the Internet.

Print publishing continues to grow, but increasingly publications are appearing in digital versions, increasingly in digital-only versions. Both commercial and non-commercial publishers produce digital publications, as do millions of other people who would not see themselves as publishers at all. 'Semi-published' materials such as pre-print papers and theses held in e-print and other archives available for restricted use within specific communities such as universities and scholarly societies

Organisational and personal records of activity, transactions, correspondence, etc. A very large part of the world's business and government records now exist in electronic record keeping systems. Email, messages to discussion lists and bulletin boards, web diaries, 'blogs' and 'cams' - dynamic, informal interactions enabled by digital technology - may also include important digital records amongst a tidal wave of data.

Datasets collected to record and analyse scientific, geospatial, spatial, sociological, demographic, educational, health, environmental and other phenomena. Learning objects used in technology-assisted education. Software tools such as databases, models, simulations, and software applications. Unique unpublished materials that may include research reports, oral history and folklore recordings.

Electronic 'manuscripts' such as drafts of works and personal correspondence. Entertainment products from the film, music, broadcasting and games industries, both commercial and non-commercial. Digitally generated artworks and documentary photographs. Digital copies of images, sound, text and three-dimensional objects from non-digital originals.

Many of these materials exist only in a digital form (even if carried on a physical carrier of some kind). With no equivalent non-digital version, their content is especially vulnerable to the influences that threaten digital materials. There are also rapidly growing collections of digital copies. Having originally been generated from non-digital sources, these might appear to be less vulnerable, but many of them are the only surviving version of originals that have since been damaged, lost or dispersed.

Continuity of the digital heritage is profoundly important. Increasingly this is a heritage that documents the actions of governments, the results of scientific research, the debate of ideas, the aspirations and imagination of communities, the histories of the current and coming world. If these are not to be lost or distorted, continuity is required: continuity of production, continuity of survival, and continuity of access. This must be achieved in the face of many threats:

— The carriers used to store these digital materials are usually unstable and deteriorate within a few years or decades at most

— Use of digital materials depends on means of access that work in particular ways

The Internet is an interesting scenario in which many of these threats are played out. In assessing the risks associated with the Internet, it is necessary to distinguish between two overlapping but different concerns. One concern is to look at the Internet as a whole. There is no central agency that can decide what happens to material made available through the Internet. Typically, users connect with a kaleidoscope of information for which no single creator, publisher, or any other agency is responsible.

A different viewpoint is to look at individual resources published through the Internet. These may also be quite unstable, but their instability reflects the decisions and actions of their owners in deleting, changing, moving, or renaming them. The loss of materials in this environment is attributable to how they are managed at a local level, exposed to many of the same threats that other kinds of digital materials experience.

While it is largely beyond the power of Internet users to control whether information remains available, it is very much within the power of those owning and managing digital objects and sites. If they are committed to maintaining access, it is generally within their power to do so. However, the Internet does present some special risks. For example:

- There is a strong novelty factor, so some publishers choose to change things frequently - sometimes the way information looks, sometimes also the content
- Many Internet resources are a virtual composite drawn from a number of sources, which may not be stored together anywhere.

Strategies for Preserving Digital Materials

Digital preservation involves choosing and implementing an evolving range of strategies to achieve the kind of accessibility discussed above, addressing the preservation needs of the different layers of digital objects. The strategies include:

- Working with producers (creators and distributors) to apply standards that will prolong the effective life of the available means of access and reduce the range of unknown problems that must be managed
- Recognising that it is not practical to try to preserve everything, selecting what material should be preserved
- Placing the material in a safe place
- Controlling material, using structured metadata and other documentation to facilitate access and to support all preservation process
- Protecting the integrity and identity of data
- Choosing appropriate means of providing access in the face of technological change
- Managing preservation programmes to achieve their goals in cost-effective, timely, holistic, proactive and accountable ways.

Preservation programmes have certain responsibilities and functions that have been defined, at least at a conceptual level. Comprehensive programmes must take control of appropriate digital materials and ensure they remain understandable and usable as authentic copies.

This generally involves taking the materials, properly prepared, along with associated documentation or metadata, into an archival digital storage system of some kind, where they can be managed to deal with the threats of data loss an technological change. The characteristics or attributes of programmes that can be relied upon to deliver ongoing digital preservation have also been described, in terms of responsibility, viability, sustainability, technical suitability, security, and accountability.

Digital information objects are generally not understandable or re-presentable by themselves: users need help to use them. Preservation depends on maintaining digital objects and any information and tools that would be needed in order to access and understand them. Together, these can be considered to form an information package that must be managed either as a single object or as a virtual package.

Preservation programmes must identify a safe place where digital materials can be stored and managed. Because the concept of the preservation programme allows for distributed arrangements and shared responsibilities, it is quite conceivable that while some programmes will create their own repositories, others may decide to look for a suitable 'safe place' operated and managed by someone else.

The processes of receiving, preparing and transferring digital materials into the archival system are usually referred to as ingest. Preparing material for entry into the archival information system is critical to the way the whole system is managed. It involves a number of important steps that may determine how easy or difficult it is to maintain the archived information packages in the system. These steps include:

— Applying collection policies and selection criteria to assess whether material is in scope so that it can be sought, or accepted if submitted
— Clarifying or negotiating rights issues with rights owners
— Checking the quality of the submitted information package, including its completeness, the functionality of its component parts, its authenticity, and whether it contains unwanted material such as viruses
— Labelling the material with unique identifiers
— Assessing the elements that must be maintained, and assigning preservation objectives
— Setting retention and review periods for the material, if appropriate
— Checking and if necessary upgrading the documentation that describes the material, including the technical and preservation metadata
— Assessing the file format(s) and deciding if they need to be changed to comply with the Programme's policy on what formats it will manage
— If necessary, changing the file formats to comply with the policy
— Adjusting the documentation to reflect any changes.

Once the digital object and its metadata have been prepared and associated with each other to form an information package, they are saved to the archival storage system. A preservation programme must provide archival storage that maintains, protects and verifies the integrity of the stored information packages, both the digital object and the metadata, whether stored as a single data stream or as separate but linked data streams.

To achieve this, the storage function must include practices that protect the data stream from unintended change, damage or loss: this will usually require regular copying of the data stream to fresh media, and when necessary copying to new media types. Storage practices must also include checking that the data stream has not been corrupted; system security; backup regimes that place copies at remote sites; and disaster recovery plans that address contingencies such as complete loss of the system's operating infrastructure.

Obviously, this requires technical capabilities to provide a suitably secure and reliable storage service. Such a capability can be achieved with modest equipment so long as the equipment and the whole system are well managed. The more material there is, and the more diverse and complex it is, the more sophisticated the storage system needs to be.

For most digital materials, preserving accessibility requires more than the data protection offered in the Archival Storage function. Only material being kept for very short periods could be stored without further attention to the means of providing access. The purpose of the Preservation Planning function is to monitor threats to accessibility, and to specify action to pre-empt or respond to them. The relevant threats mostly relate to changes in the technology that underlies access, so this function looks for such changes and takes action to maintain accessibility despite these changes.

Data management

Managing information packages in the archive generates its own data about what material is stored, what can be accessed, and about the management of the archive. This data must be managed to support use of the archive, and to support its effective administration. This function provides a user interface to the archive, allowing users to discover what is held, to request material and if appropriate to receive copies.

For many archives, access will be subject to restrictions for some or all potential users. The Access function may well require mechanisms to control access. The preservation programme must find ways to advocate good practices among producers, aimed at facilitating preservation of the material for which the programme will be responsible.

There is also a need to understand who the likely users of the material will be, so that preservation and access arrangements can be tailored to their needs and expectations. The overall operation of the programme must be managed. In part this responsibility involves the development of policy frameworks and standards covering all areas of operations; in part it involves the ongoing supply of appropriate resources and infrastructure including suitable technical systems; and in part management processes such as monitoring and reporting on the programme's operations.

Reference Model for Open Archival Information Systems (OAIS), released in 2002 as a draft international standard by the International Standards Organisation. The OAIS Reference Model is the most successful attempt to define both a conceptual model for managing digital materials of enduring value, and a vocabulary with which to discuss it. Anyone contemplating a responsibility for managing digital materials should seek to understand the concepts articulated in the Reference Model itself.

The Reference Model is a high level conceptual framework that can be used as a reference point for those designing, using and evaluating real implementations. It is important to realise that it is not an implementation specification: it does not provide a set of instructions on how to preserve digital information. Its value lies in explaining what is required at a highly conceptual level, regardless of the means chosen to achieve it.

The reliability and trustworthiness of digital preservation programmes are very important issues to many stakeholders. Producers, users, investors and the broad community have a strong interest in ensuring that digital heritage materials are managed by arrangements that can be trusted. Those potentially responsible for the programmes also have an interest in assessing what they can offer and the risks of accepting responsibility.

Preservation programmes offering long-term reliability are expected to have the following characteristics:

— *Responsibility*: a fundamental commitment to preservation of the digital materials in question. Organisational viability, including the prospect of an ongoing mandate; a legal status as an organisation that would support an ongoing preservation role; and a demonstrated ability to put together the resources, infrastructure and work teams that could manage the complexity of digital preservation

— *Financial sustainability*: a likely prospect of the organisation being able to continue to provide the required resources well into the future, with a sustainable business model to support its digital preservation mandate

— *Technological and procedural suitability*: the use of appropriate systems and procedures to do what is required to manage and preserve digital resources

— *System security of a very high order:* Procedural accountability, with clear allocation of responsibilities and mechanisms for reporting and assessing performance.

Arrangements that are able to demonstrate these attributes should be trustworthy. Development of trust may be a matter of demonstrating these characteristics over time. In the long term, certification programmes will probably be needed but at the time of writing no certification programmes for digital preservation arrangements have appeared. It remains very much the responsibility of those proposing digital preservation programmes to show why their arrangements should be trusted, and very much the responsibility of other stakeholders to determine that any arrangements on offer can provide an acceptable level of reliability.

Responsibility in Digital Preservation

Responsibility is a crucial issue in the preservation of digital heritage. The starting point for action is a decision about responsibility. Because the cost implications for an organisation can be significant, and because the requirements may be complex and uncertain, it is no small thing to accept a responsible role. The purpose of such arrangements is to provide a good prospect of preservation continuing beyond their own involvement, should that become necessary.

Fail-safe arrangements extend along a continuum, from a commitment to find someone else to take over responsibility before discarding digital materials, through to legally mandated arrangements for one agency to take over the management of data held by another agency if it fails to meet its preservation responsibilities. Responsibility for initiating and maintaining succession plans obviously lies with whomever is managing the material, but there may be other players who should accept some responsibility.

In facing the daunting challenges of preservation responsibility, it may help to consider some pragmatic principles:

— *Someone has to take responsibility*: if no one does, the chances of any particular materials surviving are very small

— *Everyone does not have to do everything*: responsibility can be shared. As these guidelines indicate, there are more than enough responsibilities for one preservation Programme. Many tasks, such as deciding what should be preserved, are best managed in partnership with others. If there is no one suitable to share responsibilities, preservation programmes should make realistic judgments about the responsibilities they can carry alone

— *Everything does not have to be done at once*: developing all the components of a large-scale, comprehensive preservation programme takes time. It is good to approach the task with a sense of urgency, but it may also be necessary to look for ways of buying time. This might require prioritising the issues that need to be addressed, or the material that needs attention. It may involve looking for easily managed materials ('low hanging fruit'). Some problems must be addressed without delay; some can be addressed in stages; and some can wait

— *Responsibility does not have to be forever*: there is definitely a place for time-limited contributions to an overall preservation programme, so long as the time limits are explicitly understood

— *Limited responsibility should not mean causing harm*: preservation programmes may need to take steps before all problems are solved and all techniques settled, but they must also try to minimise the harm of making later preservation efforts more difficult

— *Someone must take a leading role*: even when responsibility is shared, progress usually depends on at least one partner accepting the responsibility to lead.

Some people believe that new institutions will be needed to take on the task of preserving digital heritage. Presumably these agencies would offer specialist expertise and facilities dedicated to digital materials, and possibly dedicated to preservation rather than a wider range of functions which existing collecting institutions perform, like arranging and interpreting materials and promoting their use.

Many data archives fit into such a field already, as they exist solely to manage and preserve digital materials. They often have the paradoxical advantages of being able to focus on a limited range of materials and management tasks, while being able to offer services to a wider range of data-producing communities.

Just as it is too early to judge the long-term role of libraries, archives and museums, it is too early to attempt a definitive list of others who may play an important role. Universities and other institutes of research and learning have a natural interest in ensuring ongoing access to certain kinds of digital materials, and may have both the long-term viability and the technical infrastructure to play a preservation role. Publishers and creators of digital content have a range of interests in ongoing management and accessibility.

In many cases this extends beyond immediate commercial considerations to a longer-term investment in the exchange of ideas and the intellectual and cultural capital that ongoing accessibility encourages. Some publishers and creators may be willing and able to provide the infrastructure needed to maintain digital heritage materials in which they have an interest.

When preservation programmes have decided what kind of responsibility they will take, it is very important that they declare their intentions. This makes it easier for others to work with them, reduces the likelihood of effort being unnecessarily duplicated, and provides a clearer picture of what material is likely to survive and what is not.

Tools for Preservation Programmes

Standards lie behind almost everything that computers do, so they form a crucial foundation to the creation and use of digital materials. However, they have not yet been great enablers of preservation. They can be expected to make several important contributions if they are well chosen and well used. Those contributions can be seen in:

— The creation of digital materials that should be relatively straightforward to preserve. Some file formats (themselves standardised) have proven to be so widely useful that they have been adopted by creator communities as a best practice, raising the prospect that they will continue to be used for a long time. Examples include the Tagged Interchange File Format (TIFF) for images, and the

Structured General Markup Language (SGML) family of formats including HTML and XML, for structured documents

— Where such widely adopted formats are based on open source, non-proprietary specifications (as is the case with TIFF and SGML), it should be relatively easy to find or develop tools when they are needed to provide ongoing access across changes in technologies

— Agreed approaches to a number of preservation processes, including the recording of metadata, migration processes, data protection and item identification. Standards are still evolving in these areas

— Defining the responsibilities and functions of certain kinds of preservation programmes. The outstanding example of this to date is the Reference Model for an Open Archival Information System (OAIS), accepted by the International Standards Organisation in 2002.

Standards should not be seen as a preservation panacea. Even where they exist, they are subject to change, versioning and non-standard use by producers. Many format standards are in fact proprietary specifications that may not be publicly available, so it may be impossible to know whether tools for future access will be available. While increased standardisation of processes can only help preservation programmes, it is important not to wait for a single 'digital preservation standard' to emerge before taking sensible preservation action.

There are many different models that have been used as organisational structures to manage digital preservation. Some possibilities include:

— Setting up a single separate digital preservation unit to look after all aspects

— A series of specialist units looking after different aspects

— A matrix of people working in different areas, responsible to an overall programme manager

— Mainstreaming of the work through existing work areas so that it becomes part of the normal work integrated with other operations

— Embedding the programme in a particular existing work area such as IT, preservation, collection development, or collection management sections.

These different models tend to produce different emphases, reflecting various levels of comfort with IT tools, collecting objectives, preservation thinking, etc. Any model can be made to work effectively, so long as it draws on the perspectives and skills that are needed and has strong management support.

Preservation programmes should be guided by a policy framework that says what the programme is trying to do and how it will try to achieve it. In a field of such complexity and evolving understandings, a policy document needs to provide clear, long-term direction as well as regularly reviewed guidance. In implementing policy and developing action plans, it is almost always necessary to decide what issues, actions and materials should be given priority for attention, and to understand what work is critical before other work can be attempted.

There may be alternative paths for achieving the preservation commitments of the programme. Organisations should consider whether they will get a better result from doing the work in-house, or by contracting with someone else to do it, or by a combination of approaches. Many processes such as storage and documentation may be amenable to contracting, which may offer access to specialised expertise and facilities that would not be available otherwise.

In many cases, programmes may not be able to afford the initial investments involved in setting up and maintaining infrastructure, so paying for someone else to provide services may be attractive. Contracting may present some potential risks, including:

— Creating a distance between programme objectives and service provision
— The possibility of being locked into the service provider's services because the cost of seeking alternatives is greater than the cost of continuing
— Less control over what happens on a day-to-day basis
— Higher costs (they may also be lower) than in-house arrangements over the long term.
— Fewer learning opportunities that might suggest better ways of doing things.

The success of contracting may depend on the programme manager's ability to define what is needed; finding a reliable supplier who can offer the services required at a suitable price; being able to negotiate a suitable contract with adequate safeguards; and skills in managing the contract. In working with service providers, preservation managers must ensure they:

— Understand their business and what they need to achieve

— Communicate their needs

— Rigorously assess the capabilities, motivations, and understandings of potential suppliers

— Prepare and negotiate an appropriate contract

— Ensure communication channels are open so that any problems that be reported early

— Monitor performance closely and evaluate arrangements regularly. Ensure there are responsible exit strategies and succession plans in place for when arrangements come to an end.

There are good technological, economic and political reasons for preservation programmes to cooperate. Decisions about collaboration should be based on assessment of the benefits expected and the costs involved. There are a number of possibilities regarding where to look for partners, what the focus of the relationship should be, and structural frameworks that would be suitable. Successful cooperation is usually the result of careful attention to these choices, and to putting in the effort required to manage the collaboration in practice.

Technical and Practical Perspectives

It is usually necessary to decide what digital materials are worth keeping, as has been the case with non-digital materials. Many of the same approaches - selection based on criteria embodied in collection development policies, and good knowledge of the materials and their context - are fundamental for digital heritage selection. Preservation programmes also need to define the elements or characteristics of the materials they select that give them value, so that those elements can be maintained.

Deciding what should be preserved, by whom, and for how long, have been fundamental decisions in managing all kinds of tangible heritage. Such decisions are necessary because there are usually more things - more information, more records, more publications, more data than we have the means to keep. Every choice to preserve is at the expense of something else.

The selection of digital heritage is conceptually the same as selection of non-digital materials. Any existing programme with well-established procedures for assessing and selecting material for preservation will already have policies, skills and tools that can help in selecting digital materials, even though they may need some adjustment. However, digital materials do present some new challenges that programme managers must take into account in making the best selection decisions they can.

— There is often a large amount of material to be assessed

— The means of producing and disseminating digital materials are widely available, so their quality is often inconsistent

— At the same time, there may be pressure to preserve the entire traffic carried by new communication channels such as the World Wide Web, regardless of quality

— Timing of selection is usually critical, as digital materials quickly de-select themselves by becoming unusable. It may not be possible to wait for evidence of enduring value to emerge before making selection decisions

— Some digital objects may be hard to pin down. New genres may not fit into existing classifications; some digital resources consist of linked or overlapping parts; many also exist in parallel versions.

— Even when external boundaries have been defined, it may be hard to tell which elements need to be maintained if the digital object is to fulfil its essential purpose

— It may even be difficult to tell where digital materials come from, making it hard to decide who is responsible for their preservation and with whom to negotiate the rights required by preservation programmes.

There are dangers in assuming that current value assessments are a completely reliable guide to future values. For example, remote sensing data collected in previous decades has become unexpectedly important for assessing environmental change. This experience suggests it is probably better to err on the side of collecting more material rather than less, if the preservation programme can manage it.

Where digital materials can only be understood by reference to a set of rules such as a record keeping system, database or data generation system, or other contextual information, selection processes must identify the documentation that will also need to be preserved. Producers of digital materials may have a significant role to play in selecting what should be preserved. They are often well placed to understand why digital objects were brought into being, their essential 'message', and the relationships between objects and their context. If that information is not captured from the producer it may be too difficult to reconstruct it later.

Both comprehensive and selective approaches are supported by strong arguments. Advocates of a comprehensive approach argue that any information may turn out to have long-term value, and that the costs of detailed selection are greater than the costs of collecting and storing everything. Advocates of a more selective approach argue that it allows them to create collections of high value resources, with some assurance of technical quality and an opportunity to negotiate access rights with producers.

There may well be a place for both approaches, as they are likely to produce quite different collections of digital heritage that are valued for different purposes. To minimise the risk of important materials being missed, and to avoid unnecessary duplication of effort, it may be necessary to seek agreements with other potential collecting and preservation agencies about respective roles and responsibilities.

Selection policies may have to decide whether to select whole items and whole collections, or samples only. It is generally preferable to preserve whole items to retain their integrity, but it may be necessary to restrict collecting to representative samples as a way of at least evidencing the existence of some kinds of materials. Selection policy may also have to consider whether the re-use of material constitutes a new item that should also be preserved.

Rights issues may influence selection decisions. Preservation programmes often select materials that are still subject to rights, but generally would not select material if rights were so restrictive that arrangements for giving access at some future stage cannot be negotiated. If the material can never be made available for use, or if necessary preservation steps cannot be taken, there is little point in selecting it as heritage material.

Managing selection also requires the development of criteria for appraisal. Where the amount of material is so large that it is not feasible to assess items individually, it may be necessary to establish classes of material that can be assessed on the basis of representative samples. Preservation programmes often act as agents for other stakeholders: they take preservation action on behalf of someone who wants material kept for a reason.

The 'someone else' may be as broad and many-faceted as 'the nation' or 'the general community', who may mandate a programme to collect and preserve a very broad range of materials; or it may be as narrow as the members of an organisation or researchers working in a particular discipline who want their own research output preserved for later use.

The needs of the 'community' - however defined - for whom the material is being kept will drive many decisions, from what material is selected, to the kind and level of documentation that is recorded, to the level of concern with authenticity, to the strategies that are used. For example, some programmes must offer users the option of interrogating old data to produce new results, whereas others have a brief to present material in a read-only form to that it cannot be changed or manipulated.

Some programmes may even have to ensure users can run old simulations, play old computer games, or view digital art in ways that reproduce the original experience rather than a speeded up experience that later technologies may provide. Defining the essential elements or characteristics (also referred to as significant properties by some programmes) is not conceptually difficult, as the examples above illustrate. In some circumstances - such as clearly defined and constrained user expectations, and easily characterised materials that are all similar - defining and encoding the essential elements should be straightforward.

For instance, a programme may decide that users of a large collection of electronic mail messages only need to see elements that can be characterised as 'content information', such as the name and address of the sender, subject, date and time, recipients, and the message, in a standardised structure with only the most simple of formatting. A government archive with this approach could expect to apply this essential elements template to very large numbers of email records.

On the other hand, some materials are much more difficult to characterise, and expectations about how they will be re-presented for use, especially to an open-ended community of potential users, may be so hard to define in advance that it becomes almost impossible. Approaches to this issue are developing as more people encounter the problems of describing, storing and planning to re-present digital objects in growing collections over long periods of time.

Preservation programmes with few resources must still make decisions about the materials for which they accept responsibility. Because the costs of preservation are related to the amount of material to be managed, such programmes may need to be highly selective, limiting their ambitions to a small amount of highly valued material. Preservation costs are also related to the range of problems and formats that need to be managed, so it may also make sense to severely limit the kinds of materials selected to a very few formats.

Collecting agreements with other programmes may shift some of the burden of selecting materials. While these would normally be negotiated with other preservation programmes, there may be potential for agreements with producers that would lead them to make decisions about what should be collected and preserved. The preservation programme would still need to take some responsibility for quality control, as well as articulating the criteria by which material should be chosen.

Digital heritage is often created without consideration of ongoing use and accessibility. However, there are definitely standards and practices that producers can use that either help or hinder preservation. Programme managers need to look for ways of exerting a positive influence from as early in the digital heritage life cycle as possible. This often requires a willingness to work with producers.

Digital materials are created by producers who are not necessarily concerned with long-term availability: creation of 'digital heritage' may not be part of their intention. Even those hoping to make something of enduring value may not have the knowledge or the means to do so, or be constrained by other impediments in their working environment. Without some kind of intervention, it is unlikely that digital heritage materials will automatically be made in ways that will minimise costs and remove barriers to preservation. Many practices in fact make preservation much harder.

Preservation efforts that wait until problems start to appear are likely to be more costly, more difficult, and less effective than efforts that start early. Organisations that have both heritage-creating and heritage-preserving functions have learnt from experience that care invested from the start in the use of standards, documentation, good file management and other practices, pays dividends later in lower preservation and maintenance costs, as well as more easily accessed, re-used and managed collections.

While all preservation programmes do not have the same opportunities to influence production practices, all programmes should seek to influence the way materials are created, and managed, from as early in their life cycle as possible. It is important to recognise that creators of digital materials work in different environments and are likely to be quite diverse in many ways: how they approach their work, their size of operations, the organisational and technical support at their disposal, and their interest in long-term access issues.

For example, scientists collecting data are likely to have an overriding interest in how accurately and securely their data is protected; how well any proposed formats and standards fit with their working needs; the convenience of transfer arrangements; and maintenance of moral rights and access controls over their data. On the other hand, commercial publishers of CD-ROM packages are likely to be more interested in controls on unauthorised copying; the costs and risks associated with providing 'unprotected' versions to a preservation programme; the potential re-use of their content; and their licence obligations to software owners whose products they have used.

There are many ways in which those responsible for preserving digital heritage may approach working with those who create and disseminate it. Preservation programmes should proactively promote awareness of their own role. It may be advantageous to identify particular groups of producers and work with them, addressing specific issues, rather than trying to resolve everyone's concerns at a generic level. At a broader industry level, it may be helpful to develop a code of practice that sets out agreed understandings about roles and responsibilities, and defines the scope and terms of ongoing cooperation.

Many sectors have active industry groups that provide forums for discussing issues. As well as offering opportunities for dialogue with industry leaders, such forums may help in establishing new norms of thinking that incorporate a longer term perspective. It is important for preservation programmes to offer positive encouragement and feedback for the steps producers are willing to take, and to provide a level of accountability for the way preservation programmes deal with their materials.

In many situations, working with producers means a real input by the preservation programme, not just the producer. Possible areas of input may include:

— Providing written guidelines and specifications

— Providing training for staff

— Help in designing systems and workflows
— Exchange of information and working tips
— Succession arrangements for material in a producer-managed preservation programme.

Specifications and best practice guidance Guidance on good practice is likely to include advice on the following:

— *Organisational issues that will make it easier to manage digital materials:* Project planning, emphasising system design prior to the creation of any records or publications
— *Choice of carrier*: Producers should be encouraged to use 'industrial strength' products that will survive long enough for the data to be transferred to other carriers, either by the producer or on transfer to the preservation programme
— *Choice of appropriate file formats and data standards*: Unless there are very good reasons to do otherwise, creators should be encouraged to use very widely adopted, well-standardised file formats that fit their purposes. Generally speaking, data in simpler formats using open source, non-proprietary software are easier to preserve (although some proprietary applications achieve such widespread use that they may be accepted as an industry standard, especially if their specifications are openly published).

  Online materials published for public access should be readable by commonly used browsers. Structuring documents in a standard, easily recognised and durable format such as XML (Extensible Markup Language) should be considered for material of enduring value
— *Validation of formats*: It is not enough simply to choose a standard format and then to use it in non-standard ways: formats should be implemented in compliance with their standard and if necessary validated to remove any idiosyncrasies likely to complicate preservation.
— *File names should be consistent and unambiguous*: Online files should be managed for persistent access through the use of a persistent identifier and resolver service, or re-direct messages if files are moved. A number of PI schemes are in use internationally in different sectors, although none are in universal use. The DOI (Digital Object Identifier)

scheme used by commercial publishers to manage rights has the widest acceptance.

Creators should create good quality metadata for the resources they create, using a widely accepted schema such as MARC, the Dublin Core metadata elements or one of its many sector-based enhancements. The metadata will help users find and use their resources. Metadata should also be recorded that describes the technical nature of the digital objects, what is required to access them, and any changes in these details over their life cycle: this information will be needed in managing them. The metadata can be either embedded in the resources or stored in a linked metadata file

— *File management*: Preservation master files should be stored and managed separately from dissemination copies. Database management procedures should ensure that data is not overwritten before it is captured

— *System security*: Files and systems should be fully protected from damage or loss by adopting best practice security measures and by appropriate backup arrangements even for short-term storage

— *Authenticity*: All files should be identified and their provenance and history documented to provide continuous evidence of authenticity

— *Training*: Staff, contractors and others coming into contact with the digital materials should be guided by appropriate procedures and manuals, and be adequately trained, motivated and equipped to use them

— If access or copying barriers are considered necessary to protect intellectual property, they may well make preservation impossible. Arrangements will be needed to allow preservation processes such as copying to take place.

Initial steps in maintaining access may include keeping all the software required for access, as well as any specialised hardware. This will not be an effective long-term strategy but may well be necessary in the short term. There may be a need to evaluate digital materials, decide how long they should be kept and by whom, in accordance with an approved policy such as an archival disposal authority.

Digital preservation programmes with few resources may find they are unable to spare any resources to work with producers. However, it may be possible to make a worthwhile investment in reducing future costs by taking limited, targeted actions aimed at influencing the material they have to manage.

Data Protection

Data protection is a fundamental of all preservation programmes. For many programmes, authenticity is also critically important. Authenticity relates to the ongoing integrity of data, and its clear and sustained identification. Data protection strategies include allocation of responsibility, technical infrastructure, maintenance, data transfer, proper storage of data carriers, backup, system security and disaster planning. Authenticity also relies on clear documentation of the origins and history of digital materials.

Data must be stored. While it is appropriate to focus preservation attention on how best to re-present digital objects as originally intended, it must never be forgotten that the digital object has an underlying form as data. It is as data that it must be stored, managed and protected if any digital object is to be available for presentation to a user.

Heritage materials are often valued, at least in part, for their authenticity - the degree to which one can trust that they are indeed what they are thought to be. For archival records, scientific data, and many other kinds of digital materials, trust in their ongoing authenticity is critical, for without it they are of virtually no value. Authenticity derives from being able to trust both the identity of an object - that it is what it says it is, and has not been confused with some other object - and the integrity of the object - that it has not been changed in ways that change its meaning.

Maintenance of both identity and integrity implies sustained and documented links between an object as originally created and as currently presented. Evaluating, maintaining and providing evidence of continued authenticity are key responsibilities for most preservation programmes.

The nature of digital materials, and how they must be managed for preservation and access, both present challenges:

— Digital materials can be changed easily, with or without fraudulent intent, and even without any intent at all
— Changes that happen may not be obvious
— Preservation processes almost always involve making changes - transferring data from one system to another, from one carrier to

another, adding or updating metadata, creating new copies that need new file names, changing the means of presentation as technologies change, and so on.

Where digital materials have value as records that offer evidence of some kind, authenticity is extremely important. Not all digital materials are made or selected to provide evidence: for example, they may reflect creative expression, the debate of ideas, or the desire to entertain and be entertained.

Even for these materials authenticity may be an issue, as the integrity of their creators' work or ideas should be protected. Ultimately, preservation programmes must decide how much to invest in ensuring that the authenticity of material in their care can be trusted, bearing in mind that object identity and data integrity are fundamental responsibilities.

Data protection must play a key role in any preservation programme, for two reasons: i) So that there is a digital object for a user to access. This is a fundamental requirement: if data is lost or seriously corrupted it may be impossible to re-present the intended digital object at all, and the preservation process must be judged to have failed ii) So that the integrity of the data can be maintained without tampering or corruption in order for users to trust the authenticity of the re-presented object.

Role of documentation

Documentation also plays a key role, for two reasons:

— By explaining the links between objects and by clearly distinguishing between them, it provides evidence of identity

— By showing what changes, if any, have taken place, with whose authority, and to what effect, it provides an audit trail to attest to authenticity.

Of all the responsibilities of preservation programmes, storage and data protection may be the ones for which it is easiest to find suitable third party service providers. The considerable investments required for equipment and expertise may make this an attractive alternative to managing data in-house. However, the critical nature of data protection means that the preservation programme must still accept responsibility for ensuring that any contracted services deliver the necessary levels of care and control.

Data must be stored and managed with appropriate systems and on an appropriate carrier. There are digital asset management systems or digital object storage systems available that meet the requirements of digital preservation programmes. Once requirements have been determined, they should be thoroughly discussed with potential suppliers. Different systems and carriers are suited to different needs and those chosen for preservation programmes must be fit for their purpose.

The overall system must have adequate capabilities including:

Sufficient storage capacity. Storage capacity can be build up over time, but the system must be able to manage the amount of data expected to be stored within its life cycle -As a fundamental capability, the system must be able to duplicate data as required without loss, and transfer data to new or 'refreshed' carriers without loss -Demonstrated reliability and technical support to deal with problems promptly -The ability to map file names into a file-naming scheme suitable for its storage architecture. Storage systems are based around named objects.

Different systems use different architectures to organise objects. This may impose constraints on how objects are named within storage; for example, disk systems may impose a hierarchical directory structure on existing file names, different from those that would be used on a tape system. The system must allow, or preferably carry out, a mapping of system-imposed file names and existing identifiers

Error checking. A level of automated error checking is normal in most computer storage. Because heritage materials must be kept for long periods, often with very low human usage, the system must be able to detect changes or loss of data and take appropriate action.

Technical infrastructure must also include means of storing metadata and of reliably linking metadata to stored digital objects. Large operations often find they need to set up digital object management systems that are linked to, but separate from, their digital mass storage system, in order to cope with the range of processes involved, and to allow metadata and work interfaces to be changed without having to change the mass storage.

While the cost of replacing data carriers must be considered, replacement media typically offer increased storage capacity. Unfortunately, any savings are usually offset by growth in the amount of data to be stored. The market for data storage and management systems extends well beyond preservation programmes, so there are good COTS (Commercial Off The Shelf) products available.

Using COTS technology is possibly the most easily managed, low risk and cost effective approach as technical support and upgrades are provided by vendors in a competitive marketplace. Standards are sufficiently widely used in the storage market to allow mixing and matching products from various vendors so that a number of upgrade and replacement paths are available when needed.

Storage systems rely on safe and complete replication of data, rather than enduring carriers, for data protection. Data must be copied from carrier to carrier to avoid the impact of carrier deterioration. As new kinds of carriers prove their usefulness in storage systems, data is transferred from older kinds of carriers. This must happen before any hardware or software required to retrieve the data are discarded. Planning for data transfers is a management challenge, whatever the system used.

For example, a small, low use archive storing data on shelved CDs, must keep track of the age and condition of the CDs as well as signs that CD technology will have to be replaced. More sophisticated mass storage systems generally automate decisions about regular transfer of data between carriers, but managers still need to decide when carriers should be replaced with new media, and when underlying technology has been superseded. Appropriate storage and handling conditions for carriers.

Digital data carriers must be stored in conditions that do not accelerate their rate of deterioration. The main risks for data carriers are excessive temperature and humidity which endanger the carrier; dust or other particulates which may obscure access to the data; and in the case of optically encoded material, light, which may damage the optically inscribed data. Modern data tapes are of such a high coercivity, that accidental erasure by a magnetic field does not constitute a major risk.

Magnetic data tapes may be integrated into a digital storage system. Typically this would be housed in a clean computer room with controlled temperature and relatively humidity set at 18°C, and 40% RH, a continuous influx of clean, dust-free air, with daily cleaning to prevent contamination. The conditions would fluctuate no more than 2°C and 10% RH in any given 24 hour period. Magnetic data tapes stored for optimum carrier life should be stored under more stringent conditions, at a temperature between 18°C and 10°C, with a daily tolerance of no more than 1°C, and between 30 and 40% RH with a tolerance of no more than 3%RH.

Optical carriers, such as CD-Recordable, should be stored under similar conditions, in a darkened environment due to their sensitivity to light. There are suggestions that very low temperatures (approaching or lower than 0°C), may be detrimental to the life expectancy of certain carriers, however, this has not been proven.

While storing multiple copies of the same data does offer some protection against failure, preservation programmes must also consider the risks of a disaster which damages all copies stored at the same site. Storing copies at different sites is a basic requirement; to avoid the impact of region-wide disasters such as floods, earthquakes, wildfires, and war, programmes should consider the need to store additional backup copies of important data outside their own region.

Preservation programmes may also need to adjust normal backup schedules so that preservation data, which must be kept, is refreshed (i.e. rewritten) not overwritten with new data.

Data protection is such a critical responsibility that even programmes with few resources must give it a high priority. The simplified risk analysis above may suggest areas of lower risk for some programmes. It also suggests that some risks may be reduced at the cost of reducing the level or speed of access. This may be perfectly acceptable for some collections.

Changes in software and hardware add up to a loss in the means of access to digital heritage materials. This is expected to be the core challenge for most preservation programmes. Using understandings of the relationship between digital objects and their means of access, and taking account of what has to be presented to a user in providing access, programme managers must decide on strategies that will guarantee accessibility whenever it is needed.

Strategies, which are likely to vary over time and according to needs, are still evolving. The strategies discussed are grouped into those based on investment of resources from early in the life cycle of digital materials, those with short-term and with medium- to long-term effectiveness, and some alternative 'non-digital' and 'non-preservation' strategies.

Intellectual Access to Digital Information

Today most libraries, invests heavily in cataloging its collections. It probably has the largest cataloging operation in the world1 and is a source of both cataloging data and standards for much of the library community. In the world of paper-based publication, its role is second to none. One enduring role of libraries during the transition from physical to digital information will be the intellectual task of cataloging—imposing order on diverse resources with the goal of making those resources easier to discover and manage.

Cataloging is arguably among the most expensive tasks in the library. Current estimates range from $50 to $110 for the creation of a single full cataloging record. What is responsible for this high cost? While some of the tasks of cataloging—for example, recording a title—are indeed mundane (in the majority of but not all cases), others are intellectually challenging and time consuming:

— *Subject analysis*—The usability of library catalogs for finding resources "about" a particular subject depends greatly on the nontrivial task of understanding the content of a resource and tagging it with a controlled subject heading.
— *Authority control*—While the subject of assigning authorship may seem superficially simple, it is confounded by the fact that people frequently use different forms of their name, and different people frequently have very similar or identical names.

There is the problem of the multiple spellings of historical figures (is it "Shakespeare" or "Shakespere" or "Shakespear" or ?), the problem of aliases ("Mark Twain" and "Samuel Clemens"), and the seemingly random use of initials, shortened names, and the like ("Samuel Langhorne Clemens," "Samuel L. Clemens," "Sam Clemens," etc.). Authority control, in the context of author names, is the task of, first, associating these name variations with a canonical name in the cataloging record to show that the variations are indeed the same person and, second, differentiating between ambiguous and overlapping names.

The development of standard cataloging practices from the end of the nineteenth century through the twentieth century made it possible to share cataloging records, leading to a significant cost savings for libraries. "Copy cataloging" exploits the fact that the overwhelming majority of resources in an average library are not unique. Rather than produce original cataloging records for the duplicated resources, libraries can use cataloging records from other libraries.

In US, the development of the machine-readable cataloging (MARC) record by the Library of Congress, in concert with the library community, in the 1960s was a landmark event in the automation of library operations. As recalled above, preautomation catalog sharing involved the physical shipment of catalog cards to fellow libraries. The introduction of computers into the library environment allowed sharing computer catalog records among libraries by exchanging magnetic tapes.

MARC consists of both an encoding scheme for labeling cataloging elements (e.g., "author" or "title") and an exchange format for packaging the encoded bibliographic data into a record for transfer purposes. The MARC record remains a critical technical foundation of existing integrated library systems and permits the transfer of records among these systems. The Library's Network Development and MARC Standards Office leads and coordinates international efforts to further develop MARC as a standard for the efficient and long-term interchange of bibliographic information.

In recent years, the office has been analyzing the relationship of MARC to standard generalized markup language (SGML) and the use of MARC for digital media. Such a catalog could have been a natural product for a national library and, perhaps, could have provided a revenue stream to underwrite the Library's cataloging operation. In fact, the Library, for reasons not entirely obvious to the committee or the individuals, failed to take advantage of this key opportunity and ceded it to the Online Computer Library Center (OCLC) and the Research Libraries Group (RLG).

While MARC provides the markup and transfer syntax for bibliographic records, the Anglo-American Cataloging Rules (AACR2) provide the rules for the actual description of a bibliographic item. The Library of Congress plays a major role in coordinating activities in AACR2, and its Library of Congress Rule Interpretations defines common practice for the use of AACR2 in cooperative cataloging. The result, in combination with the MARC standard, is that both the meaning and encoding of cataloging records can be shared among a large number of libraries.

These activities are centered in the Library's Cataloging Policy and Support Office (CPSO), which provides "leadership in the creation and implementation of cataloging policy within the Library of Congress and in the national and international library community." In general, archival and manuscript items are handled differently from monographs and serials. Whereas the latter are cataloged at the item level, the former are described at a coarser level of granularity (for example, a manuscript box or folder). Tools for locating such items are referred to as "finding aids."

The encoded archival description (EAD) was the product of a project at the University of California at Berkeley in the early 1990s to develop a standard for machine-readable finding aids. The EAD standard utilizes SGML to mark up structured descriptions of units of archival information. The Library's Network Development and MARC Standards Office serves as the maintenance agency for the EAD standard, an excellent example of the Library stepping in to play an important role in the new metadata environment.

Challenges to Traditional Cataloguing Practices

A user of the Web who has sampled any of the numerous search engines (e.g., Google, AltaVista, Excite) might argue that digital content, networks, and full-text indexing have made human-mediated organization through cataloging obsolete. Web search engines demonstrate the great utility of such searching and the benefits of over 30 years of research in information retrieval and, to a lesser degree, natural language processing. However, there are numerous inherent limitations to the technology underlying them:

— Scalability—Most Web search engines accumulate indexes by scanning the Web and downloading full content from sites. As the volume of Web content grows, it has become increasingly difficult to keep these indexes current or complete. One study indicates that even the best search engines index only about 12 to 15 percent of Web content. Even more problematic are the limitations of the information retrieval (IR) technology used in most popular Web search engines. The nature of the Web as a corpus presents some difficult scalability challenges for IR and often leads to poor results. The sheer size of the corpus is a notable problem; a typical Web query will retrieve a very large set of potentially relevant documents. In addition, the Web corpus is usually presented as a single, unorganized collection of documents, which makes synonym clashes inevitable. Synonym clashes are well understood and can be addressed with a variety of techniques (e.g., thesauri, user feedback, local context analysis, phrase structure), but these techniques are generally not exploited by Web search engines.

— Access limitations and databases—While a great deal of useful content is freely available on the Internet, there is a growing and equally valuable portion of Internet content that is proprietary and held in protected systems. Much "valuable" content is held in databases on special servers that require a password or other means of authorization for access. These databases also provide enhanced functions beyond what can be done with simple, static Web pages. However, they do not in general support access via crawling, the method used to build most Internet search services. Thus, while Web indexers are able to access and index a large percentage of the total content on the Web, an ever-growing percentage of the most-sought-after material is not available from Internet search facilities.

— Format—Existing Web search engines are limited to textual content. They index words in documents and process textual queries—for example, "digital imaging"—returning lists of documents ranked according to the appearance of the query words in their content. Extending this approach to images will require tools to analyze image content and respond to queries such as "find images with cars in them" or, at an even more advanced level, to queries that ask for images with features similar to those of another digitized image. The tools to retrieve images, video segments, voice, and music are being actively researched but are currently beyond the capabilities of Internet search engines.

— Context—At a more abstract level, the usefulness of indexing based solely on the text content of a resource is compromised by lack of context. The best tools to help a person locate a resource are those that are tailored to the context in which the resource occurs and to the knowledge context of the searcher. For example, content-based searches of MEDLINE (the medical index at the National Library of Medicine) might be appropriate for a professional familiar with medical terminology and with the body of medical literature indexed by MEDLINE. However, a high-school student might not be able to select documents that are appropriate to his or her background and might not be familiar with medical terms, so he or she might find content-based searching to be difficult. The lack of context is a problem for both human and automatically generated representations, but different representations can often be combined to good effect.

— Markup—HTML, the main markup language of the Web, provides only a very simplified set of tags for labeling the parts of a document. These are primarily oriented to supporting the appropriate display of the document and in general tell little about the meaning of the various sections of the document. Many search engines utilize smart markup to provide more powerful retrieval facilities, allowing users to limit which parts of a document are used to satisfy the search argument. The simplicity of HTML markup severely constrains Internet search engines' use of such facilities, which are very useful for limiting and refining search results.

The creation of structured descriptive records for resources (e.g., traditional cataloging records or, more generally, surrogates) can help to address some of these limitations. Scalability can improve if surrogates are used instead of the full content for indexing. Content providers may be more willing to distribute freely descriptive surrogates for indexing, in lieu of the full content. Surrogates can be created, and standards are being developed for describing all manner of digital objects.

Finally, surrogate records may include descriptive information that is not part of the document itself (usually the result of human analysis). For example, surrogates to facilitate searching MEDLINE by high-school students might associate more common medical subject terms with the resources, thus making searching easier for this community. On the other hand, there is broad agreement among the committee members and in the general information community that the nature of resource description needs a thorough examination in the context of digital resources.

Traditional cataloging is one kind of resource description, which, in turn, is one kind of "metadata (information that describes the structure or content of a document but is not part of the document). The nature and use of meta-data are evolving to accommodate the great variety of digital objects.

Traditional library cataloging has scaled up to serve institutions of great size—prominent among them the Library of Congress. However, over the past year the number of resources on the Web has grown to the point that they exceed the number of books in even the largest of libraries and even the number of book pages in the average library. The growth rate of these networked resources substantially exceeds the growth rate of traditional physical resources. Sheer size presents considerable challenges to the economics of traditional library cataloging, in which metadata records are characterized by great precision, detail, and professional intervention.

The high price of traditional library cataloging makes it impractical in the context of such growth, and less expensive alternatives are needed for many, if not all, of these resources. There has always been a trade-off between the cost of creating metadata and its value in facilitating access to document collections. Large print collections generally cannot be accessed without some sort of metadata, so the value of the metadata is high. The appearance of digital objects in commercially interesting collections during the 1970s changed the economic model. Then, access could be provided with relatively little investment in metadata, although higher-quality metadata could still be justified for high-value materials. Now, the steady increase in the volume of electronic materials has increased pressure to reduce the cost of metadata, although manually produced metadata are still common.

The lifespan of networked resources differs dramatically from that of physical resources. The well-known problem of "dangling URLs" bedevils any librarian who is trying to incorporate Web pages into a collection. The impermanence of networked resources is rooted in the economics of networked dissemination. The cost of distributing networked content is low compared with the cost of printing and distributing hard-copy content, so there is little benefit to the publisher of maintaining older versions of a document. With no incentive to retain older versions, the management of objects is haphazard and object permanence is problematic.

Such an environment has a strong impact on the economics and incentives for producing metadata and also points out the critical need for preservation-oriented metadata and mechanisms to manage the preservation of digital objects. The breakdown of traditional publishing roles has disrupted some of the traditional mechanisms for establishing the credibility of an information source. Since metadata is itself an information resource, the credibility issue applies to the quality of metadata created by external sources (outside the traditional library cataloging community).

The creation of bad metadata can be nonmalicious: for example, an author who lacks training or who doesn't care may assign a bad subject classification to a descriptive metadata record. It can also be malicious: so-called "index spamming," whereby content creators seed metadata fields with misleading or incorrect information to affect the ranking of their pages by search engines, is a real problem on the Web. An important challenge for networked information is developing the mechanisms and policies to verify the origin of any information, including metadata.

Libraries, deals with a considerable variety of resources, including books, serials, maps, software, movies, images, and, now, digital resources.

The Library's efforts to create metadata for this spectrum of resources can be divided into two categories. First, much attention has been paid to enhancing the traditional cataloging mechanisms—AACR2 and MARC, for example—to accommodate these new genres. These efforts are motivated by the central role that the traditional cataloging formats play in the Integrated Library System and in the cooperative cataloging efforts.

Second, the Library has employed a number of other vehicles for resource description—metadata schemata tailored for individual resource characteristics. Some schemata have been coordinated with external communities; others have been developed internally. The use of other metadata vocabularies raises the issue of how these vocabularies interact to provide integrated information spaces for users of digital libraries. After all, one of the major strengths of the standardization on AACR2 and its expression in MARC records has been the uniform search interface provided by library catalogs to large and heterogeneous collections.

The field of metadata has exploded into a major area of investigation and development over the past several years. As information becomes more of a commodity item--and, as many would argue, is the largest product of the "new economic paradigm--its management is of interest to a broad spectrum of organizations. This stands in rather strong contrast to the situation in the pre-Internet era, when the standardized management of information was more or less restricted to libraries, with the Library of Congress playing a key leadership role.

This broadening of the metadata environment will include many new players and applications and require the Library to think in new ways if it is to reassert its leadership in this area. Descriptive cataloging, exemplified by the traditional library cataloging record, is but one of many classes of metadata. Real-world applications need to make use of a much broader range of metadata than descriptive cataloging. Some other metadata types are listed below to provide a sense of this range.

— *Terms and conditions*: metadata that describe the rules for use of an object. Terms and conditions might include an access list of who may view the object, a conditions-of-use statement that might be displayed before access to the object is allowed, a schedule (tariff) of prices and fees for use of the object, or a definition of the permitted uses of an object (viewing, printing, copying, etc.).

— *Administrative data*: metadata that relate to the management of an object in a particular server or repository. Some examples of information stored in administrative data are the date of last modification, the date of creation, and the administrator's identity.

— *Content rating*: a description of attributes of an object within a multidimensional, scaled rating scheme assigned by some rating authority; an example might be the suitability of the content for various audiences, similar to the well-known movie rating system used by the Motion Picture Association of America. Note that content ratings have applications far beyond simple filtering on sex and violence levels. Content ratings are likely to play important roles in future collaborative filtering systems, for example.

— *Provenance*: data defining the source or origin of some content object, for example, of some physical artifact from which the content was scanned. The data might also include a summary of all algorithmic transformations that have been applied to the object (filtering, reductions in image density, etc.) since its creation. Arguably, provenance information might also include evidence of authenticity and integrity through the use of digital signature schemes; or, authenticity and integrity information might be considered a separate class of metadata.

— *Linkage or relationship data*: data indicating the often complex relationships between content objects and other objects. Some examples are the relationship of a set of journal articles to the containing journal, the relationship of a translation to the work in its original language, the relationship of a subsequent edition to the original work, or the relationships among the components of a multimedia work (information on synchronization between images and a soundtrack, for example).

— *Structural data*: data defining the logical components of complex or compound objects and how to access those components. A simple example is a table of contents for a textual document. More complex examples include the definition of the different source files, subroutines, data definitions in a software suite, SGML or XML tagged books, or other complex works.

The need for additional metadata types and for traditional metadata for a larger volume of materials challenges traditional means of metadata creation—manual techniques cannot be scaled up to meet demand. But automated techniques are available that can help in the production of metadata (natural language processing, automatic classification, document clustering). These techniques have yet to be integrated with more traditional manual techniques; such integration will be a huge task for the library community.

References

Butler, Meredith A., "Issues and Challenges of Archiving and Storing Digital Information: Preserving the Past for Future Scholars", *Journal of Library Administration* 24, no. 4: 61-79, 1997.

Carlson, Scott, "Stanford Project Will Test an Approach for Preserving Digital Journals", *The Chronicle of Higher Education*, A45, 10 March 2000.

CEDARS Project, *Draft Specification: CEDARS Preservation Metadata Elements*, 2000.

Chapman, Stephen, and Anne R. Kenney, "Digital Conversion of Library Research Materials: A Case for Full Informational Capture", *D-Lib Magazine,* October 1996.

Chen, S. S., "The Paradox of Digital Preservation", *IEEE Computer*, 34 (3), pp. 24-28, 2001.

4

Archiving

The well-ordered world of the university library is giving way to a new era of promise and uncertainty, of technology, of new forms of engagement and redefined roles in learning. The assumptions and rationales that have been relied on in the past are inadequate as a guide to future developments. To be successful in this new environment those responsible for academic libraries need to understand:

— the changing expectations faced by universities,

— how universities are responding to these new expectations,

— how this affects the library's mission,

— how libraries can develop a strategy to be a central part of the university's response, and

— how the Association of Research Libraries can assist its members to take on new roles.

This concept of learning requires a shift in focus from the teacher's knowledge to the student's understandings and capabilities. This shift in focus leads to a new perspective on the development of quality in the academic enterprise. More than anything, it requires the faculty to bring the strength of the research paradigm into the learning process. The high quality of research in American universities is, in part, the result of the central role of assessment in the research process.

With an understanding of student learning objectives, the scholarship of teaching and learning identifies critical issues, uses research methods, and applies results to understand and improve learning outcomes. For over a decade, institutional and professional accreditation bodies have been shifting their attention from input measures (faculty, courses, books) to outcomes measures (what students learn). Universities and colleges are required to develop and implement a student outcomes assessment program. Assessment requires academic organizations (departments, colleges, universities) to:

— make expectations and standards for quality explicit and public

— systematically gather evidence on how well performance matches those expectations and standards

— analyze and interpret the evidence

— use the resulting information to document, explain and improve performance.

The focus on learning involves looking at the academic program not from the perspective of its subject matter content but from the perspective of the competencies to be developed by students. These competencies include knowledge, skills and abilities, and attitudes and values that are important to a graduate's future success. It is easy to treat these new expectations as one more example of a demand for accountability in higher education.

A closer examination leads me to conclude that they represent a recognition of the changing needs of graduates to be successful in an increasingly complex knowledge economy. Faculty have always assessed the performance of individual students within their individual courses. The focus of outcomes assessment is on the collective success of the program in developing the competencies of the students in the program.

The faculty is being asked to accept responsibility for a broader set of outcomes. To a significant extent this represents a new challenge because while faculty are knowledge experts, they are not necessarily learning experts. Students will also be required to approach the learning experience differently. They are being asked to become more actively involved in the learning process. While they have mastered the passive accumulation of knowledge, they are less comfortable with the responsibility to demonstrate their ability to use knowledge in unstructured situations.

They must become proficient as members of teams, in communicating their solutions, and effectively taking advantage of access to information and the use of technology. Finally, they must begin to develop and demonstrate maturity in how they approach their work. The focus on learning outcomes leads to a consideration of the learning process and the learning community.

From the University's perspective, they are achieved as a result of a total experience over a four (or more) year period. Each element of the educational program contributes, directly or indirectly, to their achievement. Looking at the learning process allows us to recognize the various activities that contribute to learning. On the far left of the figure we see how foundational courses (math, composition, etc), general education courses and special prerequisite service.courses prepare the student for the major.

The requirements for the major are designed to produce the learning outcomes necessary for the graduate to be successful. Across the bottom of the figure we see how the program offerings of the library, student life and technical services can contribute to the learning outcomes of the graduate.

Looking at the learning community allows us to consider how faculty, students and other learning professionals can contribute to learning outcomes. The faculty responsible for the major is in the best position to develop the complete set of learning outcomes, since those outcomes will depend on the specific objectives for the degree program.

The American Association for Higher Education's Principles of Good Practice for Assessing Student Learning recognize that "student learning is a campus-wide responsibility, and assessment is a way of enacting that responsibility. Faculty play an especially important role, but assessment questions can't be fully addressed without participation by student affairs educators, librarians, administrators, and students. ...assessment is not a task for a small group of experts but a collaborative activity; its aim is wider, better informed attention to student learning by all parties with a stake in its improvement."

The University is made up of various communities, each of which has a direct and/or indirect view of student learning outcomes. For example, faculty with responsibility for designing and delivering a general education program must define outcomes that assure students across the University will have a common foundation and also contribute to the learning outcomes that are important in many degree programs. An academic department has a direct interest in the learning outcomes for students in their majors.

A department with an important course that serves a critical role in preparing students in another department's degree program has an indirect interest in the learning outcomes for students in that major. For example, physics is an important service course for students in an engineering program. The Physics faculty can not be effective unless they are working with the Engineering faculty to produce a clear set of learning outcomes for their service courses that will help achieve the outcomes desired for the engineering students.

Within the new environment, we need to measure the ways in which the library is contributing to the learning that the University values. Like the general education program, the library has a direct and an indirect interest in the learning outcomes for all the students at the University. Like the Physics Department, the Library should be able to contribute to the achievement of learning outcomes for various academic programs across the University.

Developing a set of learning outcomes will allow libraries to determine the extent to which their interests are aligned with the expectations of other academic communities in the University. They will find that faculty responsible for the general education program as well as those responsible for many of the academic degree programs also are interested in critical thinking, the effective use of information and technology, the search process and collaborative reasoning.

The library can build on a shared view of what are important student learning outcomes. All the individual communities are being asked to prepare students in ways that go.beyond their expertise in their fields. It is this shared need to go beyond our traditional focus on what students need to know that creates an opportunity for the library. Consider for a moment the way in which a department faculty might look at the learning outcomes for their degree program and how they are achieved through the course requirements. Having agreed on what outcomes they believe are important to their graduate's future success, they can ask the faculty responsible for each course to identify the extent to which each outcome is a focus of the course.

Collectively, across the curriculum, they can determine which outcomes are covered to a major, moderate or minor extent. At this point, while they haven't yet assessed how well their students have developed on each learning outcome, they can evaluate whether enough attention is being paid to individual outcomes. The library must take the initiative in determining what the library has to offer that will help the department achieve greater success in achieving their learning outcomes.

As an example, the University of Arizona Library is offering instruction sessions based on the ACRL Information Literacy Competencies, using the Kuhlthau "Information Search Process" model. The instruction will be integrated into a general education natural sciences course offered by the Astronomy department. The library team has developed learning modules that focus on entry-level information literacy competencies.customized for use in Astronomy related studies.

They will be a required part of the course but offered at a variety of times outside the normal class period. The aim is for students to become confident and skillful information users. To pursue this strategy also requires that the library create new roles for its learning practitioners. To some extent and in some libraries this process of change has begun.

Libraries have developed organizational strategies to serve the various academic communities. But the focus to date is primarily on making information more and more accessible rather that addressing specifically the learning outcomes important to student success. The library needs to ask what kind of expertise is required to be actively engaged in the learning process and an effective partner in achieving learning outcomes. It then will be in a position to adapt roles and responsibilities of its professionals to take full advantage of the opportunity.

Collaborative Digital Reference Service (CDRS)

In United Kingdom the Collaborative Digital Reference Service (CDRS) provides professional reference service to researchers anytime, anywhere, through an international, online network of libraries and related institutions. Launched by the Library of Congress in June 2000, CDRS now includes more than 200 member libraries—academic, public, special, and national—worldwide and that number is growing weekly.

The collaboration has been very beneficial in that each library brings its professional experience, knowledge of user behavior and needs, and subject expertise to bear on the project. CDRS uses technology to provide the best answers in the best context, by taking advantage not only of the millions of Internet resources but also of the many more millions of resources that are not online and that are held by libraries around the world.

CDRS supports libraries by providing them additional choices for the services they offer their patrons. Libraries can more ably assist their patrons by sending questions that are best answered by the expert staff and collections of CDRS member institutions from around the world. An advisory board, comprised of representatives from CDRS member institutions, meets to discuss policy and future directions of the program. Business meetings with member representatives are also regularly held to get feedback, report on and solve workflow problems, discuss training and performance measures, and build esprit de corps.

The CDRS homepage posts general information and news links, information for members, and project milestones. An electronic mailing list allows members to communicate frequently with one another, get technical questions addressed, and comment on the efficacy of the network.

At no other time in history has the emergence of technology affected so significantly the core mission of a library. These technological advances have created new service opportunities for libraries and library patrons. For information to have relevance, it must be up-to-date and receive the hands-on touch of the skilled reference librarian to provide context and added value.

Through the CDRS network, LC and its partner libraries can serve researchers everywhere and, in so doing, bring control, context, greater choice, and timeliness to the world of information. CDRS includes two component parts: submission of a question and answer, and archiving the answer for future use. The workflow looks like this: An end user requests information through a CDRS member institution. The member institution sends the query to the online Request Manager (RM) software for processing and assigning.

The RM searches a database of CDRS member institution profiles looking for the institution best suited to answer the question. Once a match on an institution has been made, the query is sent to that institution for answering. After the query has been answered, it is routed back to the original CDRS requesting library via the RM to allow for closing out the case and completing other administrative tasks. The library profile is the core of the routing and assignment activity, and each institution can "code" itself as broadly or as narrowly as it chooses.

Library profiles contain basic information about the library, including hours of service (and time zones), collection strengths, staff strengths, education levels served, languages covered, geographic location of users served, whether there are special services provided and what they are--as many as 28 data fields. This information is captured in a table, where it is used by the online RM to sort, assign, and track incoming questions and to deliver answers to the end user.

Further, the profile tool is flexible enough to allow for regular updating to reflect staffing changes or special circumstances that would affect the automatic routing by the RM. For example, if the astronomy specialist is on sabbatical for several months and no back-up is available, the library might choose to remove that subject strength from its profile until the staff member returns.

Answers are edited and stored in a separately searchable knowledge base of information. The knowledge base, to be populated with the diverse and authentic information provided by CDRS librarians, will ultimately serve as a front end to CDRS, designed to "catch" and answer incoming questions if there is a ready match. If there is no match on the knowledge base, the question will be routed through the RM and assigned to a library.

There are no restrictions on the types of libraries that can participate. Size of a library or collection is not a factor in determining whether a library can become a member. The aforementioned Service Level Agreement defines the nature of the member library's relationship to the CDRS and that agreement is codified in the library profiles.

Many types of agreements are possible and are limited or expanded depending upon the strengths (e.g., subject) or limitations (e.g., staffing or hours of service) of the individual library. For example, a library may agree to ask and answer questions; only ask questions; ask or answer questions only during specified periods; serve as an editor for the knowledge base; or serve as the on-call library if the automatic Request Manager function is inoperable.

In addition, many libraries have local collections that are unique to them. These local, specialized collections make a potent contribution to CDRS overall, filling special niches that larger research institutions may not be able to fill. In addition to defining roles and responsibilities among the partner libraries, the SLAs will ultimately be used to determine what it will cost a library to be a member of CDRS.

We have encouraged maximum flexibility in developing the many component parts of CDRS. For a library to want to participate, CDRS has to be perceived to have value. Just as there are no "one size fits all" libraries, so too are there no "one size fits all" arrangements with CDRS. Libraries are structured and organized differently, they have different local audiences, and they have different policies and procedures for ensuring quality control.

To be useful to a library, CDRS must fill an unmet need and offer something that the library does not already have, e.g., adequate staff, a subject strength, or a special collection unique to a participating library that the whole collaboration then has access to. When the participating library defines the terms of that value, that library will have greater incentive to make the arrangement work, for itself and for CDRS.

Currently, libraries participating in CDRS connect with other libraries on behalf of patrons so that the libraries can conduct the reference interview before sending the question, define the parameters of the service, determine what works and what does not work, and create a service that is scalable and maximally responsive to user needs.

From the beginning, however, we have envisioned that CDRS will become a service that is available directly to patrons, recognizing that many individuals never go to their local library but still need information. In January 2001, the Online Computer Library Center (OCLC) and the Library of Congress, on behalf of CDRS member libraries, signed a cooperative agreement to guide CDRS through its next phase of development. OCLC will provide technical and development support to CDRS by building and maintaining a database of participating institution profiles that will route questions and answers through CDRS; building and maintaining a question-and-answer database system that will enable CDRS participants to catalog answers and store them in a searchable and browsable database; and providing administrative support for CDRS, including marketing the service, registering new members, and providing training and user support.

Together, the Library of Congress and OCLC will develop a viable model for a self-sustaining digital reference service and promote CDRS in the library community. The major factors that influence the level of investment an institution can make are software and hardware costs (including laptops for telecommuting librarians), staffing/hours issues, and training. Some libraries are offering experimental services that are open only a couple of hours a day and use inexpensive software, while others are committed to 24/7 service, delivered via sophisticated call center software from the corporate sector.

As when planning any new public service, it is helpful to conduct a needs assessment to look at the type of Internet connectivity that your users have and when they are using library resources. When choosing software, there are a large number of chat software programs and services on the market to choose from. Libraries also have the option of installing the software on their own computer networks or having it hosted by a commercial vendor or by a free service such as Yahoo! Chat. Each approach has its associated challenges, including response time, maintenance issues, and control over the user interface.

While expensive call center software may be out of reach for a smaller library's budget, many libraries are banding together in consortia to purchase software and to collaboratively staff virtual reference desks. The Biblioteksvagten consortium of academic and public libraries in Denmark, using Live Person, is one example. Many libraries are purchasing hosted service from companies named LSSI or 24/7 Reference that offer use of NetAgent or eGain software at a reduced price, and even librarians to staff your service, if staffing is an issue. In addition to the chat space, some of these features are:

— Users do not need special software to connect, only a Java-enabled web browser, such as Netscape Communicator, Opera, or Internet Explorer.
— A powerful client to help librarians answer questions quickly.
— The ability to show users web pages on their screen (push page).
— The ability to escort a user through a web search.
— Private messaging between librarians (independent of the chat space).

There are many challenges in setting up a chat reference service, not the least of which is selecting and installing usable software and marketing the new service to your users. The real challenges are overcoming staff resistance to a new and unfamiliar service, teaching effective online communication, and training librarians to field questions outside their areas.

All of these challenges can be addressed by training and experience with working on the service. It is important to give staff ample time to practice their skills before going online, and to provide them with a safety net for their first few shifts. It is also important to realize that not every question that begins in a chat session is best answered via chat. Sometimes it is more effective to e-mail the answer, to ask the user to come to the library, or to refer the question. Chat reference is a convenient and very effective way to extend reference services to users outside the library, and requires the same kind of teamwork that keeps the traditional in-library reference desk operating smoothly.

Digital Archives in Asian countries

Archives in Asian countries have the same purpose and functions as archives in other parts of the world. They are institutions whose major objective is the collection and preservation of public or private archives and records of permanent and historical value in order to make them available to the public. In some Asian countries the national/central archives derived from the record-keeping activities of former colonial administrations. In others they originated as branches of the national library and only recently began to be administered as separate departments with specific archival functions. Although the National Archives of India and Indonesia can trace their origins back to the last decade of the nineteenth century, most Asian archives were established in the 1950s or later and it was only in the mid-1980s and 1990s that they experienced significant development, partly owing to the evolution of information technology. Only recently have they developed national archival policies, established standards and enacted general archival legislation. The archives systems in Asia have a structure identical to systems in other regions. The central archives, at the national or federal level, are the most important and largest institution in the country, responsible for identifying records of historical value in the public sector (and sometimes also in the private sector) and guaranteeing their regular transfer to archival custody for preservation and use. Below the national or federal level the structure of archival services varies with the size of the country and its political and administrative systems. However, as a general rule the central archives also has some responsibility for co-ordinating archival services at regional, provincial, state and municipal or other local levels.

The degree of authority may vary from country to country, however, and in some countries the provision of archival services at those lower levels of government may still be rudimentary and uneven. There are, moreover, countries that possess archives only at the national level, such as Nepal, Singapore and the Republic of Korea. In almost all Asian countries, archives of private organizations or institutions are not controlled by the national/ central entity and they are not necessarily open to the public. The governmental authority under which archives are placed differs from country to country.

Archives in Asia are responsible primarily for collecting public records, that is, those records which are created by public service departments, but there are some archives which also collect records of private institutions, family records and personal records. The records come in a wide variety of forms. In addition to files of paper documents, most archives in Asia hold books, newspapers, gazettes, photographs, films, microfilms, slides, maps, plans, charts, drawings, audio and audiovisual records, architectural models and posters. A few hold electronic records. Archives in former colonial territories usually have rich and varied collections of records inherited from the former colonial administrations. For example, the National Archives of Sri Lanka contain official records of Portuguese, Dutch and British administrations, as well as records of independent Sri Lanka. The Records Management and Archives Office of the Philippines holds documents of Spanish and American administrations. In order to make records available for public access, Asian archives produce a wide variety of finding aids such as guides, inventories, catalogues, indexes, lists, registers, accession lists, transfer lists and exhibition catalogues.

Archiving, Preservation and Conservation

At the level of the national archives about two-thirds of archival buildings in Asia are purpose-built and the majority have some form of humidity and temperature control. However, many of them are more than twenty years old and storage space is limited: some buildings are completely full and unable to receive new accessions; others will be in the same situation in the near future. Most Asian archives have conservation workshops and reprographic laboratories, but the supply of skilled technicians is distributed very unevenly between them. Where reprographic laboratories exist, microfilming is the technology most commonly used for the preservation of archival material. Records are microfilmed to preserve the information which they contain and to protect the fragile originals from excessive use and consequently from damage. Documents in poor condition are consulted only on microfilm.

In many Asian archives the records are open to the public when they reach twenty-five or thirty years of age, as, for example, in the archives of Australia, China, Macao, Nepal and Pakistan. Documents containing information that can affect individual privacy have a longer period of access restriction (varying between 70 and 130 years). On the other hand, in many countries there are some areas of government which do not transfer records to the national archives. The legislature, foreign ministry, ministry of defence and supreme court are the bodies most likely to be exempt from the operation of archival legislation or even to be governed by separate legislation, and their records may not be accessible to the public. Archives of totalitarian regimes are more bureaucratic than archives of democratic regimes and this has consequences for the availability of records.

Communication through exhibitions and archival publications is also an important function of archival services in Asia. Notable among exhibition programmes are the 'Memorials' established and administered by the National Archives of Malaysia. These permanent exhibitions, which commemorate persons and events of enduring historical, cultural or aesthetic significance, attract over 1 million visitors each year. Almost all Asian archives have a regular programme of archival exhibitions and publications, the latter including bulletins, facsimile reprints of historic archives and technical publications, as well as finding aids. Some archives also participate in radio and television programmes. Users can normally visit archives to consult records from Monday to Saturday; archives are usually closed on Sunday and public holidays. But there are exceptions: the National Archives of Nepal and Pakistan, for example, are open on Sunday.

Most countries in Asia now have modern archival legislation. New legislation has been enacted since 1980 in Australia, Bangladesh, China, India, Indonesia, Japan, Macao, Nepal, Pakistan, Singapore, Thailand and Viet Nam. Except in Japan and Thailand, this legislation gives the national archives an active role in records management, records appraisal and records transfer within the public sector, as also does the legislation of Hong Kong, the Republic of Korea and Malaysia. However, most national archives in Asian countries are not concerned with records management in the private sector. Human resources and professional training Most Asian archives face a major problem in respect of human resources—an insufficiency of professional and technical staff.

The need for archival training courses at all levels is increasing in Asia, but it is not matched by the availability of places at archival schools. Staff can attend courses of archival education and training conducted by universities, colleges or institutes in only a few countries for example, Australia, China, India, Indonesia and Malaysia. Other countries have to send staff abroad, mainly to Australia, Europe and North America, to acquire such training. Since in most Asian countries there are no archival professional training courses at the intermediate or higher levels, major archival institutions conduct local basic training as the principal way of preparing their new employees for archival responsibilities. Some of these basic training courses accept trainees from other archival institutions within the country and staff engaged in managing current records within government agencies.

Australia, China, Japan, New Zealand and the Republic of Korea have national professional archival associations: the Australian Society of Archivists Inc. (ASA), the Chinese Archives Society, the Japan Society of Archive Institutions, the Archives and Records Association of New Zealand and the Korean Archives Conservation Association (KACA); but in general Asian countries do not have such national professional associations. However, most national archives are members of international associations. In particular, almost all are members of ICA and simultaneously belong to the appropriate ICA regional branch

Most of the Asian archives do not have a designated budget allocation within the general budget of the governmental authority under which they are placed. However, the National Archives of Macao, Pakistan, the Republic of Korea and Singapore assume that they receive, respectively, 15%, 16%, 0.01% and 5.6% of the total budget allocated to their parent body.

Generally speaking, archives have been involved in great changes with the use of modern information technology to automate archives management, especially through the application of computers for the arrangement and description of records. The result is faster and more accurate arrangement and description, as well as more efficient information retrieval. The use of computers in Asian archives is not widely developed, but the employment of word-processing or database systems to produce finding aids or to undertake other aspects of the management of archival material is now to be found in Australia, China, Indonesia, Japan, Macao, Malaysia, the Republic of Korea, Singapore and Viet Nam. An Asian computer network for exchanging archival information does not yet exist. However, archives can be linked to the Internet, where, for example, information about Australian Archives is already available.

Archives in Asia play an important role as an indispensable instrument for the history of both the whole continent and the individual nations. Consequently they must offer well-organized and structured services in order to give easier access to citizens and researchers. Until recently most archives in Asia were very isolated and unprivileged institutions. They have been gradually developed and provided with increased resources, as a result of the growing awareness of the important role they play in society. Yet the present situation is far from ideal. The scarcity of economic resources and the lack of proper archival policies are the main problems. The situation of archives in Asia, assume that all countries have archives at the national level, together with archival legislation which defines and establishes general policies and standards for the preservation of the national archival heritage.

Many archives use microfilming technology to preserve records and a few have now started to implement and develop computerised systems to help with the arrangement and description of archival materials. Almost all the archives issue archival publications and are members of international associations. However, there are less positive aspects: lack of specialised human resources and almost non-existent professional archival education and training. In the absence of qualified personnel the archives are experiencing difficulties in tackling the problems of records and archives management. Another major problem is the uncertain financial background -often archives institutions have very limited budgets which do not guarantee them adequate resources for the implementation of a proper archives policy.

Archives and Multimedia

Multimedia techniques are making slow progress in the Arab States. Their use calls for financial resources and a propitious administrative and human environment. Information retrieval applications are being developed in some countries and a few CD-ROMs relating to heritage have been produced including the CD-ROM on the fragments of the Sanaa Koran produced within the framework of UNESCO's Memory of the World Programme, and the CD-ROM on archaeological sites produced by the Regional Information Technology and Software Engineering Centre (RITSEC) in Egypt. The spread of multimedia in the archives sector, however, encounters the question of the medium's durability; conservation of original documents, because of their probative value, is indispensable. Multimedia at the moment, therefore, is more useful for distribution than for conservation.

Many Arab states are in dispute with their former colonial powers—France, the United Kingdom and Italy—on the subject of archives. The archives transferred to these latter countries concern mainly the nineteenth and twentieth centuries and are of a diplomatic nature, but some deal with the management of the country. As there is no international convention on the subject, each country has tried to resolve the issue in its own way. Algeria seems to be determined to obtain the originals, while other countries, countries, such as Lebanon and Tunisia, have used microfilm. It should be noted that the former colonial powers have given insufficient aid for the funding of microfilming operations. As far as records predating the colonial period are concerned, Turkey inherited the records of the Ottoman Empire, which included most of the Arab States for a considerable period (from the sixteenth to the nineteenth centuries). Some Arab countries have been able to microfilm the documents that interest them, but this operation is still subject to two constraints: the Turkish National Archives processes Ottoman documents slowly, so many are as yet unavailable; and the Arab countries need to train specialists in Osmanli (which differs from modern Turkish) so as to be able to use the documents. Many Arab governments take no interest in contemporary records, which are therefore in danger of accumulating in poor conservation conditions and deteriorating. Tunisia, followed by Algeria, however, has undertaken a broad programme to improve this situation. It should also be mentioned that the concept of the citizen's right to information is not shared by all Arab states. In practice, the confidentiality of government documents is often excessive, so it is rare to find in the Arab States studies dealing with recent history—issues, in other words, that are still fresh and may arouse public interest or even passion.

The archival situation in Africa is as varied as the multiplicity of nations that make up the huge continent. In as much as the more than fifty countries that comprise Africa vary in size from a geographical coverage of less than 1,000 square kilometres to 2.5 million square kilometres, populations of less than 100,000 to over 96 million, Gross Domestic Products (GDP) ranging from US$279 million to over US$110 billion and per capita incomes of US$60 to US$6,000, so too does the archival situation vary enormously. At one end of the spectrum are nations that have only the most rudimentary of archival infrastructures and where even the most basic of archival services are absent; at the other end are countries which have established advanced archival services and whose facilities and infrastructures compare favourably with other nations in the developed world.

While some countries in North Africa have archival institutions that date back several centuries, most sub-Saharan countries established national archives only after the Second World War. Benin, Burkina Faso, Namibia, Senegal, South Africa and Zimbabwe are among the few exceptions in sub-Saharan Africa that established national archives before 1950. Most countries have promulgated national archives or public archives acts which provide the legal framework under which national archives institutions operate and which control and preserve the archival heritage. The very few that as yet have no archives legislation, such as Uganda and Ethiopia, have draft legislation which is in the process of being formalized. The legislative instruments in general give the national archives the authority to deal with the records and archives of public entities such as central government, local government and parastatals. The degree of authority and control differs from country to country, ranging from giving advice to the right to inspect records and issue instructions for their proper management and handling.

In most of the legislation, the destruction of public records is forbidden without the consent of the national archives. Some of the legislation also defines the role of the national archives in relation to private records and historical manuscripts, and in certain cases controls have been introduced through the national archives to guard against the export of private archival collections deemed to be of national importance. Some of the legislation makes the distinction between public records and public archives, the latter comprising those public records that have been appraised and found to have a historical and enduring value and which must be preserved in perpetuity. In a number of countries the national archives also administer the legal deposit or printed publications acts which require the deposit of copies of all publications produced in the country. This in effect creates within the national archives the national reference library. The ministerial placement of national archives is varied, but the vast majority of the national archives are in the ministries of home affairs, education/ sports/art and culture, and the president's office. In a few countries advisory boards or committees have been created to assist the national archives.

The standards applied in the acquisition, processing, preservation, conservation and usage of records and archives in general are those that have been developed by the International Council on Archives (ICA). In West Africa, standards from the Association Française de Normalisation (AFNOR) and the International Standard Organisation (ISO) have been adopted. There are also standards which have been developed by other organisations such as the International Records Management Council (IRMC), the Association of Records Managers and Administrators (ARMA) based in the United States, the Records Management Society of Great Britain, and other specialist organizations. Standards also tend to be influenced by the practices of the former colonial powers, because most of the national archival institutions are based on the records of the former metropolitan entities and are reflective of the latter's administrative structures and systems. The type of training received by the records managers and archivists, and the institutions giving the training, also have a bearing on the standards used.

Almost all countries in Africa have national archives or public records offices. The national archival institutions play the key role in the organisation, management and preservation of records and archives at the national level. Their mandate tends to be allembracing because of the absence of similar facilities at the local government and parastatal levels and in the private sector, as is the case in other regions of the world such as Europe and North America. In a few countries there are municipal and local government archives, but these are the exception. In quite a number of countries the national archives have established regional offices but the functionality of these in the majority of cases is rather weak. Privatesector archives exist in some countries but these tend to be limited to large multinational corporations. In a number of countries private commercial records centres have been established. Architecture plays an essential role in the preservation and conservation of the archival heritage. The national archives in most countries occupy either purpose-built or converted buildings. But many archival institutions are housed in buildings which are inadequate. In some cases, such as Cape Verde, Ethiopia, Guinea, Lesotho and Uganda, the archives are temporarily housed in such places as the university library, the basement of a former colonial secretariat building or the national library.

Few countries, however, have adequate space for the storage of the archives and most, even those in purposebuilt repositories, are facing severe space shortages in buildings that were filled long ago. Many of the institutions are unable to receive new accessions because there is no storage space. There are also problems concerning airconditioning. Although most of the purpose built repositories originally included air-conditioning systems, these systems in several cases have broken down or become non-functional for one reason or another. This has created serious difficulties, as often such buildings do not allow for adequate natural ventilation and the archival holdings are therefore at risk.

The size of holdings of conventional archives varies enormously from country to country. At the lower end there are countries such as Rwanda, whose archive holdings are less than 500 metres, while at the other end of the spectrum countries such as Mozambique have as much as 25,000 metres. The archival holdings in most countries in sub-Saharan Africa are based on the former colonial administrations and there are many cases where the archives are only as old as the beginnings of the colonial occupation. National archives also often have historical manuscript collections or private archives comprising the records of non-governmental organizations and institutions as well as individuals. These archives can be varied and diverse: diaries and collections of eminent and scholarly individuals, archives of churches, educational institutions and sporting organizations, and business archives recording official transactions such as policies, procedures and meetings. Archival collections are also held by various other institutions and individuals: religious organizations, universities, libraries and some large corporations can contain sizeable archival holdings. In Ethiopia, for instance, the National Library and the Institute of Ethiopian Studies at the University of Addis Ababa have rich collections of historical manuscripts dating back some five centuries.

The staffing levels vary considerably from country to country. In some of the large countries the levels are sizeable, with Kenya and South Africa at the beginning of 1996 having staff complements of 226 and 229 respectively, while Nigeria in 1989 staff of nearly 600. The majority of institutions have between 10 and 100 staff. The ratio between paraprofessional and professional staff for nineteen countries between 1991 and 1996 was 91 paraprofessionals for every nine professional staff. The national archives face various problems in retaining trained and qualified staff, and the attrition rate is high. In 1987, for example, the National Archives of Mali and Guinea were to be handicapped by insufficient human resources. The high staff turnover is attributed to a number of factors including low salaries, low grading, lack of attractive career structures and the lure of the private sector. Government registry staff constitute the bulk of the records management staff in all countries. The registry staff, however, are not well trained and of low calibre. The morale of registry staff is quite low in most countries and they operate without recognition and some of the basic necessities. The low status of registries and registry staff also leaves them exposed to senior officers who openly flout and violate established procedures for handling records. There is an urgent need to upgrade the status of registries and to train and motivate the staff.

Technical Facilities

Most national archives in Africa have reprographic and conservation units or laboratories. These reprographic facilities consist mainly of microfilming equipment but there is also other document-reproduction equipment such as photocopiers and duplicators. Microfilming is used primarily for acquiring copies of documents whose originals cannot be obtained, for preservation purposes when documents are in a fragile condition or are constituted of materials which deteriorate rapidly, such as newspapers, and for the production of multiple copies of documents, as in the case of the records of the former Federation of Rhodesia and Nyasaland, which were microfilmed to provide copies to each of the three successor countries: Malawi, Zambia and Zimbabwe. Document conservation unit have been created to repair and rehabilitate archival materials from depositors that are received in a deteriorated condition.

The main method of repair and restoration utilised is lamination, although a limited amount of encapsulation is done in some countries. Most of the countries with conservation units have lamination machines and only in a few countries is the hand method used. Countries such as Ethiopia and the United Republic of Tanzania do not have conservation units. The need for conservation in a continent with such a harsh climatic environment is self-evident. Unfortunately, in the government ministries and departments of a number of countries in Africa, the condition in which records are being maintained is a cause for great concern. There are numerous detailing situations in which records were exposed to excessive heat, humidity, mould, light, air pollution, insects and rodents. Records have often been dumped in storerooms and sheds where the roofs leaked, the windows were broken and doors were only partially effective. This grave situation has given rise in the last ten years to international rescue missions which have been used to salvage the situation and avoid total disaster. Such missions have been launched in the Gambia, Uganda and the United Republic of Tanzania.

In many countries the larger part of the budget is consumed by staff salaries, leaving very little for recurrent expenditure. There are national archives which fail to purchase records storage boxes and are therefore not able to collect records from ministries. There are also cases where the funds are insufficient even to allow for transportation to collect the records. In some countries virtually all equipment in the national archives has been received as donations.

There is a severe crisis facing some African countries in terms of the management of public-sector records. The crisis is almost continent-wide, although a few countries are the exception and have records management systems that are operating very well. The reason why the registries are not operating well is that the national archives in most countries are hardly involved in the management of current public records. With a few exceptions such as Botswana, Kenya, Namibia, South Africa and Zimbabwe, the national archival institutions only concern themselves with semi-current and non-current records due for transfer to the national archives. And yet by that time, irreparable damage will have been caused to the records. Many countries have established records centres for semi-current records, but in a good number of the cases the records centres have been completely full for many years, making it difficult for new accessions to be received. As a result the records remain in the ministries and departments.

The crisis that faces many countries in terms of records management was aptly captured in one consultant's described file index systems that were rudimentary or nonexistent. In several registries records were strewn all over the floors and under shelves; file covers were often torn and crumpled, frequently with large numbers of pages missing; heaps of dirty, tattered and misfiled records could be found in corners and on tops of cupboards; there was a lack of discipline among staff who seemed to be driven more by tradition than by need; and office equipment was in short supply, the few filing cabinets available being rusty and damaged. This is by no means the scenario in all African countries, and indeed many have well-organized registries, but all the same such situations are a cause for concern.

Only in a few countries do national archives carry out regular visits to ministries and departments. While standing instructions for the disposal of time-expired records exist in many countries, these are often outdated and cover only a small proportion of the records produced by the ministries and departments. There are cases where time-expired records are not disposed of because of lack of capacity in the national archives. In most countries public records become archives and accessible to the public after thirty years. Some countries of huge backlogs in the appraisal of records and the processing of archives, thereby delaying the availability of the archives to the public. There are often finding aids to the collections, and in some cases guides have been published. Unfortunately, in many countries these have not been updated for many years and some predate the attainment of national independence.

Many of the archival institutions have search room facilities for researchers and the public. Some of these rooms have facilities for viewing stored cine films and microfilms, but in certain cases these collections are inaccessible because microfilm readers and projection equipment have broken down or become unserviceable. Both static and mobile exhibitions are occasionally mounted by some institutions while a few have educational programmes. Increasingly African governments realise that there is a close linkage between records, archives and efficient governance. This realization comes in the wake of the economic and political reform programmes that have taken place and the experiences that have been undergone. In a number of countries, such as the Gambia and Uganda, registry reform has been tied to the economic reform programme and supported actively. Attention is also being paid to voter registries in the realization that unless these are reformed there can be no true democracy.

Africa is undergoing fundamental changes in the private sector. These changes are a result of the economic transformation taking place and the liberalization of the economies. The demise of rigid import and foreign exchange controls and the privatization of many public institutions have immensely strengthened private sector activity. The most profound effect of the liberalization of the economies has been the influx of information technology into Africa. Whereas in the pre-1990 period there was only a handful of computers and other telecommunication equipment, today African markets are awash with such equipment and the private sector has been at the forefront of acquiring this technology, much more so than the public sector. An increasing number are acquiring fax and e-mail facilities and a few have become linked to the Internet.

Traditional records management, however, has not been a strong point in the private sector. Businesses remain characterized by decentralized and unorganized records management systems based on the operational units and individual offices. Very few in the private sector have received records management training other than the cursory treatment that it receives in secretarial and office management training courses. The standards of records management in the majority of businesses is therefore very low and no real attempt has been made to mobilize resources and effect improvement. The notable exceptions are the large multinational corporations, which often have elaborate records management procedures developed at their head offices. They also often have established in-house records centres and archives facilities.

The availability of unemployed archivists has contributed to the development of archives in banks and large firms in countries like Senegal. In a few countries, such as Zimbabwe and South Africa, commercial records centres have also been established. In some countries consulting firms are providing services in records and information management. Although increasing numbers of private firms are manufacturing and distributing records management materials, supplies and equipment, a large technology gap remains in comparison with the developed world. South Africa is probably the main exception in this regard. The privatization of public enterprises has also endangered the welfare of large quantities of records. Even when the national archives could cater for the archival collections of former public enterprises such as parastatals, very few of these enterprises made use of this facility or had any relations with the national archives. When privatizing, little attention has been paid to the fate of the records which in the first instance were public records and archives but now belong to a private entity. The national archives have in any case, by and large, lacked the capacity to intervene in order to ensure that the records are adequately catered for.

ICA is by far the most prominent professional archival association in Africa. It has established a network of regional branches: the West African Regional Branch of the International Council on Archives (WARBICA); the Central African Regional Branch of the International Council on Archives (CENARBICA); and the East and Southern African Regional Branch of the

International Council on Archives (ESARBICA). The ICA branches, some of which are very active, allow archivists from African countries to meet and exchange ideas as well as to foster archival development. Some of the branches hold biennial conferences which are well attended and are often preceded by intensive workshops on topical themes. The chairpersons of the regional branches are ex officio members of the ICA Executive Board, thereby facilitating an important linkage on the international front. Through the branches ICA is able to fund certain activities within the context of its medium-term plans, and the member countries of the branches obtain access to funding through the Commission on Archival Development (CAD). ICA provides subventions for publication of the journals of the regional branches. Affiliation to ICA also enables African countries to access funding through various international agencies.

Many national archives are also affiliated to such international organizations as the International Association of Sound Archives (IASA) and the International Federation of Library Associations and Institutions (IFLA). There are other international professional associations in Africa. Archivists from countries in the Commonwealth, for instance, have generally affiliated with the Association of Commonwealth Archivists and Records Managers (ACARM). Some countries such as Benin, Ghana, Mali and Senegal have established national associations of records managers and archivists, but many others find that the number of archivists and records managers is too small for the establishment of viable associations.

Africa lacks adequate training facilities for professional and technical staff. Attempts made in the early 1970s to establish regional training schools were only partially successful. While the school at Dakar, Senegal, for French-speaking Africa seems to have fared better with its two degrees (technical and professional), the school for English-speaking Africa in Ghana has now become no more than a national centre. A number of countries have as a result established their own educational facilities at the national level. Countries such as Botswana and Kenya have graduate schools in archives and information science. Training facilities have been established also at the paraprofessional level, but technical training facilities in conservation and reprography are virtually unavailable. In the absence of such facilities, it is not surprising that most archives staff have to be educated or trained overseas. For English-speaking Africa, this has mostly been done by University College London (United Kingdom) which runs a Master's programme. France has provided much of the training for French-speaking Africa, and Germany and Portugal have provided training for their former colonies.

India has also done a lot of training, especially in conservation. A number of countries, such as South Africa, run their own national programmes within the national archives or through longdistance training, as in the case of the South African Higher Diploma in Archives Studies run by Technikon SA. Other countries with their own training programmes include Senegal and Mauritius. Continuing training in Africa is provided at the national, regional and international levels through workshops and seminars that are organized from time to time. ICA congresses usually include precongress seminars which are attended by young archivists, including those from the regional branches. Workshops and seminars are also organized through a variety of initiatives and organizations and through the ICA Medium-Term Plans. The ICA regional branches also often precede their own conferences with workshops and seminars. Increasingly, African countries are turning to each other for training support and arranging for staff attachments in institutions which have achieved excellence in some of their operations. The emphasis is shifting in archival training for African professional and technical staff. The curriculum being developed within Africa is beginning to put more and more emphasis on the management of current and semi-current records and on automation. While traditional archives principles and practices are still being taught, some elements which are less relevant to the African continent, such as palaeography and sigillography, are now being dropped. The historical bias and orientation is also becoming less pronounced in accordance with a changing professional perception of the role of archivists and the demands of information technology that are requiring a different breed of archivist.

Audiovisual Archives

The audiovisual heritage is an important element within the cultural heritage and has achieved prominence in the twentieth century, the first to have been recorded on audiovisual formats. Audiovisuals are not new but have become of increasing importance as art, entertainment and information carriers. In some cases the transmission of sound and visual data has greater value and impact than the printed document - where, for example, there is a literacy or language barrier. Audiovisuals may also be the only suitable records for the oral or sonic transmission of culture and the arts, news and other current items. The spread and development of modern technologies mean an increase in the role of audiovisual data carriers for communication, information and culture. Today's radio and television rely heavily on archive material and it is estimated that more than 60% of radio and television programmes use archival or stock material for programming.

The definitions are still being formulated, but audiovisual materials are to be understood as visual recordings (with or without soundtrack) and sound recordings irrespective of their physical base or recording process. The carrier usually requires a playback device. This definition is meant to cover the maximum number of forms and formats. Audiovisual materials should not be confused with multimedia; the former provide source material for the latter, and multimedia as such are not archival material. Two features of audiovisual materials add an extra dimension to the principles of collection and preservation: a proliferation both of formats and of systems of production and playback. These cause incompatibility problems between formats and systems. Archives have to maintain original playback devices and employ technical staff who know how to use and maintain the machinery. The Recommendation for the Safeguarding and Preservation of Moving Images, adopted by the General Conference of UNESCO in 1980, provides a basic orientation for integrating and protecting audiovisual recordings as part of the cultural heritage of each nation.

Audiovisual archives are storehouses for a large proportion of the social and cultural heritage of the twentieth century. An audiovisual archive is defined as an organization or department of an organization which is focused on collecting, managing, preserving and providing access to a collection of audiovisual media and the audiovisual heritage, applying archival principles. Such archives contain huge treasures of unique material. Archives of audiovisual materials are relatively new, but they have proliferated in the past few decades. The first sound recordings appeared in 1877 and the first sound archive—the Phonogrammarchiv in Vienna—was established as a research archive in 1899, although it was not followed by others until the 1930s. Film appeared in the 1890s and archives began to be established in the 1930s. Photography had appeared earlier in the nineteenth century. Television was originally recorded on film, but video has been the principal material since the later 1960s. Although audiovisual materials have appeared so recently, time is not on their side and the longer we delay in gathering, conserving and preserving the materials, the less we shall be able to retain. It is vital that steps are taken now to collect and manage audiovisual materials properly before their fragile nature takes a further toll. Already much has been lost owing to ignorance, lack of awareness of the dangers and careless handling.

Audiovisual archives vary in type, purpose and function, and until recently most of them were singlematerial archives: moving image (film or television), sound and still-image archives, the latter frequently housed in more conventional archives of print materials. As the technologies converge so do the archives, to unite effort and conserve resources. Some archives take responsibility for all recorded materials, others take smaller bites and combine one or two of the materials. The larger archives cannot always combine materials in one department; the physical techniques required to deal with each material from the point of view of storage, handling and restoration need different expertise and materials are therefore separated by this parameter alone.

Other functions of collection management can be applied to all the materials: documentation and information retrieval, and selection. Storage vaults may have to accommodate more than one material and the resulting environmental considerations will be different from those more stringently applied to individual materials. Alternatively, an archive may decide that it must apply the optimum storage and environmental values which apply to each material: single-material archives are more fortunate in these cases. Academic archives also house audiovisual materials, many in universities for research, and latterly educational materials for distance learning. These may be small and specialized, or have substantial collections and preservation programmes. Specialized or thematic archives concentrate on a particular format, subject-matter or locality, or relate to specific cultural groups. Many examples could be cited, including the following: special events or periods in history; regional interests; specific cultural groups; academic and research disciplines; folklife collections; oral history; world music; and specific organizations.

Many of these archives have developed within larger organizations. Production archives. Film companies, broadcasting companies and record companies maintain archives primarily for use and exploitation by the parent company. Many of these preserve and restore their materials for re-use, but the archives' main obligation is to the parent organization rather than to preserving the cultural heritage. This may be left to a national archive, which obtains a selection of the production company's material by deposit. Other institutions with archival responsibility include museums, cinematheques, videotheques and national libraries. Most of these are more concerned with maintaining stock for exhibition purposes, and originals may be deposited for long-term preservation in a national archive. There are also collections of last resort which attempt to conserve copies of material in usable condition, but seldom retain archival originals or masters.

Audiovisual materials result from a huge level of investment. Consider the costs of a television channel, or a film production or sound recording company. That the material is allowed to deteriorate through lack of funding for conservation is an unforgivable waste of financial resources and human talent. Considering the huge investment in production, the financial resources available for preservation of the material are ludicrously small. Although some archives were established by private means, the ultimate responsibility for the protection and maintenance of a national heritage must lie with the nation itself, and this means government and granting bodies. It is incumbent upon government to ensure that the national heritage is protected for posterity. Archives in organizations such as broadcast associations or film production companies have commercial backing and motivation, and meet costs from their revenue. Once that commercial motive is fulfilled, however, it is generally acknowledged that, as with other records of the national cultural creativity, the cost of maintaining the collection reverts to government and granting bodies. Many valuable collections have disappeared for ever as a result of production company closures or changes in franchise when materials are not taken over by already overstretched archives.

The basic tasks of an audiovisual archive are collection, preservation, documentation and access provision. Methods of collection and acquisition vary, and include the legal or voluntary deposit of collections or individual items, the deposit of in-house productions, donations, special agreements for copying nationally produced materials, and purchase. Other archives collect their own materials in the form of oral or video history programmes, with the purpose of recording cultures, languages and music before they disappear.

Closely allied to acquisition are evaluation, selection and appraisal. The audiovisual archive acquires materials according to a particular remit, balancing new acquisitions against existing stock and the purpose and function of the archive. Storage space and resources being what they are, archives have to select material for preservation on the basis of relevance, uniqueness and quality. Wherever possible an archive should be dealing with original materials, but originals are hard to come by. There is strictly only one original film, video or master sound recording. Such originals seldom survive and there are various forms of tampering with the products - cut/ uncut versions, director's/producer's cut, censored and unexpurgated versions. Owners of original material may be reluctant to deposit their master material in an archive until they have no further use for it, by which time the technical quality has deteriorated.

Three elements in audiovisual documents have to be considered in the selection process: the artefact or carrier, the information content and the aesthetic content, particularly with film and sound recordings. The artefact or carrier will designate the form of the audiovisual and influence selection for technical reasons. Can this material be replayed in the collection which acquires it, or is the carrier so esoteric that it has only antique value? Is the carrier in good physical condition or will it need transfer and/or costly restoration before or on receipt, or indeed is the damage irreparable? There are also implications for damage and disaster to the rest of the collection; canker present in one item may spread to others if it is stored untreated and without inspection. Archives have very stringent selection policies. It is widely quoted that archives select less than 2% of the material presented.

Audiovisual archives, therefore, do not have a huge selection of material, but most of it has unique value, and such archives retain more material than many other archives. Some audiovisual collections will include several interpretations of the same work—for example, music recordings—or several records of the same event carried in different documents: a film, video or sound version.

Guidelines for archival selection exist, but they are usually those of organizations with their own parameters. Selection of material is dependent upon the function of the archive, the quality of the material and the uniqueness or rarity of the content. Audiovisual archives should concentrate on recordings of national origin. To avoid duplication of effort, material should be offered back to the country of original production or to archives with a more relevant collection remit.

Function of Archives

The main function of any archive is to preserve the heritage and the artefacts which make up that heritage. These are the major concerns of audiovisual archives. Many of the difficulties encountered result from the fragility or the volatile nature of the materials. The carriers are the weak link and the materials have to be transferred to other carriers that are more stable, with a longer life expectancy or more up to date. Audiovisual materials are made of polymers, and all polymers decay! Progress is being made to slow this decay and prolong the life expectancy of the carriers and thus the source material, but preservation measures will simply retard deterioration, not prevent it. The life expectancy of audiovisual materials is dependent on chemistry and storage and handling conditions. After 100 years much early film has been lost, especially volatile nitrate. Sound and video recordings are subject to attack from many enemies. No universal panacea has been found and the new technologies of optical disks are as prone to damage as the old. For example, there have been problems with vinegar syndrome producing tape and laser rot affecting optical disks designed to act as storage media for tape materials. Archives must copy material from one format to another to save the content, to overcome the obsolescence of equipment and systems, and to provide copies for research and other uses. There are three steps in preservation work:

- Conservation;
- Preservation; and
- Restoration.

Wherever possible the original data have to be preserved on the original format for future use by more advanced technologies of transfer and presentation. Guidelines and standards exist and can be adjusted to suit prevailing conditions—hot and humid climates call for different standards of storage and preservation than cold, temperate climates. The American National Standards Institute (ANSI), the International Standards Organization (ISO) and the British Standards Institute (BSI) all publish standards for composition of tape, and for storage environments and conditions. The international audiovisual NGOs also issue guidelines. Digitization is not yet the answer as there may be loss of quality in copying the original, even though clones will retain the quality of the copy. Digitization is often associated with mass storage techniques, but data density techniques are not necessarily reversible—hence the caution of technicians in retaining originals whenever possible.

Providing Access

If preservation is the primary concern of the audiovisual archive, access is the second. Audiovisual archiving is a culturally motivated activity, intent upon the preservation of the audiovisual heritage because of its intrinsic worth, regardless of commercial potential. Such values are still important, but most archives are now growing faster than the financial resources to support them. There is therefore a certain necessity for archives to generate some income; there is also the public service aspect—that is, to provide access to the people whose heritage is contained within the archive.

Copyright in archive material is usually vested in the owner and respected, but the archive itself requires rights to acquire, copy, use and provide access to the material. Acquisition of material is achieved by some countries through legal deposit arrangements, but this will only cover a small proportion of the material acquired by an archive—that which is published. Much of the material is unpublished. Archives have ad hoc agreements with donors for voluntary deposits but, in the case of some commercial producers, the archive's rights may be severely restricted. Archives are not in competition with producers or owners, and need some rights over material deposited with them, on which they may have spent considerable time, effort and money for preservation and storage.

Archives are not simply convenient storehouses, and have to maintain the integrity of the material. Most especially they need rights to copy the material for preservation, access and exhibition purposes, and some rights to retain the material once acquired. Once deposited, archive copies should not leave archive premises but should remain under archive control.

Detailed cataloguing of archive material is essential to provide a permanent, accurate record, especially of the unedited, unpublished material which abounds. Many archives developed their own rules, but an international initiative is now under way to produce ground rules for all audiovisual materials. Ground rules are necessary for the exchange of information in electronic databases—if everyone uses different criteria, then confusion will result and information exchange be retarded. Accurate and rapid information retrieval is the goal of indexing, and essential data elements have to be devised to make this possible, even though each kind of material will have its own set of data elements. Retrieval by subject has been made easier by the introduction of computer techniques and free-text searching—but the terms for description of subject content have to be carefully chosen, based on international thesauri, or data and material will be lost.

As electronic technology develops so the means of transmitting information—printed and audiovisual— are advanced. In a world of incompatible systems (computers are no exception), the search continues for a system capable of access by as wide a public as possible. Work has started to find the lowest common denominator for the transmission of information with the highest common quality, a sort of 'ASCII' code for all information. In addition to information retrieval, archives have to keep detailed technical records—what has happened to the material, its current format, has it been restored, if so on what system, how and why to assist future technicians.

The technical record is usually kept separate from the information record. There are many published information tools ranging from catalogues of holdings to discographies and filmographies, but national discographies and filmographies are compiled independently of the archives, because the latter's stock is not comprehensive, even when legal deposit exists, and seldom up to date. Other discographies and filmographies are selective and cover directors, performers or composers.

Audio, film and video archives was carried out by the Library of Congress on behalf of Eastman Kodak. The figures are alarming. Even with the most stringent selection criteria and limited collection resources, the holdings of just 500 archives amounted to 11,175 million feet of film, 8.5 million hours of video, and 44.5 million hours of audio, and there are many more archives than this. A recent studies of audiovisual archives in Europe alone, Map-TV - Film and Television Collections in Europe, identified some additional 1,900 archives and collections for film and television. There are approximately 40,000 radio and television stations around the world, many of which have archives; film archives exist in over eighty countries, and sound archives in fifty countries at a conservative estimate. A large part of audiovisual production will be lost for future generations without greater efforts from the international community to support the establishment and development of audiovisual archives worldwide.

Personnel working in audiovisual archives come from many different professions and scientific disciplines, and have long professional experience and on-the-job training. There is a serious gap, however, between the growing importance of audiovisual archives and the provision of professional education, a gap no less wide in developed than in developing countries. Audiovisual archivists need to be specialists with a thorough knowledge of archival principles and the special characteristics of audiovisual materials. There are two main types of audiovisual archivist:

a) collection managers, documentalists and selectors and

b) technical staff, who have to be of a high standard with thorough knowledge of their disciplines.

There are few courses available; most are summer schools and seminars, but some longer courses can be found in existing schools of library and archival studies.

The UNESCO Memory of the World Programme is an attempt to save the cultural heritage, and audiovisual materials cannot be excluded. These materials, however, are among the most vulnerable to destruction. Lost collections are a sad reminder of the ravages of time, chemistry, natural and man-made disasters, wars and conflicts, but fortunately endangered collections are currently being identified by this programme.

Audiovisual archives have set up their own federations: the International Federation of Film Archives (FIAF) was established sixty-eight years ago, the International Association of Sound Archives (IASA) in 1969 and the International Federation of Television Archives (IFTA) in 1977. All have NGO status within UNESCO. Although each has its own constituency and membership structures, the audiovisual NGOs, ICA and the International Federation of Library Associations and Institutions (IFLA) have collaborated since 1979 in a Round Table on Audiovisual Records under the auspices of UNESCO. The Round Table has been responsible for many activities including publications, the development of guidelines and training. It provides an arena for audiovisual organizations to address common issues and improve the recognition and status of audiovisual archives as vital components in safeguarding the cultural heritage. The Round Table has an important subcommittee—the Technical Co-ordinating Committee—which organizes Joint Technical Symposia across its spectrum of interests and provides technical advice and expertise.

In addition to the international NGOs there are several national and regional associations: the Association of Recorded Sound Collections (ARSC) in the United States, the Association of Moving Image Archives (AMIA), with its network of interests in North America and beyond, and the recently formed South-East Asia-Pacific Audiovisual Archives Association (SEAPAVAA). Other closely allied associations include the International Council on Museums (ICOM) and the International Council on Traditional Music (ICTM). Thus many associations are willing to assist if one knows where to look.

Accessing Unique Library Materials

The period from 1988 to 1994 has been one of dramatic change and rapid but uneven development. The growth and spread of consensus on the general principles of access to archival and primary documentary materials have been remarkable. In contrast, the state of affairs in different countries and regions varies significantly, and there are enormous resource problems to be faced.

Nevertheless, the outlines, or at least the principles, of a generally agreed system for access to primary documentation and the dissemination of information from it are now beginning to emerge. Technological change and the emergence of international electronic highways have begun to affect the way we see the situation, but from a worldwide point of view have not yet begun to influence seriously the way access to archival and manuscript material is provided.

The potential for change here is very great, and will probably be the most obvious development during the next decade. All archival and unique documents are, and always have been, subject to some kind of appraisal, and this appraisal process has, of course, been fundamental in determining what information would survive and what would be provided for use.

In the past, much appraisal has been haphazard and completely or substantially a matter of chance or, in some cases, subject to political control. From the beginning, archivists have sought to establish a general set of rules by which appraisal should be carried out. At times this has been seen as an attempt to delineate a science of appraisal.

Probably few would still make the claim that selection procedures can be so objective and so exactly based on an analysis of the information world that they can be regarded as scientific in the full sense. Nevertheless, there is a consensus, expressed in most new archival legislation, that general lines of approach can be laid down.

That a wide spectrum of human activity is worthy of being included in appraisal at the national or international levels - hence the documentation of areas such as literature and scholarship (the work of individual authors), politics (personal, central and local), government (central, regional, municipal), science and medicine (research and implementation), banking, insurance and commercial activities generally, and manufacturing industry are all to be included in appraisal and collection programmes.

One result of this understanding is that the process of appraisal is no longer seen as being essentially the preserve of government agencies or of large corporate bodies. Although no longer claimed as a science, the principles on which appraisal is conducted have been developed in important new ways over the last decade or so.

Traditional ways of approaching the task of appraisal were centred upon structural analysis: archivists would examine the surviving documentation and apply tests to it. These tests were to establish the value of the material in terms of its evidential or informational quality. More recently there has been a tendency to include appraisal tests based upon functional analysis. Here the archivists would be attempting to judge whether the documentation available did or did not present a true overall picture of the relevant field of activity; where it did not, they would seek to fill in the missing bits by alternative means.

Another development of increasing importance has been the tendency of archivists to take into consideration the costs (both financial and in terms of informational value) of retention or disposal of the material being appraised. These changes in the principles of appraisal have not yet been disseminated to all parts of the world, nor are they universally accepted, as yet, by the archival profession; but they are well established in the most advanced areas.

Overall, it is probably true that everywhere in the world it is accepted that appraisal and collection policies should cover a very wide range of activities. The effective implementation of this perception varies greatly, of course, from country to country. In 1995-96 the International Council on Archives (ICA) published the text of recent new archival legislation in two volumes of its main journal, Archivum.

This reveals that in the period 1981-94, ninety-seven countries introduced new laws, or revisions of earlier laws, on the management of archives, and at least ten international, quasi-governmental institutions did so too. The weight of this legislation varied considerably, but there is no doubt that most of it incorporated generally agreed international principles of archival operation.

Differences mostly concentrated upon the degree of centralization within a state structure and on the detailed control of government materials. Several features are worth reporting. New laws in Australia, Canada, the Netherlands and the United States show the application of new principles, advancing to new levels of activity and new quality standards.

The most advanced of the new laws explicitly define the right of citizens to access materials held in archival institutions, redefine the range of materials that fall within the purview of these services, and make provision for systematic appraisal. The most striking changes were in the legislation introduced by states created by the break-up of former imperial groupings. The most important of these were the republics of the former USSR.

During the communist period, the archival system of the USSR had been extremely centralized. By 1994 the central structure (Glavarkiv) had been dismantled and replaced by new controlling authorities at the level of the constituent republics, and in some cases at lower levels as well. The reconstitution of the central archival training facility as a new University of the Humanities will doubtless have an effect on user services and on access to archives generally.

The Russian Federation, under its own new legislation, is in the process of giving up the central control of archival services; the new legislation in Belarus, Latvia, Lithuania and Ukraine provides these countries with their own national legal framework. The states of the former Yugoslav federation show a rather similar situation.

New laws in Albania, Croatia, the Czech Republic, Hungary, Poland, Romania and Slovakia are all intended to bring their respective national systems in line with accepted international standards by allowing clearly defined rights of access not only to their own citizens but also to researchers from abroad. The new archival law in Germany reflects the union of the country after 1989, and provides for a centrally organized federal archives service, with state archives services in each of the Länder, within which a network of city and specialized archives and libraries exists.

The changes that have made this possible involved an enormous upheaval in established practices and services on both sides of the former dividing line, but have been carried out with professionalism and thoroughness. The official policy of the old regimes in all the former communist countries had allowed access to archival sources for approved researchers but there had been no clear delineation of the principle on which access was based, nor on what finding aids should be open.

The new legislation has sought to change this. Most countries now seem to have adopted some variant of the thirty-year rule (the delay between the storage of archival material and its accessibility to the public), which now can be regarded as an international norm. Interesting new developments in archival regulation can also be seen in South Africa, where the regime established after the fall of the apartheid system has begun organizing the archives to support its attempt to resolve past enmities and open its society.

This has led to the re-establishment, in professional terms, of the country's leadership of the Central and Southern Africa region, a leadership that had been impossible to exercise during the apartheid years. Bibliographic control, finding aids and descriptive standards It is clear that whatever the law may say, users cannot have access to either archival or unique library materials unless there are adequate finding aids, and unless these finding aids are openly available.

It is, and always has been, a difficult and slow job to provide these aids, and it is probable that completely satisfactory finding aids will never be available for all the documentation that has to be covered. Even in countries and sites where archivists and librarians have been steadily working at the completion of catalogues, there remain substantial backlogs, and there are cases, sometimes notorious, where access cannot be given because lists are not ready or not divulged.

These cases are not always confined to countries that have suffered from political control. A notable example is provided by the papers of Eamon De Valera, founding President of Ireland, which are nominally open to access but in practice are largely closed because of the lack of finding aids. Archivists and librarians continue everywhere to work at backlogs, and there are signs that eventually a substantial investment in computer equipment may improve the rate of progress.

There is a particular problem in the countries of the former USSR, and to a lesser extent in the countries of the former Eastern bloc in Europe. Under the previous regimes finding aids were either secret or restricted to internal use. Under the liberalized regimes that have been established since 1989, these internal lists are now being progressively released for use by researchers, but their coverage and adequacy as catalogues have often been questioned.

In these countries, enormous quantities of new archival materials, previously secret, have now been transferred to the archives services or have been released for consultation. It is clear that the task of drawing up adequate finding aids for all this documentation is so massive that even if there were no resourcing difficulties, the job would take a very long time.

Microfilming and other external projects do little to attack the main core of the problem. An additional problem is that government bodies are tempted to sell access rights to their archive materials, or even the materials themselves, in order to obtain hard currency. This has led to a patchwork of uncoordinated releases, often through American universities.

ICA, with funding from UNESCO, has begun to follow the example set many years ago by the International Federation of Library Associations and Institutions (IFLA) for the library community, in establishing description standards for the international exchange of data about archival holdings. The basic document is the International Standard Archival Description ISAD(G), adopted by the International Congress on Archives in Montreal in 1992.

ISAD(G) has now been translated into French, Italian, Japanese, Spanish and probably other languages. Training courses and workshops in its use have also been held in different parts of the world. The standard is minimal, but is serving as a skeleton upon which national or subject-based finding aids can be structured. For many countries and traditions this is an innovation, the first such standard that has had any degree of penetration from the outside world.

ICA is now working on the development of a standard for authority files covering the names of creators of archival holdings, whether official or corporate bodies, private individuals or families. This standard is not as yet fully accepted by the archival community - it will be debated at the International Congress on Archives in Beijing in 1996 - but it also follows in the footsteps of the library community.

Another standard for the description of archives and manuscripts was developed in North America in the early 1980s: the Archives and

Manuscripts Control (AMC) version of the longestablished Machine-Readable Record (MARC) bibliographic exchange format. AMC became wellestablished in the United States because it was a required format for the large public online catalogue systems, Online Computer Library Center (OCLC) and Research Libraries Information Network (RLIN), both of which have extensive but partial outreach capabilities in other parts of the world.

It has since become more important because of its use in the project to catalogue the Vatican Secret Archives, undertaken by the University of Michigan in 1988. The opening of the Vatican Archives almost coincided with the opening of the Communist Party archives in the former USSR and its satellites. The Vatican case has a broader and more technical significance, however, because of its use of the MARC AMC standard: this standard has allowed the great mass of this historic archive to be structured and managed in a way that conforms to best modern practice.

Significantly, this also marked the first international use of a previously purely American standard. A standard for the archival use of SGML (Standard Generalized Markup Language) is being developed at the University of California. If successfully completed and adopted by the archival community this standard will be of great use in under-pinning the use of the Internet for archival interchange.

There will probably continue to be a need for international data exchange for two categories of archival and unique library materials: full text (in which the content of the documents can be displayed) and bibliographic (giving information about the existence and whereabouts of archival holdings). There have been interesting innovations in both these areas.

The imaging project at the Archivo de Indias in Seville, Spain, is making available the images of original documents from the Spanish discovery and administration of America from 1492 onwards. Some 10% of the holdings of this major archive are covered by the project. The images are retrieved by a separate but linked indexing system, and can be accessed remotely (although this aspect of the project still remains for the most part unexecuted).

In the United Kingdom, large databases containing full abstracts of the personal papers of the first Duke of Wellington (a general in the Napoleonic wars and subsequently Prime Minister of Britain in the early nineteenth century) and the personal papers of Lord Mountbatten have both been made available electronically, giving access to full or almost full text. British universities also have provided bibliographic descriptions of other archives.

Unfortunately, none of these have been based upon any descriptive standard or format, nor have they yet been assimilated into the new formats required by the Internet. The wide-area bibliographic networks, OCLC and RLIN, both hold large quantities of bibliographic descriptions of archival and unique library materials. Although based in the United States, these databases also contain materials relating to other countries and, of course, can be accessed from anywhere in the world.

Since American universities and other institutions hold much important material relating to other regions, the ability of users to consult them is an important enlargement of the world's information resources. During the late 1980s it appeared likely that these databases, or others like them, would expand to include comparable materials from other countries. This promise has not, for the most part, been realized. The failure of these projects to expand fully over the world was probably caused by a lack of resources, but also by the development of alternative, and less restrictive, media of communication, and more generally by the backlog of descriptions that could be made available.

The idea that archives and unique documents are kept primarily so that users may have access to them spread only slowly through the world. Certain countries, such as Sweden and France, accepted early the principle of public access to materials held in archival or library institutions. By the middle of the twentieth century a consensus had developed that there should be statutorily supported rights of (or at least facilities for) access.

The spread of this principle received an enormous boost in the late 1980s and early 1990s, when most countries, in all parts of the world, set about revising the relevant legislation. Practical implementation of the new approach has been slower and less predictable than the acceptance of the principle. However, it is probably true that researchers now expect to be able to gain access to a wide range of documentation, and there is a growing body of literature that reports on the success or failure of such expectations.

Several nations that can be regarded as being in the vanguard of the modern information movement have enacted Freedom of Information legislation. These laws give the public rights of access to government documents, irrespective of date or of whether they have been transferred to archival institutions.

The most notable of these countries are Sweden (where the legislation has historic roots), the United States, Canada, Australia and the Netherlands. The International Archive Round Table Conference held at Austin, Texas, in 1985, and one of the recommendations from that meeting was that archivists should be professionally charged with the duty of advising their governments on questions of freedom of information and of privacy.

Since then, although the principle of freedom of information is still gaining ground (especially, of course, in the countries of the former communist bloc), the privacy side of the equation has come into more prominence. At the Austin meeting the areas in which privacy should be ensured were set out: personal registration details (birth, marriage, death); the health of individuals; income; criminal proceedings; professional life; political, religious or philosophical opinions; the basic documents providing statistical information (for example, census returns); questions of family honour; police matters; and information gained under promise of confidentiality.

Methods used to ensure privacy include control both by regulating the transfer of relevant documents to the archives and by the operation of a phased closed period. Most countries now have data protection legislation that applies these principles to databases held on computer systems. Important principles are involved. One is that under data protection legislation it is usual to give subjects the right to insist that erroneous information about themselves should be changed.

Archivists, however, must argue that there is a broader historical interest: data that are erroneous in terms of the current situation are not necessarily erroneous as a historical historical record. In some notorious cases a conflict of interest has come to the fore, for example, where persons who have changed sex during their lifetime have demanded the right to have their birth certificates altered.

Although desirable for their current rights as citizens, it is clear that to alter the certificate would be historically a falsification. It is likely that there will be further controversy on these issues in the future. Similarly, if personal information is rendered anonymous in order to promote rapid current use, this process damages its long-term historical value.

There is a need to ensure that information supplied under conditions of confidentiality is preserved archivally without being rendered anonymous. In some countries, for example Australia, this question has become politically sensitive and has led to the destruction of important census material. The major event of the last decade must surely be the actual and promised release of the enormous and detailed archives previously closed because of the nature for the regimes that generated them.

The release of this material has been accompanied by important upheavals in the archival administrations and library services of these countries. The attention of the world has been drawn to these events, which indeed have had considerable significance for everybody. In Germany the process of unifying the two previous republics into a federal structure included a radical reorganization of the federal archival system.

The two archive administrations were brought together, with a considerable change of senior personnel. The older archival holdings had been scattered by the occupation of Germany in 1945, and these were now reassembled. The enormous archives accumulated by the apparatus of state control of the former German Democratic Republic, including secret dossiers on large numbers of individuals, were brought under archival administration and a start made on making them available for consultation.

A particular problem in these countries was what to do with the archives of the Communist Party. Theoretically these belonged to a private organization, but in practice they contained material relating to the entire range of government activity, and reached deeply into the affairs of many citizens. For the most part, these archives have now been brought under the control of the national archives system, though the problems of creating and making available the necessary finding aids remain formidable.

Interestingly, this resolution of the question of the Party archives has brought into relief the parallel problem of the archives of the Church in these countries. While the state had taken over from the churches the responsibility for civil registration, church archives still contain important demographic information, and access to them is a subject of broad interest.

One particular aspect of this issue concerns the recovery of confiscated Church property, the re-establishment of monastic institutions and the specific ownership (as between different ecclesiastical groups) of buildings. There have been bilateral projects intended to assist in the preservation and accessibility of archival holdings in the former communist states.

For example, the Hoover Institute at Stanford University in the United States had an agreement between 1992 and 1995 to microfilm some of the state archives in the Russian Federation. This project was very controversial and recalls similar projects in the past, such as that of Syracuse University and the archives of Kenya in the 1960s. Though they help to preserve and make accessible parts of the world's archival heritage, it is not clear that the best way to achieve this is to remove control from the country of origin.

China, echoing its importance in world affairs, is now strengthening its impact on international archival matters, and in 1996 assumed the presidency of ICA. Despite the damage and setbacks of the Cultural Revolution in the 1960s, the country has made considerable new investment in the management of archives and unique documents, and has begun to attack the problems posed by a tradition of secretiveness.

Archives for the period up to 1949 were opened by legislation in 1980, and there has been increasing international co-operation in archival training since then. When discussing archive collections in terms of human rights, the development of archival services in international bodies and the coming together of archival services in the countries of the European Union are both significant.

The latter has been marked by a determination to recall the importance of proper archives services for democratic regimes and the rule of law, and to implement such services. An important statement made by the countries of the Council of Europe as a result of a conference in Strasbourg in 1994 included plans for the computerization of finding aids and publications, microfilming, and improving access facilities as an underpinning to the concept of a common European heritage.

A particular programme was announced for the management and opening of the archives of the Comintern (the Third Communist International), and for aid to currently disadvantaged countries - a specific programme is proposed for Albania. This European statement applies principally to archives held in traditional form. Similar problems exist in connection with appraisal, preservation and access to archival material in audiovisual form. These have been the subject of international discussion and agreement in specialist forums.

The importance of computers for library cataloguing and for archive administration is clear, and several projects and events have underlined this potential in the world arena. The project for an extended international catalogue of eighteenth-century books has now been virtually completed, and is another example of the effective use of agreed formats and cataloguing standards.

After long delays and hesitations, the Manuscripts Division of the British Library adopted a system for computer cataloguing which has, in effect, eliminated the notorious thirtyyear backlog between the acquisition of materials and the publication of the finding aids to them. This achievement alone should give cause for optimism that in the following decades similar backlogs can be removed.

The arrival of the Internet has caused a flurry of activity, and it is now possible to find on it descriptions of archive and manuscript holdings in many countries. One reason for the rush to put homepages on the World Wide Web is that, once access has been gained to the Internet by way of a provider agency (usually the archive's parent institution), archivists and librarians are not impeded by the need to learn and adapt to detailed formats and cataloguing rules.

It is a simple matter to put descriptions on the Web as free text, embellished by graphics and digital images. Comparing the structure of MARC records with pages entered using the standard Internet format, HTML, shows immediately how relatively quick and easy the latter method is, both in the technicalities of data entry and in the presentation of the material to users.

The Web is itself, moreover, directly a user interface. Nevertheless, it should be added that from a worldwide point of view the computer age has hardly hardly begun for manuscripts and archives. In many of the most important regions it is not easy for archivists and librarians to get access to hardware or software, or to keep their equipment maintained to a reliable standard. When equipment is obtained, there is a shortage of relevant training.

Software may have to be adapted to local conditions, and there is little or no standardization in either the developed or developing world. In some developed countries, such as Italy, Germany or the United Kingdom, archivists and related communities have attempted to develop specialized software, only to find that they do not have the resources to compete with the constantly upgraded commercial packages.

In less developed areas, UNESCO's CDS/ISIS software has been used to good effect, but here again the absence of pre-designed applications or of general standards has prevented rapid development of databases, and this despite the devoted efforts of a few trainers to extend the body of expertise. In other developed areas, for example Japan, archivists and manuscript librarians have not yet generally come into contact with computer systems.

Even in the most highly developed countries there are many smaller, local, specialized or poorly supported archives and manuscript collections that have not yet seriously begun to use automated methods. ICA is now actively establishing a presence on the World Wide Web, and is supporting a project under which the national archives of key countries in the developing world will be enabled to join the Internet community.

Appraising, preserving and giving access to electronic records and data sets has been an increasing preoccupation in many countries. Most progress towards a technological solution to these problems has been made in North America, and from there the expertise has been disseminated. In November 1994 an important conference in Australia, 'Playing for Keeps', assembled a body of authoritative papers which is likely to serve as a structure for action in this field. These papers deal with the management of electronic archives.

In the case of unique but nonarchival documents in electronic form, a body of expertise has already been developed, under the general aegis of the International Association for Social Science Information Service and Technology (IASSIST), operating through electronic data archives. One or more of these institutions can be found in most developed countries, and there is now a regular system for identifying, appraising, acquiring and making available data sets in electronic form.

In some countries, such as Sweden, this operation is strongly co-ordinated with the national archives service. In others, such as the United Kingdom, the operation is separate. Access to this material is increasingly provided remotely by way of the Internet or other networks.

The Memory of the World Programme, initiated by UNESCO, aimed at preservation of and access to the documentary heritage of the world. As stated in its initial document, 'access facilitates protection and preservation ensures access'. The seven introductory projects include digitization of manuscripts from the cities of Prague, St Petersburg and Moscow, and from Bulgaria and the Yemen, a newspaper project in Latin America and a programme for scientific manuscripts in Turkey.

A Memory of the World national committee now exists in ten countries, and it is clear that the programme will have important effects in preserving and making available specific sets of unique materials. So far these materials appear to have been chosen because they are considered particularly valuable and attractive; the real problem lies with the vast masses of undescribed and unmanageable archives, bearing intimately on the life of people, that have suddenly, in the last few years, been thrust upon the world stage.

Documentary heritage reflects the diversity of languages, peoples and cultures. It is the mirror of the world and its memory. But that memory is fragile. Every day, fragments, if not entire sections, of the documentary heritage disappear for ever. To guard against collective amnesia, it must remain our aim and hope to preserve manuscripts and other rare and valuable archive and library material existing in any form, whether written, audiovisual or electronic, and to ensure their wider dissemination.

For this reason, UNESCO has launched a vast and ambitious programme entitled 'Memory of the World'. The twofold purpose of the UNESCO 'Memory of the World' Programme is to safeguard and promote the endangered world documentary heritage. The scale and structure of the programme are such that intellectual, technical and financial partnerships will be required.

In this programme, UNESCO intends to act as a co-ordinator and catalyst. An International Advisory Committee guides the overall implementation of the programme and determines the award of the 'Memory of the World' label to the projects selected. At the national level, a committee is responsible for project selection and follow-up. A world list of endangered library and archive holdings will be a cornerstone of the programme.

Preservation by means of the most appropriate techniques, ease of access and wide dissemination must be the hallmarks of this programme, which is to include not only rare manuscripts and documents from libraries and archives, but also audiovisual and computerized recorded material. The 'Memory of the World' Programme has aroused great interest from the time it was launched, and requests for assistance are regularly being received by UNESCO.

Organisation of Archives

In a well-designed archival network, institutions can share the burden of archiving journals, and libraries and researchers needing to use archival materials can locate and retrieve appropriate copies from a participant in the network. However an archival system is set up, though, it must be clear who takes responsibility for the material being archived and how this responsibility is enforced.

Some authors and organizations may attempt to archive their own material. A publisher may declare that it will archive its own back issues indefinitely, for instance. Many authors have also provided preprints of their papers and journal articles on their Web sites for years. This informal practice is now encouraged by manifestos like the Budapest Open Access Initiative. "Self-archiving" can also be done by authors' institutions.

For instance, MIT's Dspace repository promises stable long-term storage for the scholarly work of its faculty. Self-archiving, however, will not suffice to preserve scholarly journals, let alone scholarly communication as a whole. It essentially relies on the self-interest of the original creators and publishers to keep the archive viable, but Web sites often disappear when an individual changes institutions or careers.

Copies of papers on individual sites are often preprints, so they may lack important revisions and supplementary information that appeared in the journal version. Publisher-run archives may disappear without warning if they are no longer cost-effective to the publisher, or if the journal or the publisher fails or is acquired by another company. Contents of archives may be changed, corrupted, or withdrawn, either by accident or intentionally. As holders of copyrights to the content they archive, publishers and authors have exclusive rights to disseminate this content unless they grant rights to archives run by disinterested third parties.

With exclusive rights comes near-exclusive responsibility for their material. Without very strong certification and backup strategies, self-archiving with this level of exclusivity is not likely to be widely trusted to preserve scholarly information for the time spans researchers and libraries have come to expect. This does not mean that self-archiving is useless, however. Self-archiving can be a backup to trusted archives run by other parties.

Responsibilities of Archives

An electronic journal archive has responsibilities to scholars and their institutions and to publishers. The archive is responsible for ensuring scholars can access journal content for as long as it is of scholarly value in a form that allows it to be used effectively for research, teaching, and learning. The archive is responsible for respecting the copyrights of authors and publishers in its stewardship of electronic journal content.

It is also responsible for helping maintain a healthy climate of scholarship and scholarly communication. It should neither hinder publishers or libraries with overly burdensome procedural and economic constraints, nor hinder scholars themselves with overly restrictive policies for access or deposit. Archives need to be granted sufficient rights to carry out these responsibilities.

Integrated Responsibility

Whether run by content creators and publishers or by third parties, archives have traditionally taken full responsibility for the content they archive. They are responsible for quality control, continued preservation, and providing appropriate access. If they themselves cannot maintain the content in perpetuity, they are responsible for finding someone else who can. While they may delegate some of their functions, such as ingestion or migration, to outside service providers, they are ultimately responsible to their clients for making sure these functions are carried out correctly and that the content is preserved for future access.

This "integrated" responsibility for preserving and providing access to content may earn the trust of users, since the buck stops, as it were, with a definite party. Publishers, too, may be more willing to grant rights to a specific agent who takes responsibility for their work. Of course, the archive must live up to this responsibility, with its attendant certification and sustainability requirements.

Distributed Responsibility

The LOCKSS (Lots of Copies Keep Stuff Safe) project at Stanford suggests a more distributed form of responsibility, similar to the distributed responsibility for print journals discussed earlier. With LOCKSS, no one institution takes responsibility for a journal. Instead, many institutions maintain sites that cache copies of journal content published on Web sites.

Content can be accessed from the cache if it is no longer available on the original publisher's Web site. Cache contents are automatically checked against each other on a regular basis, and corrupted or lost copies of items replaced with other copies. The cache correction protocol is slow and relies on records of past holdings. These features make it highly unlikely, given enough participants, that a copy of an object will be completely lost, be corrupted, or become unavailable to any site that originally cached the content. Because the protocol also checks what content a site has previously demonstrated that it owned, the protocol does not "leak" content to sites that were not authorized to see it.

LOCKSS is designed to run on low-cost machines with as little maintenance as possible, making it attractive for libraries to set up LOCKSS caches. If enough libraries continue to cache the same content, that content (at least in its original format) can be preserved reliably even if no single institution takes final responsibility for it. The system can be queried to see how many sites are caching content. Institutions that see a need for greater reliability, can arrange to put additional copies on caches run at their own site or other sites.

In its original form, LOCKSS makes a number of simplifying assumptions about what is being cached, that may not be applicable to all journal archives. For instance, LOCKSS obtains publishers' content by automatically polling their Web sites for HTML and image files, but while those sites may include presentation forms of journals they typically do not include source forms. However, the basic LOCKSS model can be generalized to cover a broader range of journal archiving strategies, especially if caching sites can individually decide what to cache and how.

Service Providers

Service providers perform specific functions on behalf of the archival system. In an "integrated responsibility" model, service providers are essentially subcontractors for the main archive. In the "distributed responsibility" model, service providers are trusted sources, as defined above. Service providers help scale up an archival system by spreading out responsibility for archival tasks. They can be useful when an archival function requires specialized expertise or resources.

For instance, if a company provides low-cost, highly replicated reliable data storage, an archive might out-source backups to that company rather than maintain backups itself. Or, if content is submitted or stored in a variety of protocols and formats, ingestion and migration of this content might be usefully parceled out to service providers, each specializing in a particular format or data provider, instead of trying to have one organization handle everything. Service providers often do not need to make the same sort of long-term commitments as archives themselves do, unless their service includes long term information storage.

However, they still need to be visible in the design and operations of an archiving system. Archive users may want to make sure they are certified for carrying out their service correctly. Publisher agreements may need to allow them to access copyrighted material, and publishers may want to be assured that they do not distribute or alter this material without authorization. The business model for the archive or archival system also needs to include some sort of compensation for the services of the providers.

Access and Distribution Responsibilities

The archive is responsible to its clients for providing authorized users with its content and metadata, and it is responsible to publishers for providing content only to authorized users. Content provided to authorized users should include:

— Copies of the journal content as originally published (byte-for-byte copy, in original formats) for journals archived in presentation form.

— Images of the journal pages in formats commonly readable at the time of access for journals archived in presentation form. This may require migration if common data formats change.

— The text of the journal content in formats commonly readable at the time of access. This may also require migration.

— Where feasible and cost-effective, other journal content, such as data sets and audiovisual materials, in formats commonly readable at the time of access.

Metadata should include at least citation information for the journals and their articles. The archive should also provide reasonable facilities for locating an article or journal with a known citation. It seems relatively uncontroversial to allow general access at least to citation-level descriptive metadata. This allows users to know what is in an archive. Richer descriptions, such as abstracts, may be more controversial, but if they encourage a user to seek out the full content and become more interested in the journal as a whole, providing such detailed metadata can benefit both archive and publisher.

Likewise, allowing access to content by the publisher and by the archive maintainers seems uncontroversial. Widening access further, though, proved more problematic. Even providing access to subscribers to the journal for content that was also available on the publisher's Web site raised concerns that the archive would compete with the publisher's own offerings. The concerns here seemed to be not just possible loss of marketing opportunities on the publisher's own Web site, but also possible degradation of image.

The look, the services, and the authority that the publisher took pains to establish on their Web site could be lost on the archive site, thus weakening the "brand" or reputation of the publisher. This seemed to be less of a concern if the archive just offered material that was no longer available on the publisher's own Web site. Concerns about image may also be alleviated if appropriate links are made between the archive site and the publisher's site. Even more controversial is allowing access to archived journal content to those who are not subscribers to the journal. JSTOR and Highwire, two established projects that archive journal content, allow such access after a certain time has passed from publication. The point at which access is opened is referred to as the "moving wall."

Some may argue that copyright law already specifies a moving wall when works enter the public domain and are available to anyone. However, this moving wall has been extended repeatedly in the United States and is now up to ninety-five years after publication for older publications and works for hire, and to seventy years after the death of the last surviving author for other works. The distance and uncertainty of copyright expiration in these circumstances makes an archive that requires public domain verification before providing access to electronic journal content equivalent to a "dark" archive for most practical purposes.

Other "trigger" events besides a fixed moving wall are also worth considering. For example, opening up access when migration is required would ease user concerns that migration might not be successful. It might also benefit publishers if they found migration too expensive or troublesome to carry out themselves. It is also reasonable for archives to be able to provide general access to content that is no longer being offered online by the publisher or the publisher's agents. The archiving agreement should not abridge the traditional rights recognized by copyright law.

These rights include fair use, first-sale rights, and unrestricted use of public domain material. All of these rights play important roles in scholarship, so archives whose purpose is to support scholarship should avoid restricting them. Some publishers digitizing older material may want to make an exception to this rule for new digitizations of public domain content from early in a journal's run. An archive should weigh this proposed exception carefully. In some cases, a short-term embargo on unrestricted use of this material may be necessary if the only likely digitizer of the content is worried about the investment going to waste, but there is little justification for extending this embargo beyond the same moving wall term that is given to copyrighted content.

On the whole, the copyrighted content of most electronic journal archives will usually be much more valuable than recently-digitized public domain content. Users are also much more likely to trust and support a comprehensive and authorized archive of a journal's run than an unauthorized provider of part of the journal's run. Rights and responsibilities for certification and evaluation. The archive is responsible for specifying a process for certification of its content and procedures, and for reporting the results of this certification to its clients, including its publisher partners.

The RLG-OCLC Trusted Repositories paper notes two basic approaches to certification: an approach based on auditing and an approach based on standards and usage. For a "dark" archive, or an archival system that uses software that is not available for public inspection, certification will generally need to involve auditing, to satisfy the concerns of constituents who cannot examine the content or the software themselves. In a more open system, such as LOCKSS, each site can examine its own contents and the software it is using.

In such cases, separate auditing is less important though it may be desirable for the designers of the system to have the code reviewed and certified by an outside party. Publishers may want to know how the content they publish is being used in an archive as well as the cost of the archiving processes. It is reasonable for an archive to share aggregated usage information with publishers as long as the form of the information sharing protects the privacy of individual readers. If publishers are subsidizing the archiving they also have a right to be informed of the costs involved.

Archives and publishers should agree in advance on the data an archive will collect, what an archive can be expected to provide, and for how long an archive should retain usage data.

Responsibilities for Sustainability

The archive is responsible for ensuring it has appropriate technology, procedures, and funding for it to continue archiving activities for as long as needed. Responsibility for funding, however, is related to the other rights and responsibilities of an archive. Self-funding is viable for most academic libraries if the archival system is sufficiently lightweight and inexpensive to run and provides commensurate benefits. We can run a LOCKSS server on a commodity PC, for example, and in its current form it requires very little maintenance.

Even a more ambitious system, such as the distributed archiving system described earlier, could easily pay for itself if its cost were similar to the original LOCKSS system and it made it easier for us to move older journals to inexpensive remote storage. Full-service "integrated responsibility" archives are much more heavyweight. According to discussions with its maintainers, PubMedCentral, run by the National Center for BiotechnOlogy Information (NCBI) of the National Institutes of Health (NIH), requires seven full-time employees to run on an ongoing basis.

The project archives fewer than thirty externally published journals, plus a few dozen very low volume journals published by NCBI, and makes extensive use of automation. PubMedCentral staff represent only a small fraction of the staff of the NCBI, itself a small division of NIH. Organizations like this, which have national mandates as collectors and providers of research information, should find it a relatively small stretch to maintain an archive of online scholarly journals in-house and to justify it in their budgets. Many publishers can fund an archive if the archive provides them sufficient benefit. The costs of funding will ultimately be passed on to someone else.

For subscription-based journals, the price of subscriptions may account for the cost of funding the archive. Journals that charge authors for publication might build charges for preservation of the article into the author's fee. Journals published by scholarly societies may have those societies fund their preservation. Costs for preserving journal material arc ongoing but publishers may be unwilling or unable to pay for archiving the material indefinitely. One solution to this problem is to structure publisher funding as an endowment. When a publisher deposits a journal volume or issue in an archive, it would also include a one-time payment to endow the future archive needs of the deposited content.

Income from this endowment would fund ongoing archiving, backup, mirroring, maintenance, and migration of that journal content in perpetuity. If the archive decided to transfer responsibility for the content to another institution or back to the publisher, the content's endowment would be transferred as well. If a publisher stopped supporting an archive, the endowments associated with previously deposited content could still fund the preservation of that content. For the publisher and journal subscribers, the endowment would provide a guaranteed source of funds to ensure the ongoing availability of journal content. Funding would not be dependent on an archive's ongoing revenue stream.

By guaranteeing long-term availability of journal content, an endowment-funded archive could ultimately save money both for the publisher and subscribers to the journal. Subscribers who can rely on preserved electronic copies may be willing to forgo print versions or keep them in less expensive storage, thereby lowering their costs. Hence, they may be willing to contribute to an endowment fund via their subscription fees. If the archive is sufficiently trustworthy and accessible, it may even be possible to discontinue print production which would lower costs and subscription fees for the publisher.

For the endowment model to work, however, costs have to be well-understood and kept under control. If the costs can be kept down to a small percentage of subscription revenue, the endowment model may be financially viable. For instance, a journal that costs $350 per volume, with 300 annual subscribers, brings in about $100,000 of subscription revenue. If endowment income were five percent per year, then each one percent surcharge for archiving would pay $50 per year of archiving costs for that volume. So if the true costs to the archive were $150 per year per volume, three percent of subscription revenues would need to go towards archiving.

Unfortunately, this may be an optimistic estimate of archiving costs, which are still uncertain and likely to change as archives develop and as technology changes. Long-term costs may be difficult to measure in the early stages of an archiving project, especially since it may be unclear what costs are startup costs and what costs are ongoing or recurrent, given the fluid nature of technology and archiving standards. Automation of as many tasks as possible may help, as long as the cost of computers continues to decrease while the cost of labor increases. The endowment model also works best when an archive's fixed costs of operation are low compared to costs that vary with the size of the archive, favoring larger archives.

For similar reasons, high endowment requirements may also favor larger publishers which might be an undesirable side-effect for libraries already worried about over-consolidation of scholarly journal publishing in for-profit conglomerates. If scholarly archives are ultimately designed to meet the needs of scholars and scholarly institutions, a funding model that relies on publishers may produce a less useful archive than one that is funded more directly by scholars and their libraries. Funding by users appears to be a viable alternative to endowments by publishers. JSTOR has found success through funding from libraries and other journal users.

Libraries pay a one-time capital development fee and an annual subscription fee to access JSTOR content. Publishers are not charged for deposits into the archive. JSTOR has proven highly popular with libraries and their patrons. JSTOR's convenient access is the carrot that encourages libraries to pay for subscriptions that cover both access services and archiving. JSTOR's success with libraries, scholars, and publishers makes a powerful case for this type of funding model. Of course, it is possible for journal archives to have multiple funding sources, but complicated funding models may produce more problems than they solve.

An archive faced with high ingestion costs could depend on users to fund its general operations and development, as JSTOR does, but charge publishers for ingesting their content unless their content came in a prepackaged, easily-validated form prescribed by the archive. In effect, the archive would offer to sell publishers a packaging service for their content. The publisher could pay for the archive to package their content, or pay some other service provider to do it, or do it on its own and avoid having to pay. In any case, the archive's own costs for ingestion would be reduced and publishers would have an incentive to provide their content in accordance with archival standards. Both of these developments would make the archive more reliable and sustainable.

Funding and control of access rights represent a tradeoff. Publishers can provide funds or they can provide access rights to users after a suitable delay. They are reluctant to provide both. Libraries and scholars, on the other hand, may be disinclined to fund an archive that does not give them access except in some far-distant or unforeseeable circumstances. Thus, archives funded primarily by publishers may tend to be "dark," whereas archives funded primarily by libraries and archives should be more open to access by their funders.

Responsibilities and rights for transfer and delegation. Archives must be ready for unforeseen changes in the scholarly or online community that may render the archive unsustainable or make it far preferable to archive content elsewhere. Therefore, agreements with the publisher should allow the transfer, if necessary, of the archival material and its associated rights to another party that agrees to assume the archive's responsibilities. The publisher, if it is still in existence, may want to stipulate some additional qualities of the new party, for instance, that it not be a commercial competitor.

Similarly, the agreement should allow third parties to act as service providers for delegated archival functions as long as the third parties do not distribute archival material or use it for any purpose other than to carry out legitimate archival functions on the archive's behalf. For example, integrated archives may need to have a third-party off-site mirror of the archive's contents in case of a disaster at the main archival site.

Archival Life Cycle

Size of the content varied greatly among journals. For example, PDFs for American Law and Economics Review, a semi-annual journal, took up little more than 2 MB of storage space per year, whereas PDFs for Brain, a monthly medical journal, took up closer to 100 MB of storage space per year. Articles in PDF form were generally easy to harvest, usually as one PDF file per article, although in some instances the PDFs were page-oriented instead and included content from multiple or adjacent items in the same file. Correctly harvesting HTML presentation forms was considerably more problematic.

Many of the HTML-formatted articles were clearly generated from source files and included numerous automatically generated links, some of which led to content that was important to the article, such as high-resolution versions of illustrations, while others led to related material that was not part of the article itself. Many of these HTML articles were produced by the same organization, Highwire Press. Ingesting material into an archive, whether manually or automatically, is far from foolproof.

When publishers manually send a journal issue to an archive they may accidentally leave out articles, send misformatted files, or even send the wrong files altogether. Occasionally, articles published on Web sites included mistakes. An early spot-check of one mathematics journal article revealed a PDF file in which the last pages could not be read as the file was initially posted. Human checks may turn up some of these errors but can be expensive to perform.

Open Archive Initiatives

The Open Archives Metadata Harvesting Protocol, an important new infrastructure component for supporting distributed networked information services. The Metadata Harvesting Protocol-a mechanism that enables data providers to expose their metadata-is seeing very rapid deployment, and enables a fascinating array of new services and system architectures for a diverse set of communities. There has been considerable confusion about the Open Archives Metadata Harvesting Protocol, mostly beginning with and stemming from its name.

The protocol no longer has much to do with archiving or archives, other than in terms of its heritage. The Open Archives Metadata Harvesting Protocol grew out of an effort to solve some of the problems that were emerging as e-print servers became more widely deployed; it originated in the community concerned with advancing the development of e-print archives. However, as work on the protocol advanced it became clear that it provided a very general-purpose mechanism that could address a surprisingly wide range of urgent needs and, in order to be useful in the widest variety of contexts, this mechanism had to be defined so that it was agnostic to assumptions about types of content, economic models, intellectual property constraints, or systems of information flow.

For better or worse, by that time the protocol was widely known as the Open Archives Protocol, and the program to develop it was widely known as the Open Archives Initiative, so the decision was made to maintain the popularly known terminology. The protocol is now often referred to as the Open Archives Metadata Harvesting Protocol in an attempt to reintroduce a bit more clarity. This Metadata Harvesting Protocol (MHP), is simply an interface that a networked server (not necessarily an e-print server) can employ to make metadata describing objects housed at that server available to external applications that wish to collect this metadata.

A server does not need to be part of an e-print program to use the protocol; indeed, it does not need to house journal papers at all. The server does not need to offer free access to the digital objects that it stores. The Metadata Harvesting Protocol can be implemented by servers housing commercial products available by subscription (like scientific journals) or available for transactional purchase, by libraries or museums offering access to digitized images, or by scientific data archives, to list only a few potential applications.

Many of the people who have been involved in the work on the MHP are also strong proponents of the broader program to open free public access to the scholarly journal literature, but they are usually careful to differentiate between the two; the MHP can certainly advance the deployment of e-print archives, but it is not limited to supporting that program. It is a much more general and more neutral technical-enabling mechanism. The term "Open Archives Initiative" is ambiguous; it refers both to a specific, organized, funded effort to advance the Metadata Harvesting Protocol, and to a separate, diffuse movement to promote the deployment and use of e-print archives involving a lot of the same people.

The Open Archives Metadata Harvesting Initiative had its roots in work done by Herbert Van de Sompel (then of the University of Ghent) working in collaboration with groups that included researchers and librarians at Los Alamos National Labs in the United States. In late 1999, a meeting was convened in Santa Fe, New Mexico to address a series of problems that he had been exploring in the e-print server world. Fundamentally, the problem was that as disciplinary e-print servers proliferated, often with overlapping disciplinary coverage and geographical affinity, there was a need to develop services that permitted searching across papers housed at multiple repositories. Repositories also needed capabilities to automatically identify and copy papers that had been deposited in other repositories.

Further complicating matters, institutional e-print archives (such as the DSpace project being carried out at MIT in collaboration with Hewlett-Packard3) were beginning to emerge that would house the intellectual output of specific campus communities; it was undesirable to require scholars to deposit their work in multiple repositories, and hence it would be necessary for disciplinary archives to be able to identify and replicate material from these institutional archives and for federated search services to be able to search across both institutional and disciplinary archives.

The Metadata Harvesting Protocol uses a very simple HTTP-based request-response transaction framework for communication between a harvester and a repository. A harvester can ask for metadata to be returned with optional restrictions based on when the metadata has been added or modified (in other words, it can obtain new or changed metadata since its last harvest interaction with a repository); it can also restrict metadata by server-defined "partitions" (think of these as gross subject-oriented subcollections housed on a server).

The server returns a series of sets of metadata elements (in XML) plus identifiers (i.e., URLs) for the objects that the metadata describes. Supporting this core harvesting transaction are a few ancillary transactions: for example, to permit a harvester to obtain a list of the names of partitions that a server has defined and which can thus be used as restriction criteria in harvesting requests. Multiple metadata schemes are supported in the Open Archives Metadata Harvesting Protocol-this is really the key architectural change from the Santa Fe Convention.

The protocol requires that all servers offer unqualified Dublin Core metadata (encoded in XML) as a lowest common denominator; however, each server is also free to offer metadata in one or more other schemes, and a harvester can request that metadata be provided in a scheme other than Dublin Core as part of the harvest request. There is also another auxiliary transaction that permits a harvester to obtain a list of the names of the metadata schemes that a given repository supports.

The underlying idea here is that we will see communities of practice evolve that define metadata schemes that are richer and more precise than unqualified Dublin Core; for example, the e-print archives community is already working on one that encodes various important data elements for e-prints, such as author affiliations, bibliographic information if the paper has been published in a journal, and even the paper's cited references in a structured form. These community-specific schemes could be handled as qualified Dublin Core, or as de novo schemes; the only requirement is that they be transportable in XML. This is a very powerful method of enabling communities with common metadata to work together while still ensuring some minimal level of interoperability for very broad federated search or other services based on unqualified Dublin Core.

It seems very likely that the MHP will drive development of community-specific metadata schemes. It will also be helpful in clarifying our understanding of the value of unqualified Dublin Core for lowest common denominator cross-domain resource discovery. Authentication and access management are not covered. A given repository can use a range of access-management mechanisms that are external to the protocol to decide which harvesters it will provide with metadata if it wishes to impose access control.

Independent of access control decisions about providing metadata, the server only includes a pointer-such as a URL or URN-to each object described by metadata that it makes available for harvest; access controls on this base object may or may not exist. In addition, any authentication that the harvester wants to conduct on the repository is handled by external mechanisms. The protocol does not address the very real issue of how harvesters will identify repositories that they wish to harvest, nor does it provide information to help determine when harvesting should occur, or how frequently. There will clearly be a need for some kind of registry of names for well-known community-specific metadata schemes.

The MHP does not address this, though it clearly must be part of the broader infrastructure associated with the protocol. The most obvious applications that are enabled by the Metadata Harvesting Protocol are those that helped to motivate the work at the initial Santa Fe meeting: repository synchronization and federated search. For repository synchronization, one compares metadata from two or more repositories and decides what objects should be copied from one repository to another. The hard part here is in the application: deciding what repositories to examine, and determining the criteria for identifying what to copy.

There is also a problem with the propagation of metadata from one repository to another; it's not clear how to determine the most comprehensive metadata set describing an object so that all of the relevant metadata can be copied over. Similarly, federated search using MHP is not hard in principle; one collects metadata from a number of sites, normalizes it, clusters it in some fashion to deal with duplicates as appropriate, and offers search services against the resulting database. In practice, all of the details are complex: what sites to harvest, how often to harvest them, how to normalize metadata (especially if one wants to do better than the lowest common denominator-unqualified Dublin Core-offered by each site), how to handle duplicate objects-these are all key design issues that need to be addressed.

MHP provides a very powerful framework for building union-catalog-type databases (in the broad sense; not just union bibliographic catalogs, but all sorts of union descriptive databases) for collections of resources by automating and standardizing the collection of contributions from the participating sites, which has traditionally been an operational headache in building and managing union catalogs. But there are many complex specifics that need to be coded into any actual implementation. A set of applications closely related to federated search deal with the potential enhancement of web search engines in at least two distinct dimensions.

One is providing a more efficient way for web search engines to crawl static HTML pages, and also to obtain metadata associated with these pages (there are other methods of getting the metadata, such as in-line META tags, but the MHP provides a much more flexible way of doing this). The second is being able to integrate various parts of what is sometimes called the "deep web" or the "invisible web" with the indexing of static web pages, including repositories of digital objects and databases that do not exist as retrievable and indexable static web pages, and also proprietary content, where the content owner may be willing to make metadata about the content available to facilitate finding it, but may be unwilling to permit arbitrary web-indexing programs to have direct access to the content in order to index it.

The Metadata Harvesting Protocol allows a server to enumerate the objects it houses and to provide metadata associated with these objects, no matter what the nature of these objects and the access constraints that might apply to them. Any application dealing with metadata created and stored on distributed sites faces issues about whether it can trust the metadata it is relying upon. This means, for example, that it is unlikely that the public web search engines will use an OAI interface to harvest arbitrary sites anytime soon; however, federated searching or customized indexing of sites that are selected in some fashion-by being part of an organizational intranet, or through some type of editorial policy that selects quality sites as part of a subject portal, for example-will likely make wide use of the protocol.

These are the most obvious applications (and the ones that will probably be available soonest), in that they directly extend or enhance existing practices. Interesting and novel applications are likely to emerge as well. For example, one can easily imagine the rise of intermediary services (reminiscent of the brokerage services in the original Harvest system) that collect raw metadata from sets of sites, consolidate and enhance it, and then redistribute it as a single feed or as custom-selected subsets to still other sites for reuse.

Creative applications designers are at the very early stages of exploring the services that the MHP can enable, and we can expect some fascinating and unexpected developments in the next few years. While the Open Archives Metadata Harvesting Protocol solves one very important set of problems, it also focuses attention on a number of other issues that will have to be addressed as applications proliferate. Some of them will require progress in standards and/or other networked information infrastructure components; others are simply not well understood at this point and will require considerable research and experimentation to allow the development of a body of design knowledge and community practice.

Many sites make metadata about their holdings publicly available today in the sense that they offer publicly accessible search services operating against that metadata, which can then result in the display of individual records. This is the case with most library catalogs; for example, they offer searching to anyone who wants to search the database, and some systems will even provide formatted displays of individual, full MARC records that are retrieved by such searches as an option. There is a great difference between this practice and simply making the entire catalog's contents, or major subsets, available for bulk downloading and re-incorporation into other databases and services.

In a world of MHP-enabled network resources, metadata becomes migratory and recombinant. Owners and operators of large databases and repositories will need to think through how comfortable they are in making their metadata generally available on this basis, and what limits, if any, they want to place on permissible reuse. In addition, this may focus new attention on metadata ownership; while nobody may much care about who reuses the odd individual bibliographic database record, copying an entire bibliographic database may be viewed quite differently.

There is no real way to encode acceptable-use policies or restrictions on metadata harvesting within the MHP; while it would not be difficult to make reference to textual statements about such policies, encoding them in a machine-understandable way is a difficult problem that calls for collaboration between computer scientists, lawyers, and standards developers, among others. Many applications will use manually-curated lists of sites to harvest, and, indeed, the editorial processes and selectivity that go into the development and maintenance of these lists will be part of the value of the application itself. As these services multiply, operators of new repositories will face the problem of bringing their site to the attention of the appropriate service operators so that their metadata can be harvested.

If we look at the operation of the public web search engines, which seek to be comprehensive, we find much more complex methods of identifying sites to crawl (the details of which vary from search engine to search engine, and are viewed as representing proprietary advantage to these search engines). They start with a base of websites that they have identified, or that site operators have submitted to the indexing services, but then they also dynamically discover new sites to index by analyzing links on sites that they visit. They also use a variety of techniques (both manual and automated) to determine how often to revisit sites looking for new material to index.

Some applications performing metadata harvesting will want to do a similar dynamic discovery of sites that are available to be harvested. This could be done in a number of ways. Certainly, for systems that harvest static HTML pages, it would be possible to program their crawlers to also attempt to do an OAI query against each site to see if it offered metadata for harvesting. It would be possible to establish a central registry of sites that offered metadata via the OAI secretariat; setting up a database that allowed sites to register themselves and interested parties to search the registry to identify harvestable sites is technically straightforward and not terribly resource intensive.

A prototype of this exists today on the Open Archives website; this is simply a list of MHP-compliant sites that have submitted their addresses to the OAI secretariat. The secretariat does some essentially mechanical validation of the sites by running a program periodically that issues OAI queries; it checks that the site is still there and provides syntactically well-formed responses to these queries. This mechanical validation is very valuable in these early days of experimental implementations. But it is important to recognize the very limited value of such a registry. It does not address how one might classify sites (for example, by the nature of their content or their subject coverage) in order for applications to decide which sites should be harvested. Developing computer-based methods of doing this, at any level of generality, is a complex proposition.

Many applications will likely be structured around the principle of offering in-depth access to high-quality information resources, which means that they will have to be concerned with the assessments of the quality of the metadata offered by the sites they choose to harvest. It's difficult to see how this can be handled at this point other than by evaluation and/or trust decisions by the individual applications. Scaling these decisions past manual editorial management of lists of sites to harvest takes us quickly to research areas such as reputation management systems, further complicated by the fact that both the harvesting services and their end users may want to be able to make choices about trust and reputation in their use of metadata.

In developing MHP interfaces to databases or repositories, a key design decision has to do with the granularity of the objects for which the site exposes metadata. For the original e-print-archive applications this was straightforward; the objects of interest were individual article e-prints and thus they made available metadata for each article e-print. But as metadata harvesting is deployed in a wider range of contexts, the answers are less clear. For many repositories we have little or no metadata at the individual object level, and instead have various forms of collection-level description (such as the Electronic Archival Description, or EAD, files); in other cases we may have both collection- and item-level records, each of which has value in its own right, but it is not clear how to link the two and it also isn't always clear that it is useful to make huge numbers of item-level records available.

OAI-enabled service would use the MHP to pull metadata for all of the individual records in a database, and would then perform computations that allow it to provide some kind of summary metadata record for the entire database as output; these summary records could then be returned to the database owner or operator or could be made available to other resource discovery services. The Metadata Harvesting Protocol is a means of making machine-processable metadata widely available for use. It will create tremendous pressure for standards programs that are now developing schemes to codify and represent such metadata, especially the Dublin Core Metadata Initiative.

MHP specifies unqualified Dublin Core as the lowest-common-denominator mandatory metadata scheme for interoperability purposes. This will likely lead to the first truly large-scale test of the real utility and practicality of unqualified Dublin Core for resource discovery. It is certainly clear that almost any metadata scheme can be "downgraded" into unqualified Dublin Core (in a non-reversible fashion), but the actual usefulness of such a coarse metadata scheme has been the subject of considerable debate and speculation.

The Dublin Core Initiative is also codifying the notion of qualified Dublin Core-a series of extensions to the base Dublin Core elements that can provide much greater precision but that can be "interpreted down" to unqualified Dublin Core in a consistent fashion by applications that are not knowledgeable about specific extensions. At a broader level, the idea of community-based metadata schemes is central to the vision of the Metadata Harvesting Protocol. There has been a great deal of work in this area over the past few years, in part driven by the promise of XML and the growing interest in the interchange of computer-processable information using the Internet.

Fundamentally, the development of these standards is a social process within a community, though it calls upon a poorly-codified body of knowledge in data structuring, descriptive practices, classification, and other areas. It is still very slow, and very expensive, to develop these community standards, and it is hard to predict which ones will be successful in terms of broad adoption or in terms of effectively meeting community needs over reasonably long periods of time. The Research Libraries Group (RLG) manages one of the largest union library catalogs in the world.

It received support to explore how this major scholarly resource could be completely redesigned to take advantage of Internet portal technologies. In its proposed project, RLG catalog records would be made accessible via the Open Archives protocol to a standard Internet search engine, such as Google, and search results would be expected to link the user not only to a set of catalog entries, but also to a set of service options that might, for example, direct users how to purchase the book, find the nearest library that owns the title, find related works by the author or on the subject, or link to an online version if one exists.

References

Coppock, T., ed., *Making information available in digital format: perspectives from practitioners*, Edinburgh: The Stationery Office, 1999.

Daniels, Anne, "PANDORA—Archiving Electronic Publications", *M/C Reviews*, 15 September 1999.

National Library of Australia, *Preservation Metadata for Digital Collections: Exposure Draft*, 1999.

Waters, Donald J., "Choices in Digital Archiving: The American Experience" in *The Impact of Electronic Publishing on the Academic Community*, Butterworth I. (ed.), An International Workshop Organized by the Academia Europaea and the Wenner-Gren Foundation, London: Portland Press, pp.133-141, 1998.

5

Metadata

The term metadata has been bandied about a great deal in the professional literature of late. With the advent of the Dublin Core, the Text Encoding Initiative (TEI) Guidelines, the Government Information Locator Service (GILS), and other such constructs, the concept of data about data and what to do with it has again become a discussion point in librarianship. As the methods available for describing information grow beyond MARC, it becomes increasingly apparent that librarians, and more specifically catalogers, have a role to play as mediators and creators of an increasingly diverse landscape of descriptive methods. As the choices for providing access increase, the experience and traditions that the cataloging profession can bring to the creation, standardization, and manipulation of metadata systems becomes obvious.

By mediating the use of metadata, cataloguers provide for these developing systems of description and access a strong influence towards standardization. Cataloging exists as an often invisible process of order making. As constituencies develop systems for ordering in the digital world, what was once a largely invisible process becomes glaringly apparent.

The University of Michigan has been the collaborative work done for the Humanities Text Initiative, a partnership between the University Library, the School of Information and Library Studies and the University of Michigan Press. Cataloging staff were brought on board to develop policies and standardize procedures for the cataloging of texts and the production of TEI headers. The goals were the development of a continuing dialogue between each of the partners and the creation of a system of headers and MARC records that provided predictable and easy access to the Initiatives electronic texts. The effort is an ongoing collaboration between the humanities text, preservation, and cataloging communities within the library. As the effort progressed towards more large-scale production, skills in UNIX programming, workflow and systems analysis, and Standardized General Mark-Up Language (SGML) were developed on the part of the catalogers while a greater appreciation for the value of standardized forms of description and access were developed on the part of the other collaborators. As workflow patterns became finalized, another change was noticed as well. Increasingly, catalogers were working with the metadata first, in the form of TEI headers, and deriving MARC-based records for the local catalog from it. This was made possible by the efforts of catalogers to standardize the forms of description within the TEI tagging. By employing AACR2 as a standard and mediating the development of tag content, catalogers played an integral role in the development of a more descriptive and standardized header that allowed for greater predictability and fidelity in searching and retrieval.

In 1994, the University of Michigan was awarded a four-year, four-million-dollar cooperative agreement to conduct coordinated research and development to create, operate, use, and evaluate a test bed of a large-scale continually evolving multimedia digital library. The NSF/ARPA/NASA Digital Library is based on a set of highly specialized agents. The descriptive component of that library, the conspectus, consists of a metadata set for the description of objects, collections, and agents within the digital library. In early 1995, members of the University Library's Original Cataloging Unit were asked to join the Conspectus Working Group to provide expertise in the creation of systems for information organization, in the maintenance of large scale information systems and to advise on the ability of metainformational constructs to scale from the research to the production level. Work has progressed over the last year and will continue to into the future to create and refine the conspectus. Catalogers actively participated in the process of defining an attribute set. An additional area of exploration involved investigating what the best process for registering or cataloging content for the UMDL would be.

The conspectus seeks to go further than simply describing the bibliographic characteristics of an object or collection to additionally encompass rights, relationships and services also associated with the collection, object or agent being described. Each of these developments came about from a creative, collaborative process between catalogers from the university library and faculty and students from the university's schools of engineering and library and information science. In the ongoing work to create this metadata component, catalogers have employed talents largely taken for granted in the areas of description, retrieval and access as well as developing new skills in ontological description.

Emergence of Metadata

As text publishing models increasingly incorporate electronic access and delivery into their paradigm, it becomes clear that metainformation/metadata becomes included in the editorial decisions involved in the creation of the texts. This is a shift from the old model of simply publishing the text and leaving the creation of metadata description in the hands of outside agencies, such as libraries or, more specifically, catalogers. This shift of work from the bibliographic control level to the publishing level is a natural evolution of text production in the electronic information age. Whereas texts previously were gathered into the library and placed under bibliographic control via catalogs, MARC-based or otherwise, now more and more providing to clients actual texts whose revision exists beyond the control of the physical library. In addition, through initiatives such as OCLC's Dublin Core and the TEI, among others, accessing texts that contain self-describing metainformation. Metadata itself is not a new thing. Catalogers have been employing it as a descriptive method for decades as MARC records in OPACs or as cards in catalogs.

The opportunities for catalogers in the developments begin with a return to viewing cataloging as a process. The experiences that catalogers have taken from the digital library programmes at the University of Michigan illustrate this. Catalogers took away broadened perspectives on new methods of information organization, fresh looks at old assumptions involving information retrieval and organization and a return to a basic understanding of the relationship between access, description and retrieval. The underlying theme behind each of these lessons has its emphasis on cataloging as a process. Too often viewed cataloging as having its culmination in a record while the largely invisible intellectual process of creating standards, vocabularies, and systems of description and classification that are inherent in that record are taken for granted. Because of this invisibility, many of those creating libraries and systems for the new digital order assume that they are approaching these issues for the first time. By approaching these developments from a collaborative perspective, not only do librarians bring to the table experience in creating metainformational systems, but gain new insight and experience in the processes employed by other disciplines. As these digital endeavors become more and more global, the cataloger's experience in languages, diacritics, and standard making become more and more valuable.

As the extent of electronic publishing grows, metadata structures increasingly assume a central focus in describing text and items. Developers of digital libraries often do not realize that librarians have been there before. A role for libraries in providing description and access for these resources will lie with the creation, maintenance and scalability of such metadata descriptions. By bringing these new metadata discussions into libraries and, more specifically, into the roles of catalogers, it becomes clear that the future of universal access will not lie with one universal system of description. The purpose is not to replace existing systems or ignore a century of tradition in description, but to continue to build upon that knowledge in the creation of new metainformational systems, to impart insight into the creation, maintenance and scalability of metadata through collaborative efforts, and to bring expert knowledge of the cataloging process and the traditions of the cataloging community to the discussions regarding metadata and standards for the digital future.

Metadata Approach to Digital Preservation

Preserving long-term access to digital information resources is one of the key challenges facing libraries and information centers today. The University of North Texas (UNT) Libraries has entered into partnership agreements with federal and state agencies to ensure permanent storage and public access to a variety of government information sources.

As digital resource preservation encompasses a wide variety of interrelated activities, the UNT Libraries are taking a phased approach to ensure the long-term access to its digital resources.

It is now common knowledge that digital information is fragile in ways that differ from traditional technologies, such as paper or microfilm. The fact that information is increasingly stored in digital form, has led to an accelerated search for effective methods of managing electronic information resources.

The huge and ever expanding multiple sources of information on the Web normally contain special formatting and are produced with a variety of software in different versions. If the original digital resource is not "born digital", it may be a digital representation or digital surrogate of the physical medium, e.g. a page of text, an object, a painting, a photograph, a sculpture, a song, a movie, etc.

The persistence of digital information resources is an important factor for any digital library development. Addressing the preservation and long-term access issues for digital resources is one of the key challenges facing libraries and information centers today.

In order to make sense of the high heterogeneity that exists among digital resources, a growing body of research has attempted to deal with the problems associated with the volume and nature of information on the Web and to look into ways to achieve consensus on a standard.

Digital Resources Management for Metadata

Metadata is a set of attributes used to describe an object. In reviewing the library and information science literature of the past few years, there is no shortage of views of the significant role of metadata in meeting the most pressing needs and challenges of digital resource management.

A number of metadata initiatives provide detailed and descriptive information about a digital resource to facilitate discovery by users. Resource description is essentially about describing information resources using a standard framework or set of principles. But because of the specific nature of heterogeneous digital resources, describing digital resources in a consistence fashion may not be an easy task, and in some cases, it is a complex process.

Those concerned with digital information management all regard metadata as an essential component of the evolving networked information environment, but each of these communities view metadata with notably different perspectives.

Metadata Interoperability

Metadata interoperability is a closely related issue and is also a focus of current metadata research. Metadata efforts often fall into the trap of trying to create a universal metadata schema. Such efforts fail to recognize the basic nature of metadata: namely, that it is far too diverse to fit into one useful taxonomy...the creation, administration, and enhancement of individual metadata forms should be left to the relevant communities of expertise. Ideally this would occur within a framework that will support interoperability across data and domains.

Roszkowski and Lukas describe an approach for linking distributed collections of metadata so that they are searchable as a single collection, and Baldonado et al. describe an architecture that facilitates metadata compatibility and interoperability.

Current developments in metadata standardization, including interoperability issues, are reported regularly on the Web. Archivists traditionally sort, organize, and catalogue a collection, producing as a final product a finding aid. The finding aid imposes a structure on the collection and indicates, generally at the folder and box level, where the physical documents may be found.

In digital conversion projects primary attention is paid to the identification and management of documents, with perhaps somewhat less attention being paid to the overall structure of the collection. The physical location of the documents becomes of secondary concern (in some cases, the physical documents are even destroyed), and of primary concern is the ability to locate the documents in a database or over a network. If the optical character recognition (OCR) is successful, then retrieval by key words can be somewhat effective.

However, if, as is often the case with older materials, the OCR is inadequate, and if the item being converted is a photograph or some other non-textual item, then some other method is needed, in any case, for finding the individual items in the collection.

The purpose of the metadata, which is made available as an "index" record, was to ensure that documents could be retrieved even if the OCR was inadequate (which it often was). The metadata also served to link the various forms of the same document (e.g., TIFF, OCR, etc.) to each other through the unique identifier that was assigned to each document. Metadata templates, which were used to standardize the information being collected, varied by document type.

Thus, for example, published articles would have information about authors, journal, publisher, place of publication, etc., while unpublished letters would include information about the sender and the recipient. Common to all document types would be information about the contributor, number of pages, location of the physical document, scanning and index dates, and index terms from NLM's Medical Subject Headings (MeSH) thesaurus, together with a controlled terminology that was special to the RMP documents.

The master copy is a high quality, lossless TIFF image from which other formats may be derived over time. When the Web technology first became available, we created a Web-based version of the system. Underlying the Profiles Web site is a system that is designed to handle the entire life cycle of a large-scale conversion project. Metadata forms the core of the system. It is the major component of the data input stage; it is used for generating various views for display on the Web; and it serves as the basis for search and retrieval.

The archivist uses the customized metadata entry system that we created to enter descriptive and administrative metadata. The descriptive metadata is typically externalized as Dublin Core, and all the metadata is intended to allow mapping to a variety of element sets as needed. The system provides a number of document management capabilities, including tracking functions. It also has built in quality control features and provides a variety of reports, including an automatically generated scan sheet.

These scan sheets accompany the physical objects throughout the digitization process, providing information and instructions for the scanner and feedback to the archivist about problems encountered during the scanning process. Once the metadata for a set of items has been entered, the process of creating the master digital object begins.

High resolution TIFF files are created as the digital master copies from which a variety of Web-accessible derivatives is created. Adobe PDF is derived from the master TIFF files for black and white documents, and 2 sizes of JPEG are derived from the greyscale and color TIFF files. Web-friendly streaming audio and video formats (QuickTime and RealMedia) files are produced from the video and audio files.

When document scanning is complete, the scanning technician deposits the scanned files into an incoming directory, indicating that the items are ready to go through the quality control process. At that point, the scanning technician returns the original items to the archivist. The metadata entry program reads the incoming directory and performs some basic checking, for example, to see if pages are missing, or if a file is named according to a non-existent unique identifier.

Items that pass this check are marked as "ready" and those that do not pass are marked as "incomplete" and are moved to a "redo" directory. The archivist checks each original item against the ready items, and uses the metadata entry system to change the status of each metadata record to either "final" (if the item passed quality control) or "redo" (if the item failed quality control).

Items that failed either the automated or manual quality control are returned to the scanning technician. Information such as which technician scanned the item, and when the item was moved through each stage of quality control and by whom, is automatically logged by the DBMS. Those digitized items that pass final quality control are moved to the archival image server or the Web server as appropriate.

The DBMS is exported and a suite of programs performs more validity checking, creates HTML pages for the metadata records which point to the Web-accessible derivatives, and creates sets of HTML pages which allow multiple views of the collection.

Metadata Records

Metadata is often called data about data or information about information. The term metadata is used differently in different communities. Some use it to refer to machine understandable information, while others use it only for records that describe electronic resources. However, in the library environment, metadata is commonly used for any formal scheme of resource description, applying to any type of object, digital or non-digital.

Traditional library cataloguing is a form of metadata, and MARC 21 and the rulesets used with it such as AACR2 are metadata standards. Other metadata schemes have been developed to describe various types of textual and non-textual objects such as archival materials, visual materials, geographic information, and science and social science datasets.

There are several different types of metadata, including descriptive, administrative, and structural. Descriptive metadata describes a resource for purposes such as discovery and identification. It can include elements such as title, abstract, author, and keywords. Administrative metadata provides information to help manage a resource, such as when and how it was created, file type and other technical information, and who can access it.

Rights management metadata is a form of administrative metadata dealing with intellectual property rights. Structural metadata indicates how compound objects are put together, for example, how pages are ordered to form chapters. Metadata can describe resources at any level of aggregation. It can describe a collection, a unitary resource, or a component part of a larger resource (for example, a photograph in an article).

Just as cataloguers make decisions about whether a catalogue record should be created for a whole set of volumes or for each particular volume in the set, so the metadata creator makes similar decisions. Metadata can also be used for description at any level of the information model laid out in the IFLA (International Federation of Library Associations and Institutions) Functional Requirements for Bibliographic Records: work, expression, manifestation, or item.

For example, a metadata record could describe a report, a particular edition of the report, or a specific copy of that edition of the report. Metadata can be embedded in a digital object or it can be stored separately. Metadata is often embedded in HTML documents and in the headers of image files. Storing metadata with the object it describes ensures the metadata will not be lost, obviates problems of linking between data and metadata, and helps ensure that the metadata and object will be updated together.

However, it is impossible to embed metadata in some types of objects (for example, artifacts). Also, storing metadata separately can simplify the management of the metadata itself and facilitate search and retrieval. Therefore metadata is commonly stored in database systems and linked to the objects described.

Metadata schemes (also called schema) are sets of metadata elements designed for a particular purpose, for example, to describe a particular type of information resource. The definition or meaning of the elements themselves is known as the semantics of the scheme. The values given to metadata elements are the content.

Metadata schemes generally specify names of elements and their semantics. Optionally, they may specify content rules for how content must be formulated (for example, how to identify the main title) and/or representation rules for how content must be represented (for example, capitalization rules). There may also be syntax rules for how the elements and their content should be encoded.

A metadata scheme with no prescribed syntax rules is called syntax independent. Metadata can be encoded in MARC, in "keyword=value" pairs, or in any other definable syntax. Many current metadata schemes use SGML or XML. XML (Extensible Mark-up Language) is an extended form of HTML which allows for locally defined tag sets and the easy exchange of structured information.

SGML (Standard Generalized Mark-up Language) is a superset of both HTML and XML and allows for the richest mark-up of a document. An important reason for creating descriptive metadata is to facilitate discovery of relevant information. In addition to resource discovery, metadata can help organize electronic resources, facilitate interoperability and legacy resource integration, support digital identification, and support archiving and preservation.

Metadata serves the same functions in resource discovery as good cataloguing does by:

— allowing resources to be found by relevant criteria;

— identifying resources;

— bringing similar resources together;

— distinguishing dissimilar resources;

— giving location information.

As the number of Web-based resources grows exponentially, aggregate sites or portals are increasingly useful in organizing links to resources based on audience or topic. Such lists can be built as static web pages, with the names and locations of the resources "hardcoded" in the HTML.

However, it is more efficient and increasingly more common to build these pages dynamically from metadata stored in databases. Another method of organizing Web information is through channels. Channels are preselected Web sites that automatically "push" streams of information to a user's browser, commonly used for continuously updated information such as stock quotes and news.

The dominant metadata scheme for webcasting is the Channel Definition Format (CDF) developed by Microsoft and its partners. Describing a resource with metadata allows it to be understood by both humans and machines in ways that promote interoperability. Interpretability is the ability of multiple systems, with different hardware and software platforms, data structures, and interfaces, to exchange data with minimal loss of content and functionality.

Using defined metadata schemes, shared transfer protocols, and crosswalks between schemes, resources across the network can be searched more seamlessly. Two approaches to interoperability are cross-system search and metadata harvesting. The Z39.50 protocol is commonly used for cross-system search.

Z39.50 partners do not share metadata but map their own search capabilities to a common set of search attributes. A contrasting approach taken by the Open Archives Initiative is for all partners to translate their native metadata to a common core set of elements and expose this for harvesting.

A search service then gathers the metadata into a consistent central index to allow cross-repository searching regardless of the metadata formats used by participating repositories.

Most metadata schemes include elements such as standard numbers to uniquely identify the work or object to which the metadata refers. The location of a digital object may also be given using a file name, URL, or some more persistent identifier such as a Persistent URL (PURL) or the Digital Object Identifier (DOI).

Persistent identifiers are preferred because file locations change frequently, making the URL (and therefore the metadata record) invalid. In addition to the actual elements that point to the object, the metadata can be combined to act as a set of identifying data, differentiating one object from another for validation purposes.

Most current metadata efforts centre around the discovery of recently created resources. However, there is a growing concern that digital resources will not survive in usable form into the future. Digital information is fragile; it can be corrupted or altered, intentionally or unintentionally. It may become unusable as storage media and hardware and software technologies change.

Format migration and perhaps emulation of current hardware and software behaviour in future hardware and software platforms are strategies for overcoming these challenges.

Metadata is key to ensuring that resources will survive and continue to be accessible into the future. Archiving and preservation require special elements to track the lineage of a digital object (where it came from and how it has changed over time), to detail its physical characteristics, and to document its behaviour in order to emulate it on future technologies.

Many organizations internationally are working on defining metadata schemes for digital preservation, including the National Library of Australia, the British Cedars Project (CURL Exemplars in Digital Archives), and a joint Working Group of OCLC and the Research Libraries Group (RLG).

Many of these initiatives are based on or compatible with the ISO Reference Model for an Open Archival Information System (OAIS) which incorporates preservation metadata along with descriptive, administrative, and rights management metadata.

Many different metadata schemes are being used in library environments. A few of the most common ones are mentioned below.

Text Encoding Initiative (TEI)

The Text Encoding Initiative is an international project to develop guidelines for marking up electronic texts such as novels, plays, and poetry, primarily to support research in the humanities. This SGML markup becomes part of the electronic resource itself. In addition to specifying how to encode the text of a work, the TEI Guidelines also specify a header portion, embedded in the resource, that consists of metadata about the work.

The TEI header, like the rest of the TEI, is defined as an SGML DTD, a set of tags and rules defined in SGML syntax that describe the structure and elements of a type of document. Since the TEI DTD is rather large and complicated in order to apply to a vast range of texts and uses, a simpler subset of the DTD, known as "TEI Lite", is commonly used in libraries.

It is assumed that TEI-encoded texts are electronic versions of printed texts. Therefore the TEI Header can be used to record bibliographic information about both the electronic version of the text and about the non-electronic source version. The basic bibliographic information is not dissimilar to that recorded in library cataloguing and can be mapped to and from MARC.

However, there are also elements defined to record details about how the text was transcribed and edited, how markup was performed, what revisions were made, and other non-bibliographic facts. Libraries tend to use TEI headers when they have collections of SGML-encoded full text.

Some libraries use TEI headers to derive MARC records for their catalogue systems, while others use MARC records for the published source texts as the basis for creating TEI header descriptions.

Encoded Archival Description (EAD)

In archives and special collections, the finding aid is an important tool for resource description. Finding aids differ from catalogue records by being much longer, more narrative and explanatory, and highly structured in a hierarchical fashion.

They generally start with a description of the collection as a whole, indicating what types of materials it contains and why they are important. If the collection consists of the personal papers of an individual there can be a lengthy biography of that person. The finding aid describes the series into which the collection is organized, such as correspondence, business records, personal papers, and campaign speeches, and ends with an itemization of the contents of the physical boxes and folders comprising the collection.

The Encoded Archival Description (EAD) was developed as a way of marking up the data contained in a finding aid, so that finding aids can be searched and displayed online. The EAD standard is maintained jointly by the Library of Congress and the Society of American Archivists. Like the TEI Header, the EAD is defined as an SGML DTD. It begins with a header section that describes the finding aid itself which could be considered metadata about the metadata; it then goes on to the description of the collection as a whole and successively more detailed information.

If individual items being described exist in digital form, the EAD can include pointers to the digital objects. The EAD is particularly popular in academic libraries with large special collections. Although it is easier to put finding aids on the Web by simply marking them up in HTML than to follow the EAD specification, libraries and archives investing in EAD creation hope that using this metadata scheme will encourage consistency in encoding and give them some measure of search interoperability.

Visual Resources Association (VRA) Core Categories

The VRA Core Categories is a metadata element set developed to describe visual materials such as buildings, photographs, paintings and sculptures. Typically, visual resources collections used in teaching art history and similar subjects do not contain original art works but rather slides or photographs of the original art.

Metadata for these materials therefore has to accommodate the description of multiple levels of related resources; for example, an original painting, a slide of the painting, a digitized image of the slide. Version 3.0 of the VRA Core Categories consists of 17 metadata elements which can be used as applicable to describe each of these versions and relate them to each other: record type, type, title, measurements, material, technique, creator, date, location, ID number, style/period, culture, subject, relation, description, source, and rights.

Like the Dublin Core, the VRA Core scheme does not specify any particular syntax or rules for representing content. However the development of the VRA Core has served as impetus for the visual resources community to continue to develop shared vocabularies and classification schemes.

Metadata Resources

Metadata is data which describes attributes of a resource. Typically, it supports a number of functions: location, discovery, documentation, evaluation, selection and others. These activities may be carried out by users or by client programs.

In an indefinitely large resource space, effective management of networked information will increasingly rely on effective management of metadata. Increased commercialisation and complexity of information resources makes this need all the greater. It is unlikely that some monolithic metadata format will be universally used. This is for a number of more or less well known reasons. There is a variety of types of metadata.

There is traditional descriptive information of the kind found in library catalogues, which typically includes such attributes as author, title, some indication of intellectual content and so on.

There is information that might help a client application make a decision based on format or on location. There are different types of user: a user as customer wishes to know the terms under which an object is available; a user as researcher may wish to have some extended documentation about a particular resource, its provenance for example.

There are different types of resource. Some resources may have a fugitive existence, existing to satisfy some temporary need and are only ever minimally described, if at all; some are important and valuable scholarly or commercial resources, where the value of extensive description is recognised. Some resources may be simple; some may be complex in various ways. There will be many different information providers, some commercial 'yellow pages' type services, some scholarly or research oriented services, in different organisational configurations with different target audiences and products.

Metadata may be closely coupled with the object it describes as an intrinsic part of its composition; or it may have no intrinsic link with it at all. At the same time, the technical and service environments in which metadata services are being deployed are the subject of rapid change and development. Thus, the nature of the problem to be solved suggests a variety of solutions.

It is helpful to consider a metadata spectrum, along which data becomes successively fuller, more structured, specialised, and expensive to create. This division into bands is presented for purposes of analysis only — as a way of presenting a view over an existing situation — and not as a set of fundamental distinctions. At one end is data used in services which currently support location and limited discovery. Terse metadata allows searching for known items, and for topics. This is the area inhabited by the webcrawlers which automatically extract data from resources. They currently provide web forms access onto proprietary databases. There are moves to enhance the metadata on which they operate and to develop frameworks for interworking.

At the other end of the spectrum is metadata which supports much richer functionality. It is often associated with research or scholarly activity, requires specialised knowledge to create and maintain, and caters for specialist domain-specific requirements. Metadata formats being developed here can express a variety of formal and intellectual relationships, and are often part of a larger framework which provides for the encoding of the content they describe.

Typically, they are looking at the creation of a variety of SGML document type definitions to cater for metadata and 'content'. Such initiatives include the Inter-university Consortium for Political and Social Research (ICPSR) SGML codebook initiative to describe social science data sets, the Encoding Archival Description (EAD), Content Standards for Digital Geospatial Metadata (FGDC) and the Consortium for Interchange of Museum Information (CIMI). The Text Encoding Initiative can also be included here, and influenced some of these other developments. There has been some interest in the Z39.50 profile for access to digital collections for search and retrieval of such metadata. This has been taken furthest with CIMI where a companion profile is being developed for specific use with museum data.

The middle band contains services which contain full enough descriptions to allow a user to assess the potential utility or interest of a resource without actually having to retrieve it or connect to it, but not so full or complex as to require very specialist staff to create. Typically, but not essentially, these descriptions are manually created, or are manual enhancements of automatically extracted descriptions, and they include a variety of descriptive and other attributes. They may be created to be loaded directly into a discovery service or may be harvested. Typically they are simple enough to be created by non-specialist users, or not to require significant discipline-specific knowledge.

Descriptions tend to be of discrete objects and do not capture multiple relationships between objects. Again, typically, they involve some selectivity in what they describe and may have more or less explicit criteria for selection. For these reasons, they may be expensive to create, again driving an interest in author- or publisher- generated description and automatic extraction techniques. Examples of services in this category are OCLC's NetFirst, and the subject-based information gateways being developed in the UK Electronic Libraries Programme and in Desire.

Against this analytic background, one can note some likely future directions, especially across the boundaries of these bands. Author- or site-produced metadata will become more important for crawlers and the middle band of services. This metadata may be harvested unselectively, or only from selected sites, depending on the service environment.

An important motivation for such harvesting is to overcome some of the deficiencies of current crawlers without a provider incurring the cost of record creation. At the same time, communities using the richer 'documentation' formats will wish to disclose information about their resources to a wider audience. How best to achieve this will have to be worked out: perhaps 'discovery' records will be exported into other systems.

These directions suggest that the middle band will become more important as a general-purpose access route, maybe with links to richer domain-specific records in some cases. Incidentally, the current interest in the Dublin Core Metadata Element Set can perhaps partly be explained by the fact that it has been positioned so that its target uses coincide with the trends outlined above: it provides the basis for a 'discovery' record; it can provide the basis for embedded content description which can be harvested by robot; and it aims to provide the basis for interoperability across richer description models.

Resource Organisation and Discovery in Subject-based Services

ROADS is a development project, also in the Access to Network Resources area of eLib. A major objective of ROADS is to provide a set of software tools for the eLib subject-based services. These tools will allow the construction of distributed services and provide some data creation and other tools. An early motivation was that it should be possible to avoid the fragmentation of the current bibliographic environment and allow users have unified access to a distributed resource. ROADS is being developed in concert by the University of Loughborough (technical development), UKOLN at the University of Bath (metadata issues, requirements), SOSIG at the University of Bristol (coordination and project management, liaison with services and information providers, requirements), and Bunyip (technical consultancy).

The development of ROADS has been guided by several strategic decisions. Wheels should not be reinvented: solutions should be based on Internet standards. Where those are being formed, ROADS experience will be put into their development. The system needs to support services in the middle band identified above, and certain decisions flow from that.

For this type of application, what is required is a description which is simple to create yet full enough for effective retrieval and relevance judgement. This implies a description which falls between the terseness of the crawlers and the fullness of a research library catalogue record. ROADS is looking at IAFA/WHOIS++ templates because they offer a basis for international consensus and because we can influence their development. There are also a range of template types: for user, for service, for document, and so on, allowing a fuller range of objects to be represented than with some other formats.

ROADS introduced the concept of 'trusted information provider', arguing that the collection of descriptions from approved authors and web-site administrators will be essential to a sustainable service. Again, a simple record structure will facilitate this and data creation and gathering tools are being prepared as part of the project.

A distributed framework is required: the user is best served by a solution which allows autonomously managed services to be accessible individually or as a navigable unit. Furthermore, we think this should be done in a network-friendly way and allow for multiple different configurations of service. This aspiration is typical of directory type applications, and we see this application as a distributed 'yellow pages' directory. The project is using WHOIS++ because it is a leading candidate for this type of service. Also because, through use of the Common Indexing Protocol, it supplies a mechanism for selecting between servers to search.

The choice of IAFA and WHOIS++ was governed by pragmatic reasons: there is no ideological adherence to them as the 'one true path'. In the timescales of the project, it was important to have something which was immediately serviceable. Importantly, the project acknowledges that there is no one solution. There will be several protocols and formats and much more on-the-wire conversions between them. It is in this context that ROADS includes a component which looks at interoperability with MARC and Z39.50. This will result in a report on semantic interoperability among USMARC, IAFA/WHOIS++ templates, and the Z39.50 BIB-1 attribute set and also a small demonstrator system. The latter will involve integrated access to a selection of bibliographic resources and a subject-based network service using Z39.50 and WHOIS++. A Z39.50/WHOIS++ gateway is being developed in this context.

At a wider level, ROADS aims to provide a collaborative framework through which the UK community can help contribute to the design and development of the future of such services. This is at the service and organisational level, and at the technical level where numerous issues are outstanding. Standards for the creation of descriptions and for the search and retrieve of such descriptions are still under development and open to influence.

Omni and SOSIG are currently in production mode using ROADS version 0. This was developed so that services would have something to work with from an early stage. It provides a simple search engine, several tools for creation and processing of IAFA records, and a web interface. The services offer a search service and can generate browsable pages by subject (class number) and other categories. ROADS Version 1 is due to go into Alpha test shortly and incorporates WHOIS++. At this stage, the services will continue to provide standalone servers accessed over the web. It includes a range of other functional enhancements. In early 1997, ROADS Version 2 will be released which will implement the Common Indexing Protocol.

At this stage, we will test the ability of the system to provide unified guided access to a metadata resource distributed over several subject specific servers. Each server will generate a centroid, an inverted index style representation of its content, which will be collected in an index server. The centroids provide 'forward knowledge' about the contents of servers in the distributed directory so that sensible decisions can be taken about navigation. A fuller description of the technical architecture of ROADS and its implementation of WHOIS++ can be found elsewhere.

Further development may be possible at this stage, and will certainly take place within the Desire project. Although ROADS aims to provide the eLib subject services with a systems framework, other users are not discouraged. As such it has a secondary aim in demonstrating the efficacy of a distributed solution in one compelling service environment. If successful it would hope to extend the scope to look at other directory applications. Users would benefit enormously from a simple to maintain, working directory service for distributing information about courses, research interests, 'white pages' data, and so on.

Problem of Interoperability

Interoperability is a critical problem in the network environment especially, the Digital Libraries with increase in number of diverse computer systems, software applications, file formats, information resources and users.

But it becomes more critical problem in Indian digital libraries, with having those much differences it has another sharing problem of resources from one language to another as resources at Indian libraries are present in many Indian languages viz. English, Hindi, Sanskrit, Marathi, Gujarati, Oriya, Bengali, Punjabi etc. Thus it has problem of interoperability between multilingual digital library resources. However there are so many true type fonts are being used to represent the Indian languages on web. But that's not sufficient tool to implement the multilingual. ISCII is also being used as a standard to represent the Indian languages on the web as well on the database part. But as we found that Unicode is the only solution, which represent the all languages being spoken in this world including the Indian languages.

It does not have any ambiguity and doesn't overlap, dealt with each and every characters of every language with unique values. To implement effectively interoperability function within the digital libraries following standards speak as tools:

Metadata Lifecycle Model (MLM)

The MLM is a methodology involving a ten-step process by which digital library projects can design and implement metadata provision. It can be reviewed again once the project requirements have been changed. The purpose of the model is:

— To achieve a consistent method of developing metadata for digital library projects, so that they might achieve greater effectiveness and better.quality.

— To conduct a content-based analysis for digital collections, which takes into account knowledge mapping and metadata research needs while adopting any existing metadata formats.

The ten-step of the MLM can be classified into four main groups as follows.

Group I Requirement Assessment & Content Analysis

— Step1: Acquisition of Metadata Base Needs

— Step2: Review of Relevant Metadata Standards and Projects

— Step3: Investigation of Deep Metadata Needs

— Step4: Identification of Strategies for the Metadata Schemes and

Group II System Requirement Specification

— Step5: Preparation of the Metadata Requirement Specification

— Step6: Evaluation of Metadata Systems

Group III Metadata System

— Step7: Preparation of Best Practice Guidance

— Step8: Development of the Metadata System

Group IV Service and Evaluation

— Step9: Maintenance of Metadata Service.4

— Step10: Evaluation of Metadata Performance

The first step of the metadata lifecycle is to interview the content experts or providers about their metadata requirements for each collection project, and analyze the attributes of collection projects through the four-layer for metadata selection.

— *Metdata scope*: Attributes of metadata are relating to thing, person, event, temporal, vocabulary control, and geographic name.

— *Legacy system*: basic information about the legacy system, including elements, structure, number of records, storage format, and input method and system. In addition, it is useful to understand the advantages and disadvantages of the system.

— *Metadata context*: Is only one metadata database constructed for this project? Are any other databases required to integrate with this metadata database, such as geographic information system (GIS)?

— *Metadata role and function*: What kind of metadata role is proposed for each project? What kind of function should be achieved by metadata, such as resources description, discovery, annotation, or administration?

After the four-layer for metadata selection is applied, the candidates of metadata schemes for a digital library are thus revealed. Current metadata trends and issues from around the world related to the profile of the digital library project can be collected and analyzed as a reference for practical application and future development.

Through this stage the collection project members could well know what kind of differences exist with other similar or homogeneous collection projects, and also re-arrange the focus of expected project goals.

Metadata scope and context are clarified, and related relationships are clearly drawn and attributed to a diversity of categories. It could ensure what kind of systems and databases are integrated by metadata mechanisms such as GIS.

The purpose of developing metadata services is to guarantee the quality assurance of metadata mechanisms. A service model is constructed to formulate the service items. The assessment of metadata record quality, including completeness, accuracy, record types, granularity levels, and records' serviceability. For example, an evaluation of the U.S. Government Information Locator Service (GILS) focused on assessing metadata quality from a set of criteria and procedures.

The evaluation of the effectiveness of adopting a metadata scheme for retrieval, such as its capacity to facilitate access to title, creator, and subject. For many digital libraries, discovery, access, and description are the typical applications of metadata. However, the case study shows that there are more functions needed, such as preservation, content rating, rights, data management, and e-Learning.

In addition, domain-specific metadata sets are the core development of metadata practices in the case study. In other words, the generic metadata set, such as Dublin Core for resource discovery, is deployed in its top level of the union catalogue.

Metadata Management

Controlling what happens to digital materials is a key preservation step. In most cases this requires the safe transfer of data and documentation to the care of a preservation programme, where they are given unique identification, and described using various kinds of metadata. Metadata enables digital materials to be found and, crucially from a preservation point of view, to be managed and re-presented accurately.

Although preservation metadata standards are still developing, programmes must describe the technical characteristics, provenance and preservation objectives of the digital materials in their care. In most cases this requires the transfer of data into the care of a responsible preservation agency. The transfer process itself is not without risks as it provides opportunities for data to be lost, changed, misidentified, or divorced from the context that gives it meaning.

Because the producers of digital materials generally have some rights in the materials they produce, transfer raises a number of legal and moral rights issues. Once digital materials have been transferred, they must be controlled and organised in effective and efficient ways. This generally includes requirements that materials can be easily located, accessed, used, managed and preserved, in accord with permissions.

Transfer and control are long-established practices in managing non-digital heritage. When applied to digital materials, these processes must be modified. An appropriate legal basis for transfer is required. It must address concerns over the ease with which materials can be re-used, as well as the need to copy data for its preservation. Transfer must affected without loss of data, often using quite different methods from those used for transfer of non-digital materials. The transfer of accompanying documentation is particularly critical for digital data that may not be understandable without it.

Most transfer strategies are variations of two basic concepts: producers pushing digital materials to the preservation programme, or the preservation programme pulling materials from the producer. Programme managers must decide which approach will be most suitable for the materials being transferred and for the workflows of the parties involved.

Many programmes impose controls at the point of transfer on the formats of the material they receive. The purpose of this is to simplify preservation by reducing the variations that have to be managed in storing the material and in keeping it accessible. Not all programmes are able to restrict the formats they accept, but they should seek to verify that formats have been used in a standard way.

Digital files must be given suitable file identifiers so they can be retrieved. Each file within a storage system must be identified with a unique file name so that it cannot be confused with any other file. It is also most important for preservation programmes to ensure that the materials they keep can be reliably found, whatever their location. The Universal Resource Locator (URL) used to identify Web-based resources, for example, does not allow users to find material once it has been moved. Thus, items can be effectively lost even though it may still exist and be well protected.

Overcoming this problem requires some form of persistent identification, built around an identifier and a means of resolving or linking to the file in its current location. There are a number of schemes proposed or in place including the Digital Object Identifier (DOI) used by publishers, and various schemes being investigated by libraries and archives, but none has yet found universal acceptance.

Preservation programmes use metadata - structured information about data resources - to describe the digital materials in their care. Preservation programmes generate large amounts of information about way material is created, transferred and used; about rights and who is authorised to do what; and other management processes. Preservation metadata describes the means of providing access, along with those elements of resource management metadata required to manage preservation processes. It is critical for any preservation programme; its careful design and management is especially important for large collections that must be processed with as much automation as possible.

Metadata is itself an information resource that must be managed and preserved, along with the material that it describes. Individually developed metadata schemes can be successful in describing collections of digital materials, but there are increasingly good reasons to use a standardised approach in line with other widely adopted schemes:

— To reduce the considerable costs of developing individual schemes

— To take advantage of available software tools that automatically recognise and record standard metadata elements from digital materials, greatly reducing the cost of metadata capture

— To allow preservation programmes to share information, making their collections visible and searchable to a much wider audience

— To allow collection materials to be moved from one repository to another without the need for wholesale rewriting of metadata

— To encourage the standardisation of preservation processes that are described and controlled by the metadata.

The reproducibility of digital materials means that transfer no longer requires removal of the material from one site in order to move it to another. Perfectly authentic copies can be transferred for preservation while 'live' copies remain with the creator. The timing of transfer may be critical. Even though material may have been selected for preservation, selection of itself does nothing to slow down processes like media deterioration or obsolescence of technology.

There is no standard way of effecting the physical transfer of digital materials. Data can be transferred on a wide range of physical carriers such as various forms of diskettes, CDs, tapes, cartridges, and disk drives; or through communication networks using means such as email attachments, file transfer protocol (FTP), and downloading from Web sites. The choice of transfer media depends on the needs of the parties involved.

Whatever means are chosen, the data must remain secure. Some transfer environments may present particular risks for specific media; for example, physical carriers may be easily lost or stolen, while communication networks may be unreliable and it may be safer to hand deliver a physical carrier. The transfer medium must allow the data to be loaded and retrieved. When both sender and receiver use the same technologies, transfer should be relatively straightforward. When technologies are mismatched, one or both parties will need to bear the cost of using different technologies.

Preservation programmes may have facilities to handle a wide range of media, or their.facilities may be more restricted. Physical carriers require specific hardware which preservation agencies may not be able to provide. In such cases they will need to decide whether it is reasonable to require transfers via specific media that they can process, or to invest in facilities to handle a wider range of media.

On the other hand, preservation programmes relying on deposit may find that transfers depend on production factors beyond their control, including changes in personnel, changes in priority, or declining levels of interest, all leading to inconsistent transfers. Pull approaches place more control in the hands of the preservation programme regarding timing and content of transfers. Some producers consider this an infringement of their rights and either block the software used to copy their files or demand rights agreements, so the control offered by pull approaches is not absolute.

Digital objects can have a number of identifiers variously used for local control, for system-wide identification, and for global access, (just as a book on a library shelf can be identified by its title, a classification number, a shelf location, an accession number, a record number in the catalogue database, an International Series Book Number, and so on). Persistent identification of some kind is needed so that items can be found even if they are moved in a storage system. Any links embedded within objects will only continue to work if linked to persistent identifiers.

It has already been noted that metadata must be not only recorded, but also looked after. There are a number of elements to this:

— *Structuring*: Organising metadata into a standardised document structure such as an XML template should make it easier to preserve

— *Linking*: The links between metadata records and the digital objects they describe must be maintained. There is much debate about the best place to store metadata to achieve this. While some metadata must be attached so that software tools can automatically process the material, there is disagreement on whether full metadata records should be stored separately, attached to, or even become part of, the objects they describe.

Separate storage allows metadata to be accessed and updated without needing to extract the linked digital objects from storage - a great advantage. On the other hand, many programme managers worry about the potential for the essential link between object and record to be disrupted over long periods of time. Managers should assess the risks they operate with and decide which approach is more suitable

— *Quality control*: Ensuring the trustworthiness of metadata records is a high priority. Quality control measures are needed whenever metadata records are created or changed

— *Protection*: The integrity of metadata records must be ensured, requiring the same preservation attention as the objects they describe.

Once the digital material has been transferred and any necessary control and description work undertaken, it must be prepared for entry into a storage system, ensuring the various part of the information package (including the content and any metadata) are linked, and a data stream created that can be safely stored on the storage media in use and can found by the appropriate file searching programmes. The package is then saved to storage.

References

Day, M., "Issues and Approaches to Preservation Metadata", Proceedings from the Joint RLG and NPO Preservation Conference, September 28–30, 1998.

Granger, Stewart, , "Metadata and Digital Preservation: A Plea for Cross-Interest Collaboration", *Vine*, no. 117: 24-29, 1999.

Networked European Deposit Library, *Metadata for Long Term Preservation,* 2000.

Research Libraries Group, *RLG Working Group on Preservation Issues of Metadata: Final Report,* 1998.

Wendler, R., "LDI Update: Metadata in the Library", *Library Notes*, No. 1286, July/August, pp. 4–5, 1999.

6

Information Automation

The term "automated digital library" can be used to describe a digital library where all tasks are carried out automatically. Computer programs substitute for the intellectually demanding tasks that are traditionally carried out by skilled professionals. These tasks include selection, cataloguing and indexing, seeking for information, reference services, and so on. The common theme is that these activities require considerable mental activity, the type of activity that people are skilled at and computers find difficult.

Automated digital libraries should not be confused with library automation, which uses computing to reduce routine tasks in conventional libraries. The underlying question is not whether automated digital libraries can rival conventional digital libraries today. They clearly cannot. The question is whether we can conceive of a time when they will provide an acceptable substitute. Quality of service in automated digital libraries will not come from replicating the procedures of classical librarianship.

More likely, automated libraries will provide users with equivalent services that are fundamentally different in the way that they are delivered. For example, within the foreseeable future, computer programs are unlikely to be much good at applying the Anglo American Cataloguing Rules to monographs. But cataloguing rules are a means to an end, not the end itself. They exist to provide services to users, notably information discovery.

Automatic methods for information discovery may not need traditional cataloguing rules. The criterion for evaluating the new methods is whether the users find what the information that they require. Consider the contrast between web search engines and conventional abstracting and indexing services or library catalogs. Almost everything that is best about a library catalog is done badly by a web search service. The selection of which materials to index by a web search engine relies on arbitrary considerations, the indexing records are crude at best, authority control is non-existent, and the elimination of duplicates leaves much to be desired. On the other hand, web search services are strong in ways that catalogs are weak.

While cataloguing is expensive, indexing the web is cheap. The leading web search engines index several hundred million web pages every month, more than the total number of MARC records that have ever been created. It is wrong to claim that conventional catalogs or indexes are superior because of their quality control, and it is equally wrong to claim that the web search services are superior because of their coverage and currency. The value to users depends on what the user wants to achieve. In contrast, web search services such as GoogleSM are entirely automated. The indexes are built by a team of computers with no knowledge of what they are indexing.

Google has the advantage over Medline of indexing hundreds of millions of web pages, and doing so repeatedly every month. It is quite useful for finding general information on medical topics, but it does not index the major scientific journals, its indexing records are crude, it has no understanding of medical terminology, and makes no attempt to separate sound medicine from quackery. It is a long way from being a substitute for Medline. On the other hand, consider the trade-off between Google and Inspec, which is the leading abstracting and indexing service for computing.

In many areas of computing, Google's restriction to open access web materials is relatively unimportant, since almost every significant result first appears on a web site and only later reaches the printed journals, if ever. In computing, substantially the same information is often available from several sources. Google provides a direct link to an open access version. Inspec references a formally published version, which is usually printed or online with restricted access. For example, a scientist judges a library catalog simply as a tool for information discovery, while, for a humanist, the catalog may be a bibliographic source in its own right.

Any predictions of the future value of web search engines compared with conventional abstracting and indexing services depend heavily on the publication and reading habits of people in different disciplines. The rate of progress in computing power is described by Moore's Law, that the number of transistors on a semiconductor doubles every eighteen months. This is roughly equivalent to saying that computing power increases 100-fold in 10 years or 10,000-fold in 20 years. Few people can appreciate the implications of such dramatic change, but the future of automated digital libraries is likely to depend more on brute force computing than on sophisticated algorithms. Many of the most successful methods of artificial intelligence apply simple methods to huge volumes of data.

An interesting example comes from the computer programs that play chess. The IBM system that is now equal to the world's greatest grandmasters is descended from Deep Thought, a student project at Carnegie Mellon University. The members of the Deep Thought team were not chess experts. Their breakthrough came from expertise in developing exceptionally fast hardware, which could analyze immense numbers of chess variations. Information discovery illustrates the complementary skills of computers and people. Humans are skilled at reading a few thousand words and extracting complex concepts. Faced with a billion pages (roughly the size of the web), they are helpless.

Computers can index every word in a billion pages and search the indexes for simple patterns almost instantaneously. The web search services represent the state-of-the-art in automated information discovery. Within each service lie a number of separate processes, each of which is carried out automatically, and each of which is constrained by the current state of computing. To build the indexes, a web crawler must decide which pages to index, eliminate duplicates, create a short index record for each page and add the terms found on the page to its inverted files.

To search the index, the search engine must convert the user's query to a search command, match it against the inverted files, rank the results and return them to the user. To anticipate the potential of automatic systems to rival the functionality of Medline in all disciplines, we need to examine the components of a system like Google and see how they could be improved. Moore's law predicts that computers will be 10,000 times more powerful in twenty years. With such computer power available, we know that the automatic search systems will be extremely good, even if no new algorithms are invented. For example, to decide how closely a document matches a query would seem to require human judgment, yet standard methods of information retrieval do remarkably well.

They use the power of computers to match simple patterns as a surrogate for the human ability to relate concepts. As humans, we use our understanding of language to observe that two texts are on similar topics, or to rank how closely documents match a query. Computers can estimate closeness of match by comparing word frequencies. One basic concept, developed by Gerald Salton at Cornell University about 1970, represents each document as a multi-dimensional vector and uses the angle between their vectors as a measure of the similarity of two documents. Evaluating the importance of documents would appear to be another task that requires human understanding, but Google's ranking algorithm does remarkably well entirely automatically. The idea behind this algorithm is simple.

Google ranks web pages by how many other pages link to them. It gives greater weight to links from higher-ranking pages. Calculating the ranks requires the algorithm to iterate through a matrix that has as many rows and columns as there are pages on the web, yet with modern computing and considerable ingenuity, Google performs this calculation routinely. As a result, Google is remarkably successful in presenting a user with the most important page on a topic or a well-respected overview. This algorithm was developed as part of the NSF-funded Digital Library Initiative. The Internet is an extremely important part of modern culture and contains many materials that should be preserved for future generations. Each month, a web crawler gathers every open access web page with associated images.

The Internet Archive preserves these files for the future and mounts them on computers available for scholarly research today. The Internet Archive is not perfect. Only HTML pages and images are collected, no Java applets or style sheets; the materials are dumped into a computer system with no organization or indexing; broken links are left broken; and access for scholars is rudimentary. Yet the simple fact is that without the automated approach of the Internet Archive, these materials would already have been lost. Attempts to catalog and collect web materials using skilled librarians and archivists have floundered on the scale of effort needed to do even a rudimentary job. Citation analysis is a long-standing success story of applying computers to library information. Inspired by the efforts of Eugene Garfield, the founder of Science Citation Index, there is a long tradition of using citations as bibliographic measures.

Hyperlinks are the web's equivalent to citations. Since they are already in machine-readable form, they are amenable to algorithmic analysis.

Google's ranking algorithm can be seen as applying the concepts of citation analysis to the web. Hyperlinks refer to items or copies of a work, but citations normally refer to the work itself or a specific manifestation. Automatic systems are becoming capable of extracting a reference from a document and linking it to the digital object that it references. Currently, the most fully automated system for reference linking is the SFX system, created by Hebert Van de Sompel and colleagues at the University of Ghent.

Reference linking is one of the building blocks that are being used to build large-scale automated digital libraries. Metadata is one of the foundations of librarianship. There are a number of projects that extract metadata from digital objects automatically. Perhaps the most remarkable is the Informedia project, led by Howard Wactlar at Carnegie Mellon University. Informedia has the extremely ambitious goal of providing access to segments of video, such as television news, entirely automatically. Thus it includes algorithms for dividing raw video into discrete items, for generating short summaries (called "skims"), for indexing the sound track using speech recognition, for recognizing faces and for searching using methods of natural language processing. Each of these methods is a tough research topic and, not surprisingly, Informedia provides only a rough-and-ready service, but overall it is surprisingly effective.

Moreover, many of the weaknesses of Informedia could be overcome by applying huge amounts of computing power. The job of a reference librarian ranges from helping users with the mechanics of using a library to tasks that require deep intellectual understanding. The ugly term "disintermediation" is used when users perform for themselves tasks that used to be carried out with the help of a librarian. Information retrieval provides a good test case. The mechanics of searching have been almost completely assumed by computing. The current generation of scholars never experienced the tedium of reading through long lists of abstracts, searching huge card catalogs and following citations laboriously from journal to journal.

Searching a card catalog required skill. Because of the labor in creating and filing cards, only a small number of entries were provided for each work. Since few users ever mastered the complex rules for the main and supplementary headings, or the intricate filing conventions, serious users turned to reference librarians for help. Automated digital libraries can clearly help with the mechanics of searching, but information seeking is more complex. In disciplines with complex organization of information, searching for information remains a skilled task. Often, knowledge of the subject matter is paramount and the experts develop their own skills.

Computing power is much cheaper than human expertise, more so every year. When money and time are available in abundance, skilled professionals have no equal. But they are always in short supply. In the United States, the National Library of Medicine is funded by the government and provides open access to Medline, but only rich lawyers can afford to use the legal services provided by Westlaw and Lexis. Because of the cost, traditional library systems are selective. Indexing and abstracting services restrict their coverage to a carefully selected set of publications. Catalogs do not include potentially useful information from monographs, such as individual items in anthologies, subheading, captions, and so on.

There are essentially no attempts to catalog the content of web sites, below the level of the whole site. Even so, these services are very expensive. Automatic systems have no trouble with being inclusive; they have problems when they attempt to be selective. Their weakness is lack of precision. They exhibit what, in a human, would be called very poor judgment. Both ISI's Web of Science and ResearchIndex provide users with interlinked scientific documents. Web of Science is a splendid service, but its production is not fully automatic, since ISI relies on skilled personnel for election and for key parts of the input process. Because the ResearchIndex methods are automatic and are applied to raw data, ResearchIndex inevitably has errors, while the skilled staff at ISI eliminate almost all errors, but at a cost. Automated digital libraries combined with open access information on the Internet offer to provide the Model T Ford of information. Nobody would claim that the Model T Ford was a peer to the handcrafted cars of its generation, and automated digital libraries cannot approach the personal service available to the faculty of a well-endowed university.

Intensive Library Automation

Libraries are very record-intensive: Not only is each title different but, for many purposes, the records needed for library operations must necessarily be very concerned with individual copies of each title. Automated Library to denote a library in which the collections of library materials are primarily on paper but in which the library's procedures have been computerised.

A circulation system must know precisely which copy of which volume of which edition of which title was borrowed by precisely which borrower and when it is due back. Attributing the loan to some other borrower will not do; nor will substituting the return of some other document, even by the same borrower, be acceptable as a discharge of the loan. Acquisition records need to show precisely how many copies of a given work were ordered from which bookseller and which, if any, have so far been received.

A library not knowing which titles it already has could not function efficiently. Serials records contain minute details of copies of issues, indexes, binding, and invoices in order to assure that each set is complete and properly acquired, bound, and paid for. Library records, then, must be specific to individual copies. In general it is desirable that library record-keeping be automated for three reasons:

— Much of the work involves the accurate updating of records in files. The tasks involved are generally tedious, repetitive, mechanical in nature, and lend themselves to computerisation, even though the records may be complex and arranged in complicated ways.

— Automation is likely to improve cost-effective performance by increasing accuracy, by reducing the rate of increase in costs in labor-intensive activities, and by increased effectiveness. It should become possible to do some tasks more thoroughly than levels of staffing usually permit with manual procedures, such as the regular claiming of unsupplied issues of periodicals, or by doing things that cannot in practice be done in paper files, notably searching for combinations of characteristics.

— Automation permits decentralised access to records. A librarian in a branch library can verify the status of an order without maintaining duplicate files, travelling to the order department, or asking other staff to interrupt their work in order to find out.

Considerations of service, of cost, and of the humane use of staff all argue for the use of computers to ease the burden and to increase the effectiveness of handling library records.

Standards

Bringing order to chaos and achieving collaboration both depend on shared understanding: on standards. Library service has long depended on shared standards, of which the adoption of standardised cataloging codes and standardised subject classification schemes are two very important examples. These two examples and most library standards may facilitate automation and make computerised procedures more cost-effective, but they have little to do with computers directly. Two standards have enormous strategic importance for the Automated Library:

— The MAchine Readable Cataloging (MARC) communications formats for catalog records define how catalog records can be communicated from one computer system to another. This national and international standard is now more than twenty years old. Although rather complicated and cumbersome, it provides a necessary basis for the economies through standardisation that is essential for the development of the Automated Library.

— More recent, much less well-known, but of comparable strategic importance, is the "Search and Retrieve" standard, sometimes called the "Linked Systems Protocol". In the first twenty years of the Automated Library one would use one online catalog or one online bibliography at a time. After finishing the use of one system, one could then consult another--one at a time and separately. But as the number of different systems increased, each using commands that were more or less different from the others, and requiring telecommunications to more or less remote sites, the advantages and the inconvenience of using not only one's local system but also other, different, remote systems became increasingly clear.

The sensible alternative, for anyone interested in using computers, was to try keep the advantages and to delegate the inconvenience. Instead of withdrawing from one's local on-line catalog in order to use another, one would prefer to command the local on-line catalog to extend the search to other on-line catalogs elsewhere on one's behalf and to retrieve and to present the results. In principle, this removes from the user the need to bother with the telecommunications and possibly unfamiliar commands needed for the other online catalogs. (Figure 1.)

In theory any remote on-line catalog can become an extension of one's local catalog with the differences in commands made largely transparent. Getting one computer to "Search and Retrieve" from another can, in principle, be extended to a variety of bibliographic files. This is a new development.

The MARC standard enables computer-based bibliographic data to be shared and the "Search and Retrieve" standard enables retrieval systems to be shared. The long term consequences of both are enormous.

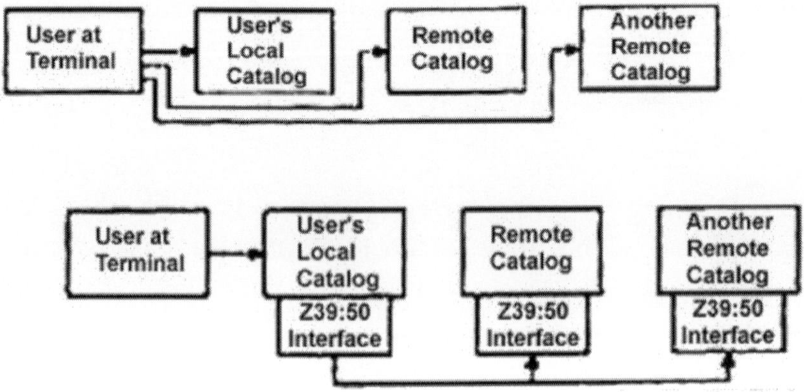

Figure 1: Search and Retrieve (Z39:50) protocol

Technological Trends

Those who predict technological trends are unanimous on certain points. If, for lack of any grounds for doing otherwise,The projections and extrapolate them forwards for a few years, reach some simple planning assumptions concerning the new information technology:

— Improved performance by computers, if continued, will result in computing power becoming extremely inexpensive, with a trend toward a computer on every desk.

— Telecommunications will become ubiquitous, convenient, and very low cost per character transmitted.

— Data storage costs become trivial.

Everything else, including labor costs, it should assume to be unchanged or getting worse. Library service is very labor intensive. About two-thirds of a library's budget usually goes for labor. Since machines can be made more cost-effective in a way that human beings can not, it appears inexorable that the cost of labor will tend to increase relative to other costs. (Fig. 2). Because of the steadily shifting relationship between machines and humans, we can expect the amount of machine use to increase steadily, relative to the use of labor for any and all activities for which machines can be used.

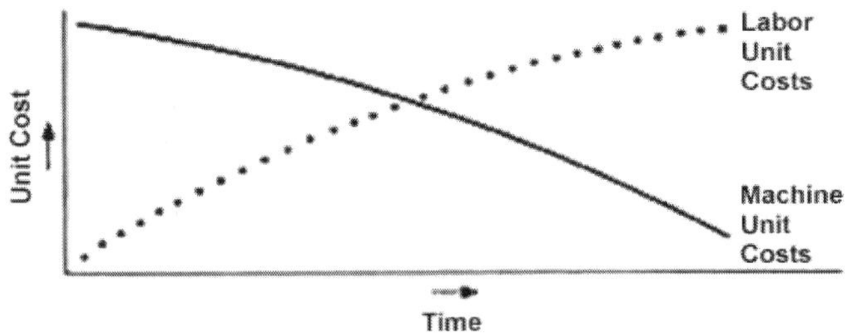

Figure 2. Costs treads: labor and machines

The effect may simply be empowerment--more machine power to increase what a person can do. The effect will also be one of substitution--what can be delegated to machines will increasingly be delegated as it becomes technically and economically feasible.

The following "drift-down" principles have been proposed by Michael Gorman:

— Nothing should be done by a professional that can be done by a technician.
— Nothing should be done by a technician that can be done by a clerk.
— Nothing should be done by a human being that can be done by a machine.

These principles do not necessarily apply in all circumstances but they do seem reasonable guidelines for improving the cost-effectiveness of library services in North America.

Paper Libraries of any size now either are or are becoming Automated Libraries. In brief, the change from the nineteenth century design of the Paper Library to the Automated Library has been characterised by:

— standardisation of data,
— remote access to files,
— the linking and combining of files,

— access to numerous different files from the same terminal,
— increased cooperative use of shared files,
— discontinuation of numerous, more-or-less duplicative local files,
— greater capability for doing things to and with the (computer-based) files, and
— increased vulnerability to technological failure.

Problems of the Automated Library

Because the collections of documents are still on paper, a localised medium, the need for local collections, the space needed for paper documents, the inflexibility of paper documents, the separation of documents from the users, opening hours for the collections, and competition for use of copies of documents all remain as much a problem as in the Automated Library as in the Paper Library.

The catalog may be used in a number of places. In particular, with remote access to the on-line catalog, the user is no longer separated from the catalog and the separation of catalog and documents is somewhat diminished since, online, a catalog can at long last be used in the bookstacks. The Automated Library represents a significant improvement but for only some of the problems and, aside for the online catalog, benefits directly those who are providing the service rather than those who are using the service.

Issues in Digital Automation

The term automated digital library can be used to describe a digital library where all tasks are carried out automatically. Computer programs substitute for the intellectually demanding tasks that are traditionally carried out by skilled professionals. These tasks include selection, cataloguing and indexing, seeking for information, reference services, and so on.

The common theme is that these activities require considerable mental activity, the type of activity that people are skilled at and computers find difficult. Automated digital libraries should not be confused with library automation, which uses computing to reduce routine tasks in conventional libraries. The underlying question is not whether automated digital libraries can rival conventional digital libraries today. They clearly cannot. The question is whether we can conceive of a time when they will provide an acceptable substitute.

Quality of service in automated digital libraries will not come from replicating the procedures of classical librarianship. More likely, automated libraries will provide users with equivalent services that are fundamentally different in the way that they are delivered. Within the foreseeable future, computer programs are unlikely to be much good at applying the Anglo American Cataloguing Rules to monographs. But cataloguing rules are a means to an end, not the end itself. They exist to provide services to users, notably information discovery. Automatic methods for information discovery may not need traditional cataloguing rules.

The criterion for evaluating the new methods is whether the users find what the information that they require. Consider the contrast between web search engines and conventional abstracting and indexing services or library catalogs. Almost everything that is best about a library catalog is done badly by a web search service. The selection of which materials to index by a web search engine relies on arbitrary considerations, the indexing records are crude at best, authority control is non-existent, and the elimination of duplicates leaves much to be desired. On the other hand, web search services are strong in ways that catalogs are weak. While cataloguing is expensive, indexing the web is cheap.

The leading web search engines index several hundred million web pages every month, more than the total number of MARC records that have ever been created. It is wrong to claim that conventional catalogs or indexes are superior because of their quality control, and it is equally wrong to claim that the web search services are superior because of their coverage and currency. The value to users depends on what the user wants to achieve. In US, for medical research, no web search engine can approach the National Library of Medicine's Medline service. Medline has over 11 million references and abstracts. It is built by a team of indexers who have knowledge of bio-medical research, using indexing rules and MeSH subject headings that have been developed laboriously over decades. In contrast, web search services such as GoogleSM are entirely automated.

The indexes are built by a team of computers with no knowledge of what they are indexing. Google has the advantage over Medline of indexing hundreds of millions of web pages, and doing so repeatedly every month. It is quite useful for finding general information on medical topics, but it does not index the major scientific journals, its indexing records are crude, it has no understanding of medical terminology, and makes no attempt to separate sound medicine from quackery. It is a long way from being a substitute for Medline. On the other hand, consider the trade-off between Google and Inspec, which is the leading abstracting and indexing service for computing. In many areas of computing, Google's restriction to open access web materials is relatively unimportant, since almost every significant result first appears on a web site and only later reaches the printed journals, if ever. In computing, substantially the same information is often available from several sources.

Google provides a direct link to an open access version. Inspec references a formally published version, which is usually printed or online with restricted access. For my purposes, Google's broad coverage and convenient links more than compensate for its weaknesses. A scientist judges a library catalog simply as a tool for information discovery, while, for a humanist, the catalog may be a bibliographic source in its own right. Any predictions of the future value of web search engines compared with conventional abstracting and indexing services depend heavily on the publication and reading habits of people in different disciplines. The rate of progress in computing power is described by Moore's Law, that the number of transistors on a semiconductor doubles every eighteen months. This is roughly equivalent to saying that computing power increases 100-fold in 10 years or 10,000-fold in 20 years. Few people can appreciate the implications of such dramatic change, but the future of automated digital libraries is likely to depend more on brute force computing than on sophisticated algorithms.

Many of the most successful methods of artificial intelligence apply simple methods to huge volumes of data. An interesting example comes from the computer programs that play chess. The IBM system that is now equal to the world's greatest grandmasters is descended from Deep Thought, a student project at Carnegie Mellon University. The members of the Deep Thought team were not chess experts. Their breakthrough came from expertise in developing exceptionally fast hardware, which could analyse immense numbers of chess variations. The potential for automated digital libraries lies in the simple observation that:

— Simple algorithms plus immense computing power often outperform human intelligence.

— Moore's Law tells us that the computing power will be available.

— The state-of-the-art in automated digital libraries

— The introduction of automated digital libraries is a continual process, much of it happening outside conventional libraries. Here are some current examples.

Information discovery illustrates the complementary skills of computers and people. Humans are skilled at reading a few thousand words and extracting complex concepts. Faced with a billion pages (roughly the size of the web), they are helpless. Computers can index every word in a billion pages and search the indexes for simple patterns almost instantaneously. The web search services represent the state-of-the-art in automated information discovery. Within each service lie a number of separate processes, each of which is carried out automatically, and each of which is constrained by the current state of computing.

To build the indexes, a web crawler must decide which pages to index, eliminate duplicates, create a short index record for each page and add the terms found on the page to its inverted files. To search the index, the search engine must convert the user's query to a search command, match it against the inverted files, rank the results and return them to the user. To anticipate the potential of automatic systems to rival the functionality of Medline in all disciplines, we need to examine the components of a system like Google and see how they could be improved. Moore's law predicts that computers will be 10,000 times more powerful in twenty years. With such computer power available, we know that the automatic search systems will be extremely good, even if no new algorithms are invented. To decide how closely a document matches a query would seem to require human judgment, yet standard methods of information retrieval do remarkably well. They use the power of computers to match simple patterns as a surrogate for the human ability to relate concepts. As humans, we use our understanding of language to observe that two texts are on similar topics, or to rank how closely documents match a query.

Computers can estimate closeness of match by comparing word frequencies. One basic concept, developed by Gerald Salton at Cornell University about 1970, represents each document as a multi-dimensional vector and uses the angle between their vectors as a measure of the similarity of two documents. Evaluating the importance of documents would appear to be another task that requires human understanding, but Google's ranking algorithm does remarkably well entirely automatically. The idea behind this algorithm is simple. Google ranks web pages by how many other pages link to them. It gives greater weight to links from higher-ranking pages. Calculating the ranks requires the algorithm to iterate through a matrix that has as many rows and columns as there are pages on the web, yet with modern computing and considerable ingenuity, Google performs this calculation routinely.

As a result, Google is remarkably successful in presenting a user with the most important page on a topic or a well-respected overview. This algorithm was developed as part of the NSF-funded Digital Library Initiative. The Internet is an extremely important part of modern culture and contains many materials that should be preserved for future generations. Each month, a web crawler gathers every open access web page with associated images. The Internet Archive preserves these files for the future and mounts them on computers available for scholarly research today. The Internet Archive is not perfect.

Only HTML pages and images are collected, no Java applets or style sheets; the materials are dumped into a computer system with no organisation or indexing; broken links are left broken; and access for scholars is rudimentary. Yet the simple fact is that without the automated approach of the Internet Archive, these materials would already have been lost. Attempts to catalog and collect web materials using skilled librarians and archivists have floundered on the scale of effort needed to do even a rudimentary job.

Citation analysis is a long-standing success story of applying computers to library information. Inspired by the efforts of Eugene Garfield, the founder of Science Citation Index, there is a long tradition of using citations as bibliographic measures. Hyperlinks are the web's equivalent to citations. Since they are already in machine-readable form, they are amenable to algorithmic analysis. Google's ranking algorithm can be seen as applying the concepts of citation analysis to the web. Hyperlinks refer to items or copies of a work, but citations normally refer to the work itself or a specific manifestation.

Automatic systems are becoming capable of extracting a reference from a document and linking it to the digital object that it references. Currently, the most fully automated system for reference linking is the SFX system, created by Hebert Van de Sompel and colleagues at the University of Ghent. Reference linking is one of the building blocks that are being used to build large-scale automated digital libraries. ResearchIndex is a digital library of computer science materials, created entirely automatically by Steve Lawrence and colleagues at NEC. It makes extensive use of citation analysis and reference linking. It downloads papers from the web. If they are in PostScript or PDF, it converts them to text. It parses the papers to extract citations and the context for the citation. It provides users with services such as searching the entire text or the citations, listing the references within a paper, following the citation links, or displaying the context in which references appear. An interesting aspect of ResearchIndex is that it provides a way for users to submit corrections, automatically of course.

Metadata is one of the foundations of librarianship. There are a number of projects that extract metadata from digital objects automatically. Perhaps the most remarkable is the Informedia project, led by Howard Wactlar at Carnegie Mellon University. Informedia has the extremely ambitious goal of providing access to segments of video, such as television news, entirely automatically. Thus it includes algorithms for dividing raw video into discrete items, for generating short summaries, for indexing the sound track using speech recognition, for recognising faces and for searching using methods of natural language processing. Each of these methods is a tough research topic and, not surprisingly, Informedia provides only a rough-and-ready service, but overall it is surprisingly effective. Moreover, many of the weaknesses of Informedia could be overcome by applying huge amounts of computing power.

The job of a reference librarian ranges from helping users with the mechanics of using a library to tasks that require deep intellectual understanding. The ugly term "disintermediation" is used when users perform for themselves tasks that used to be carried out with the help of a librarian. Information retrieval provides a good test case. The mechanics of searching have been almost completely assumed by computing. The current generation of scholars never experienced the tedium of reading through long lists of abstracts, searching huge card catalogs and following citations laboriously from journal to journal. Searching a card catalog required skill. Because of the labor in creating and filing cards, only a small number of entries were provided for each work. Since few users ever mastered the complex rules for the main and supplementary headings, or the intricate filing conventions, serious users turned to reference librarians for help. Automated digital libraries can clearly help with the mechanics of searching, but information seeking is more complex.

In disciplines with complex organisation of information, searching for information remains a skilled task. Often, knowledge of the subject matter is paramount and the experts develop their own skills. For example, carrying out legal research online is a basic skill that every law student learns. Historically, most doctors needed the help of a medical librarian to carry out an in-depth search. Now, even in medicine, the tools available to the user are sufficiently good that most searches can now be carried out directly by the user. It seems that automatic tools are steadily reducing the need for reference librarians in these fields. For many years, we have had computer systems that can search enormous collections of text for the phrase "space station", or simple variations. For this purpose, computers clearly out-perform human searching for both speed and accuracy.

Computing power is much cheaper than human expertise, more so every year. When money and time are available in abundance, skilled professionals have no equal. But they are always in short supply. In the United States, the National Library of Medicine is funded by the government and provides open access to Medline, but only rich lawyers can afford to use the legal services provided by Westlaw and Lexis. Because of the cost, traditional library systems are selective. Indexing and abstracting services restrict their coverage to a carefully selected set of publications. Catalogs do not include potentially useful information from monographs, such as individual items in anthologies, subheading, captions, and so on. There are essentially no attempts to catalog the content of web sites, below the level of the whole site. Even so, these services are very expensive. Automatic systems have no trouble with being inclusive; they have problems when they attempt to be selective. Their weakness is lack of precision.

They exhibit what, in a human, would be called very poor judgment. Both ISI's Web of Science and ResearchIndex provide users with interlinked scientific documents. Web of Science is a splendid service, but its production is not fully automatic, since ISI relies on skilled personnel for election and for key parts of the input process. Because the ResearchIndex methods are automatic and are applied to raw data, ResearchIndex inevitably has errors, while the skilled staff at ISI eliminate almost all errors, but at a cost. A library subscription to the Web of Science costs $100,000 per year. Automated digital libraries combined with open access information on the Internet offer to provide the Model T Ford of information. Nobody would claim that the Model T Ford was a peer to the handcrafted cars of its generation, and automated digital libraries cannot approach the personal service available to the faculty of a well-endowed university. But few people could afford a hand-built car, and few people have easy access to a major research library. The low cost of automated digital libraries is already bringing scientific, scholarly, medical and legal information to new audiences.

The library and information services were recognised as a key service within the newly established knowledge management group that also consisted of e-business strategy, data warehousing, management and analysis services and web services. In Australia, an integrated structure for the Department of Human Services (DHS) libraries was endorsed in July 2000 paving the way for new library innovations supporting a departmental knowledge management approach. The Department of Human Services has adopted a knowledge management approach that supports key organisational outcomes. There are five major strategic directions that scope out the future for the DHS. They are:

— Improving services for better outcomes;
— Increasing the state's capacity to promote quality of life;
— Redistributing resources in a changing environment;
— Strengthening a culture of working together;
— Providing sound management.

These strategic directions are underpinned by the strong focus on leadership, service excellence, accountability, valuing staff, innovation and enthusiasm, respect for customers and staff and acting with integrity. During 1999 the knowledge management group of functions aligned under the management of the Director for Knowledge Management (KM), Iolanda Principe. Functions currently contained in this group include:

— e-business and e-records management strategy;
— knowledge strategy;
— library and information services;
— organisational information services (data warehousing, management and analysis);
— web services.

Since this time, a Framework and Guide for Knowledge Management in the Department of Human Services was written in June 2001 and recently endorsed by the department's executive management group. This framework outlines key definitions, principles, objectives and responsibilities for KM within the department. It is designed as a practical guide for staff in the department in implementing a KM approach within their business unit while mapping out an organisation-wide approach. The principles articulate a range of elements from valuing employee knowledge as a key asset, to sharing knowledge and working collaboratively through to employees having the right to access the information / knowledge they need through appropriate systems.

The key KM objectives are:

— Leveraging the use of existing departmental knowledge;

— Fostering the creation of new knowledge;

— Enhancing the retention of knowledge (especially when people leave); and

— Improving knowledge transfer to clients.

Within this framework, the development of a knowledge centre has been identified as a key initiative for the KM program. This knowledge centre is a focal point for knowledge skills and the facilitation of knowledge flow within the organisation and requires the transformation of the current library and information services to fulfil this function. The KM framework is focussed on:

— The evolution of knowledge workers;

— The links between organisational strategic directions and KM;

— The links between knowledge / information / new economy initiatives (state, national and international) and KM within the DHS strategic plan;

— Effective measurement or evaluation of KM strategies and initiatives;

— Demonstration of KM best practice;

— Capturing organisational intellectual capital and effectively measuring how this occurs particularly within an organisational cultural context.

The DHS in South Australia is leading the way in the successful implementation of knowledge management within the public sector. The current challenges for the library are:

— Support the development and meet the needs of knowledge workers.

— Provide access to knowledge for improved decision making and innovation.

— Enhance the department's capacity to capture its knowledge and its ability to use this knowledge to further strategic objectives.

Individual training for library staff focussed on specific skill set acquisition Library culture that supports learning and innovation for strategic benefits. The current challenge for the library within this emerging knowledge enabled department is how to further this shift and overcome the barriers identified above. With clear evidence that customers want more tailored services delivered in an appropriate and timely way, it has become clear that the library must shift from a passive knowledge facilitating role to a pro-active knowledge broker role.

There are numerous creative and innovative ways in which the library can achieve these value added services and become a re-intermediary knowledge agent. For example, in working with departmental projects, the library can provide its expertise with the support of additional resources from the project allocations.

This also requires that library staff work with its customers beyond the library walls. This type of work already happens informally on an individual and ad hoc basis and, consequently, is not currently captured by existing library measurement tools. What is a knowledge centre? It:

— identifies sources of important knowledge, both inside and outside the company

— catalogues and indexes material so that retrieval is efficient and effective

— maintains and sustains the knowledge repository (the knowledge bank)

— provides a one stop shop for multiple information needs

— knows who can help - pointers to people as well as information

— runs a client advisory service - offering expertise on sources, their availability, relevance, quality and overall usefulness to the business.

While it can be argued that the library already does this to some extent now, within the KM framework, the shift for the library to a knowledge centre relies on extending what it already does well and formalising some of the informal or intangible knowledge processes that occur. The library team has an extensive knowledge base about the work being carried out in the department.

In addition, there have been several initiatives that assisted the library team to position itself for these and other changes in the future. They are:

- Enhancing partnerships with customers through knowledge need assessment processes;
- The development of a Balanced Score Card for the library and information services;
- Evolving library culture for innovation and learning;
- The realignment of Communications and Public Relations, Health Promotion South Australia and Knowledge Management groups.

A key activity in the integration of library services for the DHS was the implementation of a qualitative focus group process to identify customer needs. The strategic benefit of these initiatives is that knowledge workers now have improved access to quality, evidence based knowledge. Specifically, this knowledge is available easily and quickly, potentially seven days a week, 24 hours a day. The next challenge is to ensure that future customer participation processes enable clearer identification of knowledge worker and organisational needs and that innovative service delivery strategies are implemented to meet these needs. The balanced scorecard is one tool that will assist in this process. The DHS in South Australia has adopted the balanced scorecard as a key reporting tool for the measurement of strategic and intangible outcomes. The scorecard methodology enables the measurement of objectives that target organisational change, and, specifically, innovation and creation.

Critical to the successful integration of the library service, so that is truly reflective of knowledge management principles, is the evolution of a learning culture, that is, modelling the KM approach within the library team. As a first step, the team has undertaken customer service and team building activities. Through the provision of a tailored training program, the library staff have been able to:

- Identify the issues that prevent us from embracing change;
- Identify the existing gaps in skill set and knowledge that are required to become a knowledge enabling service for the department;
- Improve the way we communicate with one another and, consequently, with our customers;

— Extend our collective understanding of the department's strategic directions and need to integrate and extend our business to support innovation;

— Create a culture of learning within the library team so that we are better positioned in the future to adopt new technologies and innovative service delivery solutions.

Learning to share the knowledge within the team and creating an environment where it is safe experiment with new ideas will enable us to more effectively contribute to the organisational knowledge base. For the library it means a new opportunity for closer partnerships with key departmental knowledge workers who have skills and expertise in:

— Communication systems and strategy;

— Publicity, promotion and marketing and customer relationships;

— Capacity building for organisational change and knowledge creation, capture and retrieval; and

— Organisational publishing (ie creating knowledge assets).

The benefit for the library, in the first instance, is a more cohesive departmental approach to capturing organisational knowledge through improved publishing policies and protocols. Currently, the library strongly advocates for its involvement in these processes to ensure legal deposit requirements are met and copies are available, not only within the department, but also nationally and internationally. The potential within this expanded group for further service delivery innovations and the enhancement of relationships with customers is great and an opportunity the library will take up eagerly. Specifically, the library will also be looking to expand its expertise in processes for engaging with customers through partnerships with the staff in these functional areas. The challenges and barriers have been clearly defined previously. The library has commenced its journey, beyond its traditional library role, to support the organisation's knowledge management approach. The initiatives that have contributed to this reorientation have also been described. Future directions for the library that will build on these initiatives, at least in the short term, are:

— Establishment of a service delivery strategy that articulates the knowledge centre approach and shift to knowledge broker and enabling service including the building stakeholder and customer partnerships

— Development of improved processes for the mapping of future customer and organisational knowledge needs;
— Adopting reporting tools that measure the strategic and intangible benefits of library service delivery innovations, eg the Balanced Scorecard;
— Continuing reorientation of library culture to foster learning and knowledge for innovation within the library team;
— Participating as key partners in the KM program and initiatives to build the organisational knowledge base that captures both explicit and intangible knowledge.

Delivering and Preserving Information

Libraries have experienced a strong shift in focus over the past decade towards digital formats for information resources. In a growing number of libraries, there is now an attitude that user demands will be met through digital media and electronic dissemination as much as through paper-based media. Universities are investing to provide improved teaching and learning resources via digital media. Other institutions, including the British Library and the US Library of Congress, are developing large technical infrastructures. The implementation of technical infrastructure and the improvement of access to the digital world is seen as hugely important for regions such as Africa, which lacks overall investment in social economic growth, and Latin America, where development has been limited by the relatively lower economic status of the library. These shifts at the library or institutional level are a reflection of the macro economics of the global economy, which contains a much larger informational and digital element than ever before.

Today, many institutions have realised they must put in place information policies, services and technologies with a firmer long-term economic strategy than might previously have been considered. The business plan driving MIT's development of DSpace is one such example. DSpace is MIT Libraries' innovative institutional digital repository designed to manage, host, preserve and enable distribution of the scholarly output of MIT's faculty. There is a clear intent to roll out the DSpace model to many other institutions. Another major economic institutional issue is the long-term preservation of large documentary collections. Almost all libraries have to think about preservation in both analogue and digital worlds. Even if they do not themselves preserve materials, they need to be sure that some institutions are doing so if they are to direct their users to them.

The purchase of digital resources remains a difficult balancing act of apparently conflicting interests. Publishers want to retain and enhance profitability. Electronic availability of journals is not relieving the cost to libraries. Electronic journals are often treated as a value-added service, rather than a replacement technology. Thus the library budget appears to be shrinking for the same amount of information resource. Meanwhile, user demand for more digital content direct to desktops continues to grow. Purchase of a digital product is likely to mean less money for a paper-based one, and thus the balancing of costs against opportunity has arguably never been harder. As important as it is to monetise the increasing costs of print versus electronic journals, there are wider economic and international issues, such as information inequalities, that electronic journals can address given new pricing structures and the opportunities possible in the digital arena. Traditional publishing and distribution mechanisms do not deliver information products in an equitable way because a library in an economically developing country just cannot afford the same level of information provision as one in a rich country.

Digital resources, by breaking the relationship between the cost of production and distribution from that of intellectual property charges, offer an opportunity to deliver more equitable information services. To take advantage of the new economic possibilities of digital resources, the World Health Organisation has negotiated a deal with publishers of approximately 1000 leading medical and scientific journals to offer electronic subscriptions at 'free or deeply-reduced rates to institutions in the developing world' for an initial three-year period. It is clear this is an enormous information benefit to the developing world. It also offers economic benefits to all parties that are only possible in the digital arena. Digital distribution costs to the publishers are virtually nothing, but they gain significant market knowledge and customer loyalty in a new and developing world market. The opportunity for cooperation and central or consortia negotiation enables bodies, such as the World Health Organisation, to predict costs against significant benefits and to manage these effectively in a predictable way with easily apparent value.

References

Barr, Pelham, "Book Conservation and University Library Administration", *College & Research Libraries* 7, July 1946.

Battin, Patricia, "From Preservation to Access: Paradigm for the Nineties", *IFLA Journal* 19, pp. 367-73, 1993.

Bearman, David, "Reality and Chimeras in the Preservation of Electronic Records", *D-Lib Magazine,* April 1999.

Berger, Marilyn, "Digitization for Preservation and Access: A Case Study", *Library Hi Tech* 17, no. 2: 146-151, 1999.

Cloonan, Michele Valerie, "The Preservation of Knowledge", *Library Trends* 41: 594-605, Spring 1993.

Lynn, Stuart, M., "Digital Preservation and Access: Liberals and Conservatives", *Syllabus 8*, November/December 1994.

Marcum, Deanna B., "The Preservation of Digital Information", *The Journal of Academic Librarianship* 22: 451-454, November 1966.

7

Digital Cataloguing

Cataloguing in some form or other is still the key to access - indeed it is even more important if users are to find the knowledge and information they need amongst the tidal wave of raw data. However, cataloguing is an expensive business, and the economic pressures will be made worse by the increase in publishing in both digital and print formats.

This will force the even wider re-use of records than is already occurring, but efficient re-use is only possible if records are prepared to common standards. The Web and digital publishing communities have realised the importance of standards, and there is a flurry of activity to develop them. Unfortunately there is a multiplicity of standards in development, and it can be difficult to find one's way through the maze.

Cataloguing standards -leaving aside communications and catalogue search protocols such as Z39.50 -can be categorised as:

— data dictionaries (lists of data elements)

— formats (how the data are carried)

— identifiers (to uniquely identify documents, authors etc)

— cataloguing rules (by which data are presented consistently to facilitate retrieval).

The data dictionaries with greatest significance for libraries are Dublin Core, which originated at a conference hosted by OCLC in Dublin Ohio, and ONIX (Online Information eXchange) which has emerged from the book trade as a subset of the wider EPICS (EDItEUR Product Information Communication Standards) data dictionary. EItEUR is the international organisation concerned with developing standards to support trade applications, but who are also keen to ensure collaboration with the library sector.

In the formats category we have MARC (MAchine Readable Cataloguing), which has been building up its capability to accommodate records for digital documents. Meanwhile the new kid on the block is XML (eXtensible Mark-up Language) with its specially designed metadata format, the Resource e-scription Framework (RDF) for embedding records in XML documents.

Identifiers are important to uniquely identify an item to facilitate the reuse of common components and to minimise data traffic. The library world has through the International Federation of Library Associations (IFLA) been working towards a standard identifier to allow the unique identification of persons and the re-use of accurate name authority data packages. However, this requires name authority registries in each country, and there has not been the resource to achieve that. Meanwhile in the trade sector rights management is a hot topic.

Publishers, authors and other rights holders naturally want to derive revenue from the electronic market in their digital documents, and the unique identification of rights holders is essential to support this. The potential profits from this marketplace could mean that the network of registries foreseen by IFLA might be funded by trade organisations. This convergence of purpose is useful to illustrate what may become an increasingly familiar phenomenon.

The final component of the information architecture is the cataloguing codes used to provide the intellectual structure for the data. Without that structure the data loses much of its meaning was originally developed for resource discovery of digital documents on the Web. It comprises 15 data elements and is meant to be simple and cheap to apply, especially by the originators of the documents. The ONIX subset emerged from the Association of American Publishers discussions on how to get e-commerce applications under way in the trade sector. It is driven in particular by the needs of on-line booksellers where rich metadata, e.g. reviews, blurbs, extracts and images, is necessary to make up for the inability of customers to browse the books in the flesh. ONIX is implemented in XML.

Version 2.0 has been published, which can accommodate multimedia publications and e-books. ONIX is being adopted by an increasing number of trade bodies, for example in the US, UK, Germany and Latin America, and by international bodies like the ISBN network and the International OI Foundation as their preferred metadata standard for descriptive data associated with the International Standard Book A study was commissioned recently to examine the potential for ONIX to be used in the library sector.

The fact that ONIX is based on the IFLA Functional Requirements for Bibliographic Records model means that there is basic compatibility with library applications. Indeed the trade sector can be commended for not trying to reinvent the wheel and for drawing on the best of what the library world can offer. Librarians who were consulted as part of the study were enthused by the potential for trade-library collaboration, and saw ONIX as having tremendous potential for acquisitions functions and for enriching catalogue records. Indeed some foresaw ONIX as having the potential eventually to replace MARC as the format for carrying cataloguing data. Obviously extension to wider library applications will require more data elements, e.g. preservation data, but the format is expansible. This raises the question for libraries -which data dictionary does one choose? Are Dublin Core and ONIX competing or complementary? For a time there was concern that they were competing. However, the messages one hears more recently are of convergence, e.g. with the adoption of qualifiers by DC, and of dialogue between the communities. Which one predominates in the library sector will depend on the capabilities of library systems, on the availability of records in the different formats and on the investment that is put in to developing the systems and schemes.

In this situation it is obvious that interoperability will be paramount, and that realisation is gaining ground. The preexisting format in widespread use in libraries is MARC. It is well established in the library sector, but not so well in the trade sector. This makes cross sector collaboration more difficult.

The main drawback of MARC is the number of national variants and the apparent competition between UNIMARC and MARC21. The difficulties of exchanging records are pushing countries like the UK and organisations like LIBER to pursue harmonisation of formats.

The predominance of the US in research -and to a degree in publishing -means that the target format of choice is becoming MARC21. The UK is almost certainly going to harmonise its UKMARC format with MARC21, provided the role for non-US organisations in the governance of MARC21 satisfies the UK community. XML, the major new format that carries out the same function as MARC in a digital environment, grew out of the Standard Generalised Mark-up Language (SGML) originally developed to support computer typesetting, and the Hyper-text Mark-up Language (HTML) developed for writing Web pages. Combined with Java script XML is an even more powerful web authoring language.

If libraries were to invest in changing their systems to MARC21 only to find that within a few years MARC is replaced, say, by ONIX or Dublin Core records encoded in the XML format. One leading light, closely involved with developing the MARC format, saw MARC lasting at least 15 years in to the future and probably longer, because of the huge investment by libraries in systems and data. Crosswalks between formats were seen as the way of achieving interoperability, and continuing development of the format would accommodate new applications and data types.

Rules for Cataloguing

Cataloguing rules are the area where there is arguably the least international standardisation. This could be a barrier that remains when format issues etc are resolved. The Anglo-American Cataloguing Rules (AACR) is the most widely used code, but its influence is confined largely to the English-speaking world.

However, the growing interest in AACR from other regions, including LIBER members, has prompted a review by the Committee of Principals for AACR, which is looking at internationalisation of the code's development and governance. The virtual library environment means that not only must cataloguing rules cope with digital documents, but they must be also be capable of facilitating access to items from a collection that now expands well beyond the physical confines of one institution.

Another area of change being considered is whether one continues to catalogue the work in hand (currently prescribed by AACR) or the intellectual work, where the physical manifestation acquired by the library is recorded at a secondary level. This has been characterised as the "content versus carrier" debate. The FRBR favours a tiered approach working from the intellectual work at the highest level, as does ONIX, since it has adopted the FRBR model. So work is well advanced to adapt at least one major cataloguing code to a hybrid print and digital environment.

What's more, provided AACR does increase its international appeal by being more welcoming to non-English speaking communities, it may offer a common code in which catalogue data can be more readily exchanged. However, the difficulty of overcoming cultural differences between national codes should not be underestimated. Cataloguing is often singled out for scrutiny in trying to pare costs. Cataloguing has adapted to these pressures by collaboration, and there are many success stories, e.g. OCLC, the Research Libraries Group and the Consortium of European Research Libraries. However, even more collaboration will be needed to contain costs in the digital environment. Indeed, as libraries try to cope with constrained acquisitions and operating budgets, collaboration becomes a major driver in itself.

For instance in the UK university and national library sectors much work is being devoted to developing collaborative acquisition, retention and preservation schemes, and cataloguing systems need to be able to cope with the demands this collaboration places upon them. Collaboration is also a major force in the trade sector. Book publishers, music publishers and video companies want to ensure their products are readily available from the on-line retailers. So they, too, are collaborating. For collaboration to work interoperability is paramount.

The trade does not want to have to re-key data between applications. Nor do libraries want to convert records between formats as they exchange records. Lastly, but of greatest importance for a service industry, are the users and their needs. Users want a hybrid library; they don't want to search separate catalogues for print and digital documents. Neither are they interested in the distinction between what their library holds locally and what is on Web. So they are driving libraries towards providing seamless services, where again interoperability is the key.

Historically, librarians have organized the world's information. For centuries, they have successfully managed, classified, and filtered information of many types by creating surrogates. This is true of traditional materials as well as new electronic resources. But now as the amount of accessible electronic information increases, the cost of accessing this information will increase and the communities unfamiliar with library science are beginning to grapple with the problem of metadata and the organization of large collections of data. So there has been a general push to apply and develop techniques to make these resources searchable and more widely accessible. Now, the requirement is that every electronic item should have a catalog entry or its equivalent. But all electronic resources can never be humanly cataloged. It's just too expensive and also librarians are so overburdened that they can barely keep up with their traditional workload, let alone begin to catalog and organize the vast amounts of information available electronically. Clearly, automated tools to apply library science ideas like classification and filtering to electronic resources at high speed and low cost are needed.

The whole scenario of information management can be divided into two worlds. These two worlds-the seemingly unorganized Web and the organized world of libraries- have much to offer one another. The Web can offer automated tools for searching raw information and the library world can offer experience organizing and understanding information of all types. By combining their talents and techniques, these two communities can bring powerful resources to bear on the problems of accessing, maintaining, and supplying electronic information. But this is not an easy task. Even though using latest technologies, searching the raw content of every document still seems to be almost impossible since it's not uncommon to retrieve hundreds of documents for a given search.

MARCit

MARCit is an aid to easy cataloging of web sites, working with a web browser. Cataloging a site involves viewing the site with the browser, clicking on the MARCit icon, adding other information to the cataloging screen, saving the cataloging to a file, and importing the file into a library automation system. A user's manual, which can be downloaded, is very helpful and written so that it can be understood by a non-technical person. The web browser opens when MARCit is opened. Then, while viewing a web site, one can click on the MARCit icon.

The URL and title information appear in the MARCit screen directly from the web site. Several fields are cataloged automatically; other fields can be filled in manually. The software allows the cataloger to rate the site. Different records can be saved to different files. A saved file can be emptied, renamed, and deleted without leaving MARCit. The method used for importing the file into the library's online catalog depends on the automation system used. After cataloguing Internet resources, if the user searches for items on "Monalisa" for example, s/he might find a web site dedicated to Monalisa's art. The user can then access the site and get the information needed.

The user doesn't have to wade through the millions of hits a search on Monalisa might yield with a search engine. MARCit makes cataloging such sites simple. The librarian who catalogs it can also rate each MARC record. Users seeking the best information available can use the ratings as a valuable guide to quality sites. MARCit has been designed taking into consideration that accessing the information would be easier and more efficient if a librarian has designed it.

Cataloguing in Digital Order

In this century, the development of film, video, microfilm, and photocopying technologies have all required changes and accommodations in the law, in library practices, in publishing and distribution, in patterns of consumption and use.

None of these developments, however, has produced the uncertainty, confusion, and anxiety that has been occasioned by the increasing adoption of digital technologies, for none of these earlier developments challenged the order of the book, the order built around one central type of physical artifact and its modes of production, conservation, and consumption. But now, virtually every aspect of this order is being questioned: How must publishing change when "publications" can be instantaneously distributed on the Net? What models of compensation are appropriate to these new modes of production and distribution? Whose interests must be given priority? What happens to the notion of edition -- a set of "identical" artifacts produced by a publisher -- when one-of-a-kind, customized documents can be produced on a large scale? What happens to the notion of author, and the distinction between author and reader, if hypertext documents become, as some suggest, fluidly modified, collaborative efforts? How must copyright change to accommodate these other shifts, or should it be replaced by a different regulatory system?

Perhaps the greatest uncertainty, from the perspective of cataloging, is just what the new digital materials will be. Our current order carves up the bibliographic universe into discrete, stable, and long-lived units. But now, there is the potential at least for a great deal more variability and mutability of materials, and for a less rigid boundary between items. New genres, new categories of description, new institutions and practices have not yet arisen to stabilize this material. All of this together would constitute a new order, or substantial changes to the old order, as yet unrealized.

Currently there is no lack of visionaries willing to sing the praises of this new order, and to proclaim their vision of the future as good, right, and inevitable.

Having examined aspects of cataloging and the larger order of which it is a part let us explore the question of cataloging materials on the Net. From a cataloging perspective, the Net is the wrong unit of analysis, for the Net does not constitute a library in any interesting sense. It may be part of the technological infrastructure which could support a library, but it is not a library — not in the sense of an institution which oversees and provides access to a collection. Moreover, the materials on the Net do not constitute a library collection — not in the sense of a selection of items organized to serve a particular clientele. Instead, we should probably talk about cataloging digital materials on the Net.

There is of course a tremendous amount of activity in this area at the moment:

— Relatively large scale catalogs of and indices into Internet resources have been created and are being extended. Yahoo and Alex, each with thousands of entries, are but two of the many catalogs now coming into existence.

— There are ongoing experiments and feasibility studies in cataloging digital documents, such as the Catriona project funded by the British Library and a project organized by OCLC, called "Building a Catalog of Internet Resources."

— New standards are being created, and existing ones modified, to represent digital documents and "meta-data" about digital documents. The Text Encoding Initiative (TEI), for example, has created a standard for the digital encoding of texts in the humanities, which includes a proposal for an electronic text "header" for documents, permitting the equivalent of title page information to be represented, as well as other forms of meta-data. The Working Group on Document Identifiers within the Internet Engineering Task Force (IETF) is working to standardize Uniform Resource Characteristics (URCs) to represent meta-data.

— A number of conferences and workshops have been organized to explore cataloging and related issues. These include the CETH Workshop on Documenting Electronic Texts in May, 1994; the Seminar on Cataloging Digital Documents held at the Library of Congress in October, 1994; and the Metadata Workshop organized by OCLC in March, 1995.

— A great deal of information about approaches to cataloging digital documents is appearing on the Net. The Cataloging Services Department of the University of Virginia Library, for example, has a Web page with pointers to many cataloging related resources.

— Individuals, groups and institutions are creating their own home pages. These often contain lists of "favorite" Net resources that visitors to their home page may want to view. Using Web browsers such as Mosaic, people are also creating and maintaining "hotlists" of Net resources to which they can have easy access.

Digital collections will need to be organized and maintained if they are to remain stable and usable. To those within the library community this point may seem too obvious to make, since it is one of the central premises on which the modern library movement has been built. Yet it is not widely understood outside this community, to judge for example from the way the Web is often talked about. There seems to be a fairly wide-spread presumption, tacitly held, that materials can maintain their identity and their currency without continual intervention, without continual work.

Moreover, it seems certain that the work of stabilizing and maintaining digital collections will require a great deal of systematic human activity. Certainly, powerful technologies will be involved as well as human labor, as is the case now. Again, this is obvious enough to librarians; technologists, by contrast, tend to see the technical infrastructure but not the "invisible" social infrastructure by which most things, not just library collections, are maintained.

There can be no doubt that people will continue to make lists of digital resources which they will want to make available to others. Some of these will have broad scope and utility (e.g. Yahoo and Alex), while others will be of limited scope. Whether we call these lists "bibliographies" or "catalogs,"there will be an ongoing need to maintain them, to keep them current and stable; and whether or not we call this ongoing maintenance work "cataloging," it will no doubt be supported by a complex, and largely invisible, sociotechnical infrastructure.

Of course to say that there will continue to be catalogs still leaves open many important questions. What sorts of materials will be cataloged? How will digital catalogs differ from those we have today? Will they be maintained by professional catalogers or by laypeople? What skills will be needed to create these new catalogs? How will such skills be acquired? To what extent will these catalogs be based on existing standards, such as MARC and AACR? Will there, or could there be, a universal catalog of digital materials?

There can be no answers to most of these questions at this time; they will emerge in relation to, and will partly constitute, a stable digital order. Some, however, may already be amenable to analysis and may yield at least partial results, but they will require to bring knowledge from multiple work communities. Take the question of a universal catalog of digital materials. While there is something quite appealing about this vision, research in anthropology suggests that there is an inevitable tension between the desire to generalize, to make universal, and the need to tailor to local conditions. The current use of OCLC and RLIN displays both tendencies: these utilities provide sharable catalog records which are then copied and modified for local use by member institutions.

Digital Collection and Issues in Cataloguing

As with any new technology-based idea, there has been considerable controversy over the definition and possibilities of the term "digital library." To the computer science community, the new technical possibilities beckon enticingly. However, as traditionalists in the library community might point out, important issues are being ignored. According to Levy and Marshall, there is the "digital library" narrowly-construed and more broadly-construed. They argue for the broadly-construed digital library. Their vision argues for rich access to a variety of materials, all of which can be used in an interpretive and collaborative manner:

> We argue... that the design of digital libraries must take into account a broader range of materials, technologies, and practices — transient as well

> as permanent documents, fluid as well as fixed materials, paper as well as digital technologies, and collaborative as well as individual practices.

Miksa and Doty argue for the narrowly-construed digital library. This view idealizes the role of the collection and the additional indexing above the raw material:

> ...the idea of the library includes the construction of a set of arrangements that overcomes the disparateness of the individual sources by relating them to one another in terms of a single, operational, intellectually structured whole.

Both of the arguements attempt to confront the boundaries of the collection, and those boundaries are in different places for the two papers. Miksa and Doty emphasize the collection and intellectual access to it. Levy and Marshall's emphasis is on access and use of the collection by a community, and since their emphasis is on practice, the collection is used in conjunction with other information sources.

The apparently dichotomous nature of the digital library architecture has broad consequences for its maintenance. However, most technical architectures will be some combination; it will be argued below that this is likely for institutional reasons. In this section, we show that some technical architectures muddy the question of broad versus narrow. It is entirely possible to have both types of libraries simultaneously.

The library community has been very successful in maintaining traditional libraries and has developed many practices and ideals to do so. Among them are the ideas of unified collections and access methods. In fact, one could argue that many core library activities, such as circulation, technical services, and even shelving, were created by the library to maintain access to its collection over time.

It is essential to note that this set of practices and ideals maintain the traditional library as institution and as community of practice together over time. This equilibrium is in the process of being disturbed or destroyed with the intrusion of new technical possibilities.

Only some of the practices of the traditional library will carry into the digital world, perhaps only for a narrow conception of the digital library. Furthermore, the hypertext and computer science communities have no such traditions and practices for the broadly-construed library.

If we wish either vision to be successful, the above question must be answered. Some of the answer will be institutional and some of it will be technical. The mix that is possible, however, will be dependent on the types of desired collections as well as the potential control mechanisms for those collections.

In the management of most resources, managerial control can play many roles. In the digital library, different control mechanisms over the collection are possible, and these control mechanisms will influence the possibilities and necessities for maintenance. These control mechanisms are influenced by collection types, as an examination of different collection types demonstrates.

Collection Types

Libraries have always managed their collections, selecting and removing items from their shelves. This has been viewed as a critical function of library management. According to the collection management literature, the practices of collection management are dependent on the type of library collection. For example, Drew and Dewe distinguish ephemera in special collections from other items, and Kovacs distinguishes among types of libraries. We will argue here that new types of collections in the digital library will lend themselves to new types of maintenance issues.

In a traditional, or paper-based, library, there is considerable control over the collection. Versions of publications are stable. More importantly, because the collection is physically contained, there is considerable control over the collection. Library staff can decide what is and what is not in the collection. Maintenance of the collection is within the purview of the institutional members.

At one opposite is the World Wide Web. The Web nodes often change, in content, location, and even existence. On the other hand, the content in a location does not shift rapidly; it tends to remain relatively stable. There is no control by any given individual over the entire Web. An individual has control only over his nodes and the selection of pointers to others' nodes (URLs) that provide the capability for extended collections.

At another opposite is Usenet or similar computer-mediated communication (CMC) systems. The locations do not change, but the contents of any given location change constantly. The control over the collection for this type is also very low for any given individual.

In the middle of both dimensions is the organizational information repository. Since the information resides within an organization and since the organization generally provides a sanctioned organizational member to manage the system, there is considerable control over its collection. Nonetheless, organizational memories tend to be more dynamic than traditional library collections; for example, they may include informal information, time-sensitive information, or bulletin board mechanisms.

Collection Maintenance

The variation in collection control determines the type of institutional and technical maintenance possible. Collections that are closer to those in traditional libraries can use more traditional control and maintenance mechanisms. Digital libraries that incorporate more individualistic, dynamic, and informal information may need to find new maintenance mechanisms.

Digital libraries, if self-contained in a manner similar to traditional libraries will be able to draw upon traditional methods and practices. Traditional libraries, as noted above, have developed methods for maintaining their core set of institutional ideals, their community of practice, and their collections of materials. Although many maintenance practices will need to be adapted — such as preservation and circulation control as extreme examples — the existing practices can serve as the bases for new norms and practices. We have argued above that such norms and practices are required for the long-term viability of the digital library as institution. Therefore, if the adaptation of current practices is successful, then the narrowly-construed digital library will stand a much greater chance of success in the long run.

These traditional practices, however, have had their limitations. They were based on a constrained collection; i.e., a selection from the bibliographic universe. A traditional library could never cope with much ephemera; it would require too many resources. To adequately index, catalog, and otherwise conform to the institutional ideals for the broad range of ephemera would be overwhelming. In the past, there were strong institutional reasons to constrict the bibliographic universe.

Going digital, however, changes the cost structure, and collection and maintenance costs need to be revisited. It is not necessary, for example, in a digital universe to hand-index all materials; there are other methods of access.

There is considerable evidence that this change in the cost structure is affecting organizational memories. However, the dynamism and volatility of organizational memories tend to be close to that of traditional libraries. That is, organizational members can reliably return to the same location in the organization's information repositories to find the same materials. However, the widespread interest in Lotus Notes, which combines electronic messaging and document storage, argues that combining formal organizational materials with informal is valuable.

Nonetheless, because institutional adaptation is much more manageable and amicable than extreme change, we expect that there will be pressure to have digital libraries as discrete and contained collections. The resource limitations of any social institution argue for defining a discrete collection as well. Of course, it will be possible to incorporate these narrowly-construed libraries in architectures that promote broad access.

In addition, the broadly-construed digital library lacks practices that will maintain itself over the long run. The same incentive that promotes use of the Web or of Usenet — namely that there is no intervening institution between the author and his potential audience — also brings its own disincentives to systematic use. As discussed, both the Web and Usenet have high levels of volatility. The location of Web nodes can change without notice. Usenet groupsdo not change locations, but the message traffic changes constantly.

The individualistic orientation of both the Web and Usenet argues against easy control over the collection. Without institutional control, each individual using the collection must deal with the maintenance issues himself. If the informal materials are dynamic or volatile, then there is a constant maintenance problem.

Requiring every user to provide for collection maintenance raises the costs considerably. Users must determine whether materials will continue to be available, accessible, and even understandable.

Collection maintenance, then, will be a critical limitation of the broadly-construed digital library. If the broadly-construed library, with its access to multiple sources, is to be viable, users cannot have a high maintenance cost over the long run. It will be necessary to reduce the cost of long-term use, and without mediating institutions, this reduction will need technical solutions.

References

Hunter Eric J. and KGB Bakewell. *Cataloguing.* 2nd ed. London : Clive Bingley, 1983.

Kuhlman, A. F, Administration of Serial and Document Acquisition and Preparation. *In* Randall, W. M., ed.: *The* Acquisition *and Cataloguing of Books.* Chicago, University of Chicago Press, 1940.

Norris, Dorothy M.: *A History of Cataloguing and Cataloguing Methods, 1100-1850.* London, Grafton and Co., 1939.

Taylor, Arlene G., David P. Miller, and Arlene G. Taylor. *Introduction to Cataloguing and Classification.* 10th ed. Westport, Conn: Libraries Unlimited, 2006.

Wynar, Bohdan S. *Introduction to cataloguing and classification.* 6th ed. Littleton, Colorado : Libraries Unlimited. 1980.

8

Net Infrastructure

Inter-related nature of the Internet, infrastructure indicators are vitally important for Internet Service Providers (ISP) and policy makers. For infrastructure providers and users, these indicators play an increasingly important role in underpinning Internet self-governance and self-regulation. For each of the key reasons expressing why self-regulation is preferred by the Internet community, information to inform that process is essential.

If one ISP does the 'wrong thing', in terms of its inter-action with the Internet, it can impair the network and service performance for all ISPs. This can range from problems with day-to-day network quality management right up to, in the worst case, bringing traffic flows on the Internet to a standstill.

Just as policy makers have needed indicators for regulation in traditional communication sectors, the Internet industry needs infrastructure indicators for self-regulation. For policy makers familiarity with Internet infrastructure indicators is important in a number of areas.

One aspect is the increasing number of regulatory issues being placed before governments, not only in relatively unfamiliar issues at the core of the Internet (e.g. the debate over domain names) but also in areas where the Internet is converging with other communication platforms (e.g. public switched telecommunication network and broadcasting regulation).

Moreover, a better understanding of Internet infrastructures is an important element underpinning wider issues bearing on electronic commerce. They can provide a better understanding of the challenges for the private sector in upgrading infrastructure and of comparative national performance.

They also provide an important input into a better understanding of how the Internet is becoming more critical for overall economic and social development in OECD countries. The main criteria for inclusion of indicators in this document is that the data were generated by network surveys (e.g. queries of Internet Protocol network databases and objects connected to Internet Protocol networks) or by entities that play a role in administering core Internet infrastructure.

In respect to the first criteria, online or electronic network measurements would qualify but an off-line survey or e-mail based surveys are not included. The exclusions are not because such surveys may not provide valuable information but rather because the off-line survey methodologies used are generally well known.

In addition, their exclusion assists to narrow the scope of this document to a manageable level and to focus on indicators that often rely on the policy maker to bring together data from different sources to generate the indicator. The second criteria includes data that are collected by the managers of core infrastructure surrounding the Domain Name System (DNS), such as second and third level domain registration, Internet Protocol (IP) number assignment, Autonomous System Number (ASN) assignment.

Some useful Internet Websites on this subject, with the summaries of attempts to draw together the results of official and commercial surveys, are those of HeadCount and NUA. How reliable the underlying results are for each country depends on the individual surveys and there is, of course, no harmonisation of methodologies.

At the same time some of the Internet's core administrative entities, in some countries, are collecting useful data from among their members. In this context a leading example is KRNIC, the organisation which administers domain names and IP addresses in Korea, which surveys Korean Internet Service providers (ISPs) to determine their number of business connections and dial-up subscribers. KRNIC is then able to publish national Internet subscriber statistics for Korea.

IP addresses and autonomous system numbers. As appropriate, references are made to governance and regulatory issues where these indicators are being used to inform debate or form a tool used by industry for self-regulation.

Whereas surveys of hosts, servers and so forth are undertaken by the Internet's technical community, tools are available for policy makers to generate infrastructure indicators. These include the use of traceroutes to provide an indicator of market position and a better understanding of traffic exchange in backbone networks.

In addition, the use of search engines to provide information on the implementation of webcasting technologies and the topography of Internet hyper-text links to leading electronic commerce sites. By way of example, a matrix of all the hyper-text links between domains for the OECD area is made available. Accordingly, it is possible to see the emerging pathways of electronic commerce between OECD countries.

Finally, readers may find the references to electronic glossaries at the end of this document a useful aid in respect to Internet terminology. The most common indicators used to measure Internet development are the surveys of Internet hosts undertaken by Network Wizards and RIPE (Reseaux IP Européens).

Network Wizards define an Internet host as a domain name that has an associated IP address record. This would be any computer system connected to the Internet (via full or part-time, direct or dial-up connections), such as oecd.org and www.oecd.org.

The Network Wizards survey includes all Top Level Domains (TLDs) and generic Top Level Domains (gTLDs) and is undertaken every six months. The RIPE survey is undertaken monthly but is limited to TLD registrations in their service area. While both surveys are much appreciated by the Internet community the results need to be qualified and have several limitations.

The first qualification that needs to be made is that host data do not indicate the total number of users who can access the Internet. The second caveat is that these surveys do not reach every host on the Internet, as access to some hosts is blocked by company fire-walls. Recognising the limitation of this second factor Network Wizards changed their methodology for the survey undertaken in January 1998 to enable access to a greater number of hosts.

Notwithstanding this change, surveys of Internet hosts may only be interpreted as the minimum size of the 'public Internet', as it is impossible to determine the number of users accessing services via each host. The

Netcraft Web Server Survey is a survey of web server software usage on computers connected to the Internet.

Netcraft collect and collate as many hostnames providing an http-service as their survey can find, and systematically poll each one with an HyperText Transfer Protocol (HTTP) request for the server name. A host name is the first part of a hosts' domain name. In the July 1998 survey Netcraft received responses from 2 594 622 web servers. The growth rate for the first half of 1998 was 41 per cent. Some 96 per cent of these servers are in the OECD area.

By far the largest number of web servers are under.com which has 60 per cent of all web servers. As for Internet hosts, it is possible to provide penetration by domain and to weight this by the number of gTLD registrations. The country providing the most responses, on a per capita basis, is Denmark. This is because there are a lot of small virtually hosted sites in Denmark.

Netcraft report, that while this is a characteristic of many countries, it is particularly so in Denmark and the Netherlands. TeleDanmark and Cybercity operate two of the largest virtual hosting sites in Denmark. Internet surveys of hosts and servers provide one indicator of Internet development and may be used as one potential indicator of comparative Internet development between countries.

The main limitations are not reaching all hosts or servers, and the structure of the domain name system being such that there is no guarantee that all hosts under a particular domain are located in a certain geographic location. For example, the reachable hosts of a user in France, registering under a gTLD, would appear under domains such as.com or.net rather than.fr. Nor is it necessarily the fact that a host using a second level domain under.fr will be physically located in France.

That being said the OECD's observations, from an series of traceroutes to Websites under TLDs, are that by far the majority of hosts using TLDs are located in the country concerned. The availability of gTLD registrations by country presented the first possibility of redistributing Internet hosts under domain names such as.com to individual countries.

The most simple option, used to prepare this report, was to weight the number of hosts under gTLDs according to the number of gTLD registrations from a particular country. In other words if 5 per cent of the total gTLD registrations are from a particular country then 5 per cent of the total number of hosts surveyed under gTLDs are reallocated to that country. This methodology could, no doubt, be subject to a number of caveats. Nevertheless it seems reasonable to assume that this approach gives a more accurate distribution of Internet hosts, in OECD countries, than allocating all hosts under gTLD registrations to the United States.

The results of the weighted methodology are most striking in the case of Canada where, for mid 1997, there was a 72 per cent increase in the number of hosts over the number of hosts surveyed solely under.ca. Other countries recording significant increases at that time, albeit from smaller base numbers of hosts, were Turkey, Spain, Luxembourg and France.

All these countries recorded a relatively large increase in the number of hosts relative to the average OECD increase of 21 per cent. The countries for which this made very little difference are those where users mainly rely on national TLD registrations, such as Iceland, the Czech Republic, New Zealand, Poland and Finland.

The Netcraft Server surveys also provide one of the best available indicators of the growth of electronic commerce on the Internet. Whereas the best known search engines only cover http sites, Netcraft also undertakes a secure socket layer (SSL) survey. The SSL protocol was developed by Netscape for encrypted transmission over TCP/IP networks.

It sets up a secure end-to-end link over which http or any other application protocol can operate. The most common application of SSL is https for ssl-encrypted http which enables electronic commerce to take place. In August 1998, Netcraft received responses from more than 424 000 web sites using encryption. However most of these responses are excluded, in terms of electronic commerce web sites, because they do not have third party certification.

Sites without a third party certification are not expected to be engaging in electronic commerce because of the warning message that gets generated. The key element for electronic commerce is third party certification with matching certificate. Netcraft say plausible reasons for the large number of responses, where the name in the certificate did not match the site's domain name, might include web sites run from virtual hosting configurations where the provider sets up all customers with https services, with customers buying certificates when they start to make use of the facilities.

Netcraft adds that sites where the certificate issuer is not a known certificate authority, typically indicate that that site has generated and signed its own certificate, which is acceptable for prototyping, or where trust is not required outside a limited group of people, such as a company, or collaborative project. This is likely to be more commonplace on internal networks than on externally visible Internet sites.

The major electronic commerce uses of secure server software are for encrypted credit card transactions over the Internet. The most common non-retail use of SSL is subscription access to privileged information. For example many of the leading United States investment banks disseminate research over SSL, and there are some applications for virtual private networks or closed access communities.

By excluding sites without third party certification it is possible to get an indication of the number of electronic commerce sites in each OECD country. Unlike the Internet host and general Netcraft web server survey, the SSL survey does not use the domain name system to categorise location but uses the actual address of the business.

In August 1998, there were over 22,200 web sites engaged in electronic commerce via SSL in the OECD area. This number had grown by 128 per cent over the previous twelve months. The United States is a clear leader with three quarters of all electronic commerce sites but its overall share is falling as electronic commerce picks up speed in other countries. Albeit starting from smaller bases, the number of electronic commerce sites grew by more than 300 per cent over the previous year in some OECD countries.

Australia, Canada, and the United Kingdom have the highest number of electronic commerce Websites after the United States. In relative terms the United States also leads the OECD with more than six electronic commerce sites for every 100,000 inhabitants followed by Iceland, Australia and Canada.

Domain Name System

The Domain Name System (DNS) maps Internet addresses. To function as part of the Internet a host needs a domain name that has an associated Internet Protocol (IP) address record. This includes any computer system connected to the Internet via full or part-time, direct or dial-up connections.

DNS servers perform the necessary function of translating back and forth between names and numbers. These servers contain databases of IP addresses and corresponding domain names and they are interrogated each time a user wants to send an e-mail or request data over the World Wide Web.

A top-level domain name (TLD) can either be an ISO country code or one of the generic top level domains. To register a second level domain name or a third level domain name a user needs to apply to the domain name registry with the delegated authority for the TLD or gTLD. Some registries publish data on the number of registrations on a monthly basis while others publish intermittently.

The Internet Hosts surveys undertaken by Network Wizards and RIPE also provide, as a by-product, an indicator of the number of registrations under each domain. The main importance of DNS indicators are that they can be used to inform discussions over the different policies and prices of TLD and gTLD registries.

Whether the registration process under a certain domain name is subject to industry self-regulation or government oversight, the availability of DNS data is important to ensure transparency in registration management for service providers, business users and consumers. This is particularly important in those cases where a monopoly or monopoly power exists in the registration of second and third level domain names.

These tools can provide useful information for constructing certain Internet indicators. While this information is not always reliable, and some users would like to see additional information or functionality included, the various 'Whois?' databases are valuable resources for the Internet community.

The United States White Paper "A Proposal to Improve the Technical Management of Internet Domain Names and Addresses Discussion Draft", contained a number of suggestions for the type of information that should be included in domain registration databases and it will be up to the new DNS authority to work through guidelines in this area.

Internet Protocol (IP) addresses are the numbers used to identify computers, or other devices, on a TCP/IP network. Networks using the TCP/IP protocol route messages based on the IP address of the destination. The format of an IP address is a 32-bit numeric address written as four numbers separated by periods. Each number can be zero to 255. For example, 193.51.65.17 is one IP address used by the OECD.

On a stand alone private TCP/IP network, IP addresses can be assigned at random as long as each one is unique to that network. If that private network connects to the Internet it requires a registered IP address to avoid duplication. The current version of IP (IP version 4 or IPv4), which was standardised in 1981, created a pool of 4 294 967 296 IPv4 addresses.

Originally blocks of IP addresses were directly allocated by the Internet Assigned Numbers Authority (IANA). While in some cases the IANA still makes direct assignments to organisations most allocations are now made to three regional bodies-APNIC (Asia-Pacific Network Information Center), ARIN (American Registry for Internet Numbers) and RIPE NCC (Reseaux IP Européens Network Co-ordination Centre).

These organisations subsequently re-allocate or assign IP addresses to individual organisations, such as ISPs or national bodies co-ordinating IP address space for a certain country. As a general rule, end users receive IP assignments from their ISP. Notwithstanding this some ISPs receive addresses from upstream or backbone ISPs and some end users receive allocations directly from a registry or directly from the IANA.

The question of the whether the institutions allocating IP addresses at various levels have monopolies, in terms of guiding their self-governance practices, is important. Reform to the IANA is ongoing at the time of writing which takes into account its monopoly position.

Whether the three regional registries have a total monopoly position is less clear because ISPs can, and do, apply to different registries (including allocations made to industry sectors such as the Cable Television Network based ISPs). In addition, apart from convention, there may be nothing to stop an entity with a very large net block from reselling this resource in competition to the regional registries.

Certainly many entities at the sub-regional registry level 'resell' IP numbers. The best sources of data on IP addresses are the three regional IP address registries. However, the policies and practices of each organisation mean the dissemination of IP allocation and assignment is carried out in different forms.

A further indicator to assist in the understanding of IP address allocations is work which has been undertaken by the Cooperative Association for Internet Data Analysis (CAIDA) to enable visualisation of IP address occupancy.

Such depictions of the address space can also provide inputs for analysis of public policy (equity) issues, as well as information for evaluating engineering and operational aspects of the commercial Internet. Some of the main self-governance issues, relating to infrastructure, facing the Internet community are in the management of the existing IPv4 address space. These include:

— co-ordination of the three existing IP address registries;

— proposals to create new regional registries;

— the criteria for allocation of IP addresses;.

— the pricing structure used by registries for this resource.

Issues such as these can generate vigorous discussion within the Internet community and raise governance questions of a similar nature to the controversial DNS debate. Perhaps the main differences with IP address issues are that the main players are ISPs, rather than the much larger community which took an interest in DNS, and the absence of intellectual property concerns associated with trademarks and domain registration.

Notwithstanding these differences, because the existing allocation of IP addresses are a monopoly, at least in one sense, the IANA and regional registries need to observe standards of openness, transparency and public accountability. An essential part of this process, and a pre-requisite for self-governance, is the publication of data and indicators in a readily accessible form to the Internet community.

While the management of IP addresses is best done by the private sector, policy makers need to have an understanding of the IP address system because of its potential to spill over into matters placed before governments. The most significant case in point is the ongoing problem of IP address portability and the competition questions raised.

For example, if a relatively small ISP can not get a direct allocation of IP address space from a registry they need to borrow numbers from upstream ISPs. If a small ISP then wishes to change its upstream (i.e. backbone provider), it has to return the borrowed IP numbers to the larger provider. In effect this means the smaller ISP has to renumber its network, which can be expensive and disruptive for its customers, if it wants to change backbone providers.

This issue was raised in the context of the proposed merger of Worldcom and MCI which was considered by competition authorities in the

United Sates and Europe. The concern voiced by some relatively small ISPs, arguing against this merger, was that if a dominant player in the backbone market abused that position they would face a high cost to shift providers because of the lack of number portability.

At the same time, the technical reasons for not encouraging portability for small address assignments and the attendant increase in the size of the routing table this would cause need to be borne in mind. According to some experts the portability problem will not be solved by the introduction of IPv6.

Autonomous systems numbers (ASN, ASes or AS numbers) acts as a label for a set of IP addresses and are used by ISPs to specify the global routing policy for those IP addresses. On the Internet packets of data are passed between devices known as routers. Part of this process involves consultation of the routing table to determine the best onward path.

A routing policy indicates 'reachability information', and hence enables traffic to pass between the networks of different ISPs. For example, if an ISP has two connections to 'the Internet', it is often useful to spread traffic out over those two links. This policy is then propagated in order to insure that traffic (both incoming and outgoing) flows in the correct direction and that reachability of the addresses of an ISP providing services can be assured.

In practice this means that most end users and small ISPs do not receive an individual AS number but instead use their upstream service provider's AS number. If an ISP only has one connection to the Internet (i.e. it is singly homed), it only has one way in which traffic can flow, thus it does not need an AS number. However, the downstream ISP will still be exchanging traffic with the Internet, albeit under the AS number of their upstream provider.

The distinction between being single-homed and multi-homed refers to the number of connections a small ISP, or content provider, has to the Internet via different backbone infrastructure providers. If an organisation is connected to the Internet via one ISP it is single-homed, but if it receives connections from two, or more, ISPs it is multi-homed.

Internet backbone routers need to maintain the complete routing information for the Internet. As the Internet has expanded, so too have the number of routes between AS numbers. This rapid growth has been a cause for concern among the Internet's technical community because it was felt that there was a limit to the amount of global routing information able to be accommodated by backbone routers.

In mid-1997 an accident occurred which demonstrated the 'high-watermark' for the 'core Internet' and the fragility of the Internet. This was due to one Autonomous System accidentally re-announcing the entire Internet through itself resulting in a sudden doubling in the number of global routes to just over 80,000.

As a result backbone routers around the world were overloaded as they did not have enough memory to cope with the additional routes. As these same routers tried to reboot, and establish peering, they once again received the information for more than 80 000 routes, and again ran out of memory. This problem recurred until filters were manually installed or the originator of the excess routes fixed the source of the problem.

This accident demonstrated both the current upper limit of the routing resource and the need for industry to have information and indicators to assist in self-regulating Internet traffic exchange. In other words, downstream ISPs, and smaller IP networks, used the AS number of their upstream backbone connection to the United States. However, the recent increase in allocation of AS numbers in the Asia Pacific has drawn some analysts to the conclusion that there is a corresponding increase in intra-national and intra-regional connectivity.

In the Asia Pacific this process is believed to have been spurred by the devaluation of a number of currencies (increasing the cost of international bandwidth) and the desire to improve network performance via localised (intra-national and intra-regional) traffic exchange. Further analysis of the policies for the AS numbers in appropriate databases, such those of APNIC and routing registries, could provide a tool for better understanding the amount of intra-national and intra-regional connectivity.

Due to the nature of the Internet, measurement of performance across different networks can be much more difficult and controversial than the public switched telecommunication network (PSTN). Measuring the performance within one network is relatively straightforward and many ISPs are comfortable enough to place near real-time indicators on the World Wide Web. This strikes an immediate contrast to the PSTN where such information was generally reserved for engineering purposes, and only made public in regulatory filings or annual reports.

Accordingly, it is possible to see in near real time how, for example, MCI's Internet backbone is performing or the performance of links to

Singapore Telecom's Internet exchange point (STIX). Measurements include the latency of round trip times over different parts of networks and the loss of packets during times of congestion.

Where the problematic aspect of measurement arises, is in constructing indicators to measure performance across different ISP networks, core Internet infrastructure (such as DNS) and the networks and sites of users. This can, of course, give rise to different interpretations of where the reasons for good and poor performance arise. There are several motivations for an increasing number of ISPs and Internet exchange points to put performance-related data on their Websites.

Publication of such data can be used for marketing purposes and to provide customers with an additional service. At the same time many of these indicators can be constructed by independent entities or by users themselves for their individual connections. As such there are a growing number of Websites that measure the "Internet Weather" from the perspective of their network or their Website. These are also companies that specialise in measuring the performance of particular backbone providers and ISPs, as well as services such as e-mail.

In large part initiatives in the area of Internet network performance measures are best done by the private sector, albeit some government funded basic research institutions are currently playing an important role. However if self-governance and industry co-operation evolves as the standard model for Internet traffic exchange, by contrast to the often heavily regulated interconnection in the PSTN, then the availability of performance indicators across different networks is essential.

One issue that may arise for competition authorities or regulators is the claim that if one ISP held a majority share of the backbone market it might downgrade performance (i.e. traffic exchange) to other ISPs to encourage their customers to directly connect to the dominant player's network. Where there is a strongly competitive backbone market this problem should not arise.

However, in those countries where this is not the case, perhaps due to the existing or legacy effects of telecommunication monopolies, industry regulators may be called on to arbitrate very complex disputes between ISPs. On the other hand, the more indicators make transparent the relative performance of different networks the less likely such problems are to occur.

Traceroutes enable users to follow a path taken by packets of data via intermediate routers between IP addresses. A traceroute can be initiated from a user's PC, with a connection to the Internet, to a particular IP address (or a host/domain name such as www.oecd.org). The second option is to use one of the many sites on the World Wide Web which enable a user to traceroute from that web-site to an IP address using their browser.

Boardwatch Magazine has compiled a comprehensive guide to traceroutes and how they work. Essentially traceroutes work by sending packets to an Internet address and getting intermediate routers to send a return message to the source. The return message identifies the IP address of each router and the round trip time, in milliseconds, between the original router and each intermediate router.

While the use of traceroutes as a tool for the Internet technical community to monitor the performance of peer networks is the leading application, traceroutes have also been used by some knowledgeable users to learn more about the performance of their ISP and their backbone provider. Users can learn, for example, how traffic to their nominated Websites traverses the Internet, and the network providers involved, in a much more transparent way than the public switched telecommunication network.

For policy makers traceroutes also represent an important tool for better understanding and informing debates on national and international traffic exchange. For example, some traceroutes demonstrate that traffic follows a certain path not because it may be the most efficient but because of the legacy or existence of infrastructure monopolies. In other words traffic may travel a certain route because capacity on a more logical route to provide connectivity is either unavailable or priced at uncompetitive rates.

In addition, traceroutes to the most accessed Internet sites in different countries can be used as an indicator to better understand the relative positions of players in backbone markets. Prior to consideration of this application, other interesting technical features, albeit sometimes erratic in terms of success, are:

— Traceroutes can indicate the capacity of a link between two routers either through the ISP incorporating this information (in the name of the router) or via traceroute software that endeavours to identify the capacity of each link.

— Traceroutes can be conducted between any two known hosts on some web sites.

— Some within the Internet community voluntarily incorporate latitude and longitude information in their routers and would like to see this practice generally adopted by all network managers.

— Users can employ traceroutes to provide an indication, or 'non-authoritative verification', of whether a Website is actually in the location specified on a Website or implied by a top level domain name or 'Whois? record'. In a number of cases bearing on electronic commerce or law enforcement and industry self-regulatory initiatives a user's first action is to use tools such as traceroutes to provide additional information about the source of data and possible recourse to ISPs or other authorities.

Worldcom and MCI forwarded the view that Internet revenues represented the best available indicator of market share. On the other hand critics of this view held that accurate data were not available either for the total Internet market or by relevant Internet market segment. Similarly, for policy makers considering the competition aspects of the merger, data were not available on Internet traffic such that an assessment of the market shares of various players could be constructed via that avenue.

An alternative methodology is to use traceroutes to the most accessed Internet sites to gain a better understanding of backbone markets and Internet traffic exchange. The basic idea is to undertake a series of traceroutes from a Website served by a certain backbone provider to the most sought after content and portals. It is then possible to see for how many of these sites a backbone provider can carry the traffic on an end-to-end basis and for how many of those sites they need to hand traffic to another provider.

Together, a merger of Worldcom and MCI's backbone networks would have meant the new entity could carry the traffic internally to 62 of the leading 100 sites. Worthy of note is that this market position paralleled many of the market share estimates forwarded by those opposed to the merger of Internet backbones of these companies. Yet, at the same time, the data also showed a high degree of multi-homing by major content providers in the United States with 53 of all sites being multi-homed and 35 of Worldcom customers being multi-homed.

Another factor could be that the Websites in the United States bear far high traffic flows, than counterparts in other countries, and therefore require a higher degree of multi-homing. It might also be simply a sign that the Internet market in the United States is more mature than in other OECD countries. One other potential indicator of the commercial maturity of the US Internet market relative to Australia, Germany, Sweden and the Netherlands is the high proportion of university Websites that figure in the top 100 Websites for these countries.

In other words, users in universities still account for a high proportion of Internet traffic and accordingly lift the ranking of university Websites relative to commercial Websites.

One implication of this might be to bear in mind that academic backbone networks, while continuing to grow and provide important services, will either commercialise to capture mass market growth or form an increasingly smaller part of the total backbone market. There are also interesting features that apply to the four individual countries, albeit in each market a variation on the methodology has been explored.

In Sweden a series of traceroutes was also conducted from CERN in Switzerland to test the market positions from outside the country. The results were that SwipNet, owned by Tele-2 provided carriage for 41 per cent of the commercial sites (i.e. excluding Sunet the University network). Telia and Telenordia provided carriage for a further 39 per cent of commercial sites.

However, the most striking feature of this traceroute series was the amount of traffic between Denmark and Germany that traversed the United States. For one quarter of the traceroutes from TeleDanmark, to the leading sites in Germany, traffic was initially exchanged via MCI's network in the United States and then found its way back to Germany via the Netherlands or other European countries.

Whereas most large backbone providers which peer hand off traffic to another backbone network, as soon as the network determines they do not have a direct connection to the Website concerned and another path is available, Telstra's backbone network carries this traffic virtually the whole way.

Interestingly, this also leads to incoming international traffic being handed to Telstra, at an international exchange point, even if the ISP concerned has a direct backbone connection to Australia. Consider the series of traceroutes from CWIX (the Cable and Wireless US IP backbone network) which only carries traffic between CWIX and Optus (a Cable and Wireless Australian subsidiary), when it is to an Optus or Ozemail customer's Website.

This international pattern of traffic is interesting in terms of Telstra's position on the financing of international infrastructure. If CWIX (and Optus) carried the traffic from the United States to Australia, Optus would have had to pay Telstra for the domestic traffic exchange to reach the Telstra customer's Website. The interesting point is that it may be less expensive for CWIX to pass the traffic to MCI, than carry it directly to Australia and have it exchanged locally by Optus.

There are a number of companies that seek to rank the most accessed sites on the World Wide Web. Lists of the most accessed web sites are of interest to a variety of different groups. For the companies wanting to advertise on the Internet it is useful to have an indication of the relative popularity of different Websites.

For users such rankings are sometimes used as a directory service in different categories. For policy makers the main interest in Website rankings is the indication they might give for the location of the most popular content and as an input to determining the leading players providing access infrastructure to that content.

The OECD has used Web21's lists of the most accessed Websites in different categories both to highlight to location of popular content, and its impact on traffic patterns, as well as the benefits being generated for pluralism and cultural diversity at a national and global level.

Such lists have also been used to determine which ISPs have the most significant backbone networks in terms of carriage of traffic to these high volume sites. A number of companies undertake studies endeavouring to rank Websites by the amount of traffic or visits they generate. Web21 produces the "Hot100" in different categories (e.g. news, sport, business, overall) and by different countries.

Categories of content are useful when policy makers are endeavouring to better understand the location of popular content, such as webcasting radio stations and the potential impact on policy in respect to convergence between different communication platforms. Country categories are useful for examination of traffic exchange, via traceroutes, between major backbone providers in national markets and their relationships with major international backbone markets.

By combining tools such as traceroutes and lists of the most popular Websites indications can be constructed for different markets in terms of infrastructure availability, competition policy and the extent of trends such as multi-homing.

Web21 collects data from a number of different sources but primarily use the logs from proxy servers and caches. These logs are sent on-line to Web21 on a daily basis and represent the surfing patterns of over 100 000 surfers world-wide. Approximately 60 per cent of these users are in North America and 40 per cent outside the United States.

Knowledge is another company which ranks web sites by getting users to download proprietary software via the Internet onto all computers they use to access the Web. These user's surfing patterns are then tracked by the company and made available on the net by different demographic categories.

According to the Internet Advertising Bureau (IAB) the top 10 Websites receive 67 per cent of total Internet advertising expenditures. A portal is the term given to that part of a Website which acts as a gateway, or launch point, through which users navigate the World Wide Web. A portal can be the page a user sees each time they log onto the World Wide Web, such as the home page of an ISP or AOL (America Online).

Accordingly, one measure of the usage of a portal is the number of subscribers served by a certain ISP, or other online service, although this is not precise as users can create their own portal or set their opening web page to another Website. These latter users will often define portals, such as Yahoo! or Excite, as their default Websites or use the default page of their browser (e.g. Netscape, Microsoft).

These portals, which commenced service primary as search engines or directories have since moved to providing multiple applications designed to provide users with a variety of tools in one location (e.g. e-mail, news, personalised news, search engines, directories etc.). Similarly, Netscape and Microsoft have incorporated an increasing number of portal-like functions into their browsers as well as selling hyper-text links and advertising space to other portals.

Accordingly sites such as Yahoo and Excite are amongst the most accessed Websites on the Internet. It is this popularity, and the belief of many analysts that portals will become increasingly important to making the Internet more user friendly for electronic commerce, that has attracted increasing attention. Portals that were fairly recently in the preserve of sophisticated Internet users are now the best known sites on the Internet, a trend not missed by companies engaging in electronic commerce.

Another approach to investigating portals is to examine the number of hyper-text links to the gateway pages of these Websites and their origin. Many electronic commerce sites pay search engines, or other portals, a fee for each transaction referral. This can be done with, for example, 'click-through' banner advertising.

In addition the total count of hyper-text links includes internal Website hyper-text links to a particular URL (e.g. back to main page hyper text links, links to the web designer's page and so forth). It is also probable that if this measure became used as an indicator of popularity it would be relatively easy to distort.

This is useful for examining hyper-text links between domains, including TLDs and gTLDs as discussed below, but in the context of an examination of portals it is interesting to link to the main URL of a company rather than its entire domain. Nicheworks has an interesting visualisation tool for Websites and links, showing the example of the Chicago Tribune's Website.

By most measures 'Yahoo!' emerges as the most accessed Website on the Internet. Accordingly it is not a surprise that a count of the number of hyper-text links to http://www.yahoo.com/, reveals that it has the most links directed to it to on the World Wide Web. Excite and Lycos are the search engines that have the next highest number of hyper-text links followed by Alta Vista.

Netscape and Microsoft also have Websites which attract some of highest numbers of links on the World Wide Web. Apple and IBM make up the remainder of the group of companies with more than 100 000 hyper-text links to their main URLs. Results of other sites have been chosen to give an indication of the very large difference in the number of hyper-text links to 'new media' Websites and those to some traditional media.

There is a vast difference in the number of hyper-text links to Websites needed to navigate the Internet (either via search and directory functions such as Yahoo! or equipment and software such as Netscape and Microsoft) for content and services than to the Websites of traditional print media. As an aside it is also possible to use this tool to get an indication of the amount of 'adult content' relative to all content on the World Wide Web.

Here it can be noted that the leading 100 Websites providing adult content make up only around 0.05 per cent of all content on the Internet. The proxy measure for content here is to count the number of outgoing URLs from these Websites relative to the total number of outgoing URLs from all domains. This does of course not deny the importance of using self regulatory tools, such as screening technologies, because of the ease with which adult material can be located intentionally or accidentally by children.

However it is interesting to compare this figure with the amount of content under.edu (used by institutions of higher education in the United States) which makes up more than 16 per cent of all Internet content. Taken together with the content under.us (used by schools in the United States) and the educational content under top level domains, the amount of educational content helps put a more balanced perspective on the different types of content available on the World Wide Web.

It is also interesting to examine the number of hyper-text links to the traditional gatekeepers to the online world. Significantly only AT&T and NTT exceed 10 000 hyper-text links to their main URLs. In the not too distant past telecommunication carriers with government mandated monopolies owned every 'portal' from the actual line connection to the PSTN, through to every piece of customer equipment and the cover and contents of telephone directories.

Today, the majority of these markets have been liberalised in OECD countries, meaning that telecommunication carriers need to compete not only at the level of physical infrastructure but also for portals. Consider, for example, if as Internet telephony is increasingly incorporated into electronic commerce Websites, the additional communication revenue may accrue to the Internet telephony provider nominated by the owner of the portal.

Even for the telecommunication carrier that becomes an ISP, and therefore has the opportunity to create a portal via the launch point for subscribers, there is no guarantee that these users will not opt for portals like Yahoo! and Netscape. One indicator of the take up of different audio, video and other software tools on the World Wide Web is to use a search engine to count the number of applications.

As Internet searches can be conducted under a particular top level domain name, by using HotBot, it is possible to get an indication of the use of these technologies. By including objects found under gTLDs and the TLDs associated with OECD Member countries, there appeared to be around 600,000 audio and more than 200,000 video applications in July 1998. While the usual caveat applies, as to the allocations under gTLDs not being country specific, the data shown under TLDs might be taken to represent a very large sample for any given country.

Accordingly by using search engines, analysts have one indication of the number of webcasting sites under a domain associated with a certain country. In future this may be an important source of information to assist policy makers dealing with convergence issues. This innovation created new pathways for electronic commerce and, by doing so, raised the question of whether indicators of the topography of linkages between domains could be useful for policy makers.

While the nature of the Internet's DNS makes it easier to apply some analytical tools to individual domains (i.e. yahoo.com), than to geographical areas (e.g..nl for the Netherlands), it is possible to construct matrices of the linkages between all the TLDs associated with OECD countries and gTLDs. The largest number of hyper-text links between top level domains are intra-domain links. However, an important factor is the relative development of the Internet in different countries. Attractive content has to exist under a certain domain, and be accessible (i.e. some users link to the same content under one domain rather than another based on infrastructure performance), before users will link to a URL. Linkages between domains provide a interesting indicator for further analysis of comparative performance even though allowances need to be made for gTLD registrations across different countries. The differences from traditional communication patterns may suggest more about Internet use and how electronic commerce is developing than the similarities.

Technologies in Networking

Information and Communication Technologies (ICTs) can be classified as analog and more recent digital technologies. Some of the most important traditional analog ICTs are radio, television, video and audio conference (although they can also be digital). Some of the more recent digital ICTs are computers, digital networks and all the applications that can be run on them.

Probably the most important digital ICTs are the Internet and two of its applications: electronic mail and the WWW. Internet, also known as "the network of networks" or simply "the net", is a set of computers linked by phone lines, coaxial cables, optic fiber, satellite, etc., which can interchange information in a wide variety of formats; text, graphics, audio and video.

Internet makes possible the interconnection of Universities, research centers, libraries, enterprises, government dependencies, and non-government organizations. Electronic mail and the World Wide Web are two of the most popular Internet applications. Electronic mail (email) is a system that allows the interchange of messages between users of computers connected to the net.

Like postal mail, electronic mail allows sending private messages from person to person, without the messages being read by other persons. The World Wide Web (WWW or just Web) is a multimedia and hypertext technology that works through the Internet.

The term "World Wide Web" is intended to be a metaphor about the complexity of the Internet connections covering the World. Knowledge should not be regarded as simple information. Knowledge implies an internal process in which an individual forms a personal point of view or interpretation of the world.

In some cases reading or hearing is enough to "know" something. In most cases, to get to know something implies a dialogue in which an individual negotiates his or her understanding of the world with other individuals of the community. ICTs are mostly used to communicate and share information but they can also be used to learn.

Some of the ICTs that are relevant to share knowledge are electronic mail, discussion groups, tele-, audio- and videoconferences, radio, television, recorded media (audio- and videocassettes, CDs and DVDs), chat, IRC and ICQ. Some of these technologies are more suited to share information.

Some others are more suited to support a dialogue in which a networked community can share and construct knowledge. If ICTs are to be used in order to learn it is necessary to analyze their pedagogical characteristics. Building a computer network requires:

(i) special hardware (repeaters, hubs, bridges, switches, routers and gateways);

(ii) software (TCP and IP protocols, Domain Name Systems (DNS), different clients and servers, firewalls and proxies); and

(iii) telecommunications media to physically connect a network to the Internet (Dial on demand routing, Frame relay, Asynchronous Transfer Mode (ATM), POTS, ISDN or ADSL, Satellite dishes, and - very soon - 3 rd generation wireless access).

Just as happens in a human relation, relationships between computers are ruled by protocols that allow two computers to "shake hands" and "interchange information". TCP and IP are two of the main protocols used by computers connected to the Internet. Other protocols of the TCP/IP stack are the HTTP protocol, used to transfer pages from the Web, the FTP protocol, used to transfer files through the Net, the SMTP protocol, used to send electronic mail, and the POP3 protocol, used to receive email.

A Strategic Plan is very important to set the philosophy and direction for the use of ICTs within the organization. The organization should have a vision for the use of ICTs: it should know what it has, where it wants to go, and how it is going to get there. Key concepts to consider are the design of the workplace, the development of hardware and software, the definition of user roles, server start-up, and security.

In order to implement networking and learning programs in Africa and Latin America, a Strategic Plan for ICTs should include the following actions:

— Decide what should be shared and learned, and how this objective is to be achieved using ICTs.

— Implement an ICT Strategic Plan between different countries in Africa, Latin America and any other regions that are to be involved.

— Implement a telecommunications network in order to transmit and receive voice, data, and/or video from/to countries in Africa and Latin America and the other regions and organizations involved.

— Implement a Strategic Plan for LAN/WAN maintenance and operation of the computer centers of the remote sites.

— Define standards to implement remote classrooms, networks and infrastructure in African and Latin American offices.

— Guide and supervise the equipment acquisition process and the technology use in remote sites.
— Select Internet Services links, relationships with others networks and international consortiums for the development of remote offices.
— Promote and supervise the use of new technologies in remote offices.
— Develop a continuous process of research, evaluation, and implementation of new technologies.
— Incorporate technologies into different academic programs.
— Participate in the developing of strategic projects using new technologies.
— Employ qualified personnel in the areas of server administrators, Unix, Windows NT, e-mail servers, satellite equipment (broadcast and receivers), structured cabling, telephony systems, ISDN, TCP/IP protocols, and videoconferencing.

The establishment and maintenance of global or even regional networks for communicating and learning is a major undertaking that requires a significant investment in material and human resources. Consequently, any new networking or teaching/learning exercises should consider carefully the opportunities of sharing existing networks, such as the global system under construction by the World Bank or the regional system established through the Virtual University at ITESM.

Finally, an important and difficult challenge for both new and established networks is to address language and cultural differences in the design of communications and teaching/learning projects. This is especially relevant to projects involving a broad-based multidisciplinary and/or participatory approach, which is increasingly the case for projects dealing with sustainable development.

References

Ekman, Richard, and Richard Quandt (eds.), *Technology and Scholarly Communication*, Berkeley: University of California Press, 1999.

Flanders, Julia, "Trusting the Electronic Edition", *Computers and the Humanities* 31, no. 4 (1997): pp.301-310, Summer 1998.

Gilheany, S., "Preserving Information Forever and a Call for Emulators", *Proc. Digital Libraries Conference and Exhibition: The Digital Era: Implications, Challenges and Issues*, Singapore, 1998.

Neavill, Gordon B., "Electronic Publishing, Libraries, and the Survival of Information", *Library Resources & Technical Services* 28: pp.76-89, January/March 1984.

Bibliography

Ackerman, Mark S., and Roy T. Fielding, "Collection Maintenance in the Digital Library", *Proceedings of Digital Libraries* 95, Austin, TX, pp. 39-48., June 1995.

Barr, Pelham, "Book Conservation and University Library Administration", *College & Research Libraries* 7, July 1946.

Battin, Patricia, "From Preservation to Access: Paradigm for the Nineties", *IFLA Journal* 19, pp. 367-73, 1993.

Bearman, David, "Reality and Chimeras in the Preservation of Electronic Records", *D-Lib Magazine,* April 1999.

Berger, Marilyn, "Digitization for Preservation and Access: A Case Study", *Library Hi Tech* 17, no. 2: 146-151, 1999.

Butler, Meredith A., "Issues and Challenges of Archiving and Storing Digital Information: Preserving the Past for Future Scholars", *Journal of Library Administration* 24, no. 4: 61-79, 1997.

Carlson, Scott, "Stanford Project Will Test an Approach for Preserving Digital Journals", *The Chronicle of Higher Education*, A45, 10 March 2000.

CEDARS Project, *Draft Specification: CEDARS Preservation Metadata Elements*, 2000.

Chapman, Stephen, and Anne R. Kenney, "Digital Conversion of Library Research Materials: A Case for Full Informational Capture", *D-Lib Magazine,* October 1996.

Chen, S. S., "The Paradox of Digital Preservation", *IEEE Computer*, 34 (3), pp. 24-28, 2001.

Cloonan, Michele Valerie, "The Preservation of Knowledge", *Library Trends* 41: 594-605, Spring 1993.

Conway, Paul, *Preservation in the Digital World,* Washington, D.C.: Commission on Preservation and Access, 1996.

Coppock, T., ed., *Making information available in digital format: perspectives from practitioners*, Edinburgh: The Stationery Office, 1999.

Crowe, W. J. & Sanders, N. P., "Collection development in the cooperative environment," *Journal of Library Administration*, 15(3-4), 37-48, 1992.

Daniels, Anne, "PANDORA—Archiving Electronic Publications", *M/C Reviews*, 15 September 1999.

Day, M., "Issues and Approaches to Preservation Metadata", Proceedings from the Joint RLG and NPO Preservation Conference, September 28–30, 1998.

Demas, S., "Collection development for the electronic library: A conceptual and organizational model," *Library Hi-Tech*, 12(3), 71-80, 1994.

Ekman, Richard, and Richard Quandt (eds.), *Technology and Scholarly Communication*, Berkeley: University of California Press, 1999.

Flanders, Julia, "Trusting the Electronic Edition", *Computers and the Humanities* 31, no. 4 (1997): pp.301-310, Summer 1998.

Fox, E. A., *Source Book on Digital Libraries*, Virginia Tech, Department of Computer Science, TR 93-35, 1993.

Gilheany, S., "Preserving Information Forever and a Call for Emulators", *Proc. Digital Libraries Conference and Exhibition: The Digital Era: Implications, Challenges and Issues,* Singapore, 1998.

Gopal Krishan, *Digital Libraries in Electronic Information Era*, Authorspress, New Delhi, 2000.

Granger, Stewart, , "Metadata and Digital Preservation: A Plea for Cross-Interest Collaboration", *Vine*, no. 117: 24-29, 1999.

Hulser, Richard P., Digital Library: Content Preservation in a Digital World, *DESIDOC Bulletin of Information Technology*, 17, 1997.

Hunter Eric J. and KGB Bakewell. *Cataloguing.* 2nd ed. London : Clive Bingley, 1983.

Kuhlman, A. F, Administration of Serial and Document Acquisition and Preparation. *In* Randall, W. M., ed.: *The* Acquisition *and Cataloguing of Books.* Chicago, University of Chicago Press, 1940.

Lynn, Stuart, M., "Digital Preservation and Access: Liberals and Conservatives", *Syllabus 8*, November/December 1994.

Marcum, Deanna B., "The Preservation of Digital Information", *The Journal of Academic Librarianship* 22: 451-454, November 1966.

National Library of Australia, *Preservation Metadata for Digital Collections: Exposure Draft*, 1999.

Neavill, Gordon B., "Electronic Publishing, Libraries, and the Survival of Information", *Library Resources & Technical Services* 28: pp.76-89, January/March 1984.

Networked European Deposit Library, *Metadata for Long Term Preservation,* 2000.

Norris, Dorothy M.: *A History of Cataloguing and Cataloguing Methods, 1100-1850.* London, Grafton and Co., 1939.

Rajashekar, T.B., *Digital Libraries, Information Studies,* October, 1995.

Research Libraries Group, *RLG Working Group on Preservation Issues of Metadata: Final Report*, 1998.

Taylor, Arlene G., David P. Miller, and Arlene G. Taylor. *Introduction to Cataloguing and Classification.* 10th ed. Westport, Conn: Libraries Unlimited, 2006.

Waters, Donald J., "Choices in Digital Archiving: The American Experience" in *The Impact of Electronic Publishing on the Academic Community,* Butterworth I. (ed.), An International Workshop Organized by the Academia Europaea and the Wenner-Gren Foundation, London: Portland Press, pp.133-141, 1998.

Wendler, R., "LDI Update: Metadata in the Library", *Library Notes*, No. 1286, July/ August, pp. 4–5, 1999.

Wynar, Bohdan S. *Introduction to cataloguing and classification.* 6th ed. Littleton, Colorado : Libraries Unlimited. 1980.

Index

S

T

V

W